TWILIGHT OF THE BLONDES

TWILIGHT OF THE BLONDES

A Tigress Publishing Book

ISBN: 978-1-59404-042-9
1-59404-042-7
Library of Congress Control Number: 2011926788
Printed in the United States of America

Book Design: Steve Montiglio
Editors: Peter Atkins and Rosanne Royer

10 9 8 7 6 5 4 3 2 1

Requests for such permission should be submitted to:
Tigress Publishing
1301 First Ave. #1807
Seattle, WA 98101

This is a work of non-fiction. It is based on the author's
recollections of a life-changing decade. Some names and
identifying details have been changed to protect the privacy
of individuals

This book is dedicated to my beloved husband,
Dennis, who said he would never read it.

Preface

The Shifting Sands of Time and Memory

Someone once said, "When we are young we learn, when we are old we understand."

A woman's twenties can be a heartbreaking time as she travels down a road filled with many potholes. In an effort to save my faltering marriage to my handsome, charming, musician husband, I did what many desperate people do. I ran to Hollywood where I believed he would become a star and we would find happiness together.

That was not what I found. My job at Ciro's night club exposed me to leering moguls, movie stars and mobsters who prowled the Sunset Strip and brought about its downfall. I fled homeward to Seattle, knowing who I was and where I was going, even as the fate of my marriage hung in the balance.

The pain and joys of my days in Hollywood still haunt me. Remembrance can be both a curse and a blessing. I have looked back on a turbulent decade of my life, when I learned much about myself and others. Only now do I understand.

⌒ *Karoline Morrison*

Some women are born blond,
others become blond,
and many have
blondness thrust upon them.

The long sobs of the violins of autumn
pierce my heart with monotonous languor
⌐⌐ Paul Verlaine

1

I always hated L.A. in the fall.

The fronds on the palm trees don't turn red and gold. There is no frost, and most of the pumpkins are fake. Kids are still going to the beach on weekends to surf and hang out, and shrubs still bloom in the Hollywood Hills. It's not your Norman Rockwell autumn.

It was November 1962 and for months Paris had been telling us about the fall and winter fashions. *Vogue* magazine was showing long leather greatcoats, suede boots, and angora sweaters tucked into full wool skirts with wide leather belts. Hah! Not in L.A. Both men and women were wearing shorts or chino pants and then shivering after 5 p.m. And nobody owned an umbrella, in spite of the downpours that can hit out of the blue. That's what newspapers are for—to be held over your head while you dash to your car. To own an umbrella would be to admit you're not a true Southern Californian, not a native son or daughter. But come to think of it, who was? Nobody I ever met.

I missed Seattle. I missed the cold November wind that comes whipping off Puget Sound, giving me an excuse to

1

wear my black Cossack coat. I hadn't brought the coat with me, but I did somehow manage to pack my long, slim Italian umbrella. An umbrella is as much a part of a Seattleite's persona as it is a Londoner's. We take autumn seriously.

For the past two months I had been trying desperately to recapture the glory days of the fifties, when, like Antonia in Twelfth Night, "A witchcraft drew me hither." I had been away for quite some time, and it was taking a while to adjust to Hollywood in the 'sixties.

Shaking my head to clear it, I walked into the rear of the checkroom where I kept a sweater. Draping it over my shoulders, I stepped outside the nightclub where I was working the hatcheck and cigarette concession. Talk about a line of work whose time had come and gone! I might as well have been selling buggy whips. The only men who wore hats anymore were mobsters and a few older guys from the east coast. Most people had either quit smoking or were trying to. I hadn't had a cigarette in over two years. Yet here I was trying to turn back the clock to the fabulous 'fifties when the Sunset Strip was swinging, everybody smoked, and blondes ruled.

I looked up at the lighted *Club Largo* sign on the building and the marquee that proclaimed "Comedian Buddy Lester Appearing Nightly." Buddy was the less successful brother of comedian Jerry Lester. That, to me, typified the Largo—strictly second string. I should fit right in. Here I was, the former "Queen of the Sunset Strip" (as the *Hollywood Reporter* had once called me), now working at this semi-dive on a street that was suffering from entertainment blight.

The Largo was hanging on like some dinosaur too stupid to know that it had become extinct. All of the great clubs of the past were gone—the Interlude, the Crescendo, the Mocambo, and Ciro's. They had succumbed to changing

2

times and changing entertainment habits. Television and Las Vegas had provided the *coup de grace* to an already ailing industry. Why pay top prices for food and drink when you can watch the same entertainers on color TV? Or go to Vegas and have your entertainment underwritten by gambling losses?

The stream of cars passing by in both directions made me think of my own travels between Seattle and Hollywood over the past years looking for something I still hadn't found. I recalled a newspaper cartoon my dad had saved from the Great Depression. It showed two freight trains passing each other going in opposite directions. Each train had a hobo riding on top of a boxcar calling out the same message to the other: "Go back! Go back!"

Tilting my head back, I sniffed the cool evening air and pulled my sweater closer over my brief costume. Paul, a blond valet parker and Troy Donohue wannabe, called to me from the valet podium. "Keep your fingers crossed, Karoline. It looks like we could get some rain."

"Let's hope so," I said. "We could use it."

Funny, I thought, *Checkroom girls and valet parkers pray for rain as fervently as farmers do in the Corn Belt. For us, too, rain means prosperity.* When it rained, few club goers scoured the surrounding area for a parking place. And most women wore coats or stoles that they wanted to have checked. Men showed up in raincoats slung over their shoulders, Sinatra-style.

I went back inside reluctantly, preferring the smell of car exhaust to the odor of stale smoke, whiskey and Chuck Landis' cologne. Chuck was the owner-manager of the Largo. Though he had given me the cigarette-hatcheck room concession at no charge, he was one of my least favorite people. Dark-haired and stocky with beetle brows, he'd once been described by someone as having all the charm of a North Korean. His attitude toward women was that they existed solely for the gratification of men's desires—whether it be bed or breakfast.

I hung my sweater back in the checkroom and adjusted my brief costume, then walked over to the entrance of the Greco-Roman styled main room. It was still early. The first show wouldn't start until ten o'clock, and it was barely eight-thirty. There were a few people having dinner.

Tourists, I thought. None of the natives would have dinner in a place like the Largo. The band had started playing "businessmen's bounce" tunes. No one was on the dance floor. Not surprising. Who was dancing ballroom style anymore? The young hip crowds were hitting the disco and go-go joints that had opened on the Strip—places where they could do the twist and gyrate to rock-n-roll.

When the band began playing "Strangers in the Night," a couple got up from their table and walked onto the dance floor. He was wearing a double-breasted pinstripe suit with a tie that sent out shock waves even in the dimly lit room. She was in a rose crepe dress with a peplum and Joan Crawford shoulders. She probably wore it to USO dances during the war.

I watched them glide around the floor, back straight and arms held in stiffly regulated positions. I knew I was seeing graduates of the Arthur Murray franchised studio in Kansas City or Little Rock. The other patrons ignored them, preferring to concentrate on their over-priced dinners. But I kept watching them. Did I pity or envy them? Probably both. Although the woman's dress and hairstyle were hopelessly out of date, her partner gazed at her with adoring eyes. I think what bothered me most was that they seemed to be having fun. Fun! They didn't know it was no longer "in" to have fun. Especially in public. I couldn't remember the last time I had had fun. Maybe I had forgotten how.

I walked back to the checkroom and asked myself for the hundredth time what I was doing back in LA. I wasn't having fun and I wasn't making much money. The dream that brought me to Hollywood the first time had ended in the late 'fifties. I'd woken up to that reality some time ago, so why was I here? Albert Einstein once said that if he was given five minutes to come up with an answer, he'd spend three of those minutes making sure he understood the question. Apparently, I needed more time to understand my question.

On my way to the back of the checkroom, I stopped in front of the full-length mirror where I put on my costume each night. Even in the dim light I could see dark roots starting to show against my current shade of blond. I remembered hearing that Marilyn was buried with a narrow scarf tied around her hair to hide her roots. I tugged up the top of my strapless costume and at the same time wondered why I was worried about it. My Sunday school teacher was unlikely to pop in.

I hated my costume with its short, frilly skirt and big bow on the top. My 38C chest did not need the extra ornamentation. Worst of all were the black mesh tights. Not only did they make me feel like a French maid in an old vaudeville skit, they grew extremely uncomfortable as the night wore on. Imagine walking around in high-heeled shoes lined with chicken wire! Sitting down, which I rarely did, was like sitting on a waffle iron. Who invented these things, anyway? The Marquis de Sade? Still, like Popeye, "I yam what I yam." Maybe, like an early Christian hair shirt, these damned mesh tights were penance for my sins, whatever they might have been.

These dark thoughts were interrupted when I heard a vaguely familiar voice call my name. "Karoline? Are you back there?" My heart leaped. *I know that voice. It's someone from the old days. Bob Kane? George Hamilton? Phil Berle? George Schlatter? A friend? A lover?* I hurried to the front of the checkroom, pitifully anxious for some contact from the past. I stopped, puzzled, at the counter. There was no one there. My best Marilyn smile faded. Then I looked over the top of the counter and saw the last person on earth I expected.

"Turk? Is that you?" I asked, knowing that it was.

"How many dwarfs do you know?" he replied. "Sure it's me. I heard you were back in town, working here. I thought I'd drop in and see how you're doing."

Little Turk, as he was known to the showgirls and cigarette girls working the Strip in the 'fifties, was a regular visitor backstage at Ciro's during my years there. He was about four feet tall with medium brown hair and eyes that held a look of ancient suffering. He was probably now in his early thirties. Selling was his game. He drove a van that had been adapted to the requirements of his small stature and was filled with a treasure trove of bargain priced items. He'd park his van around the back of Ciro's and someone would sneak him into the dressing room backstage. The dancers, the camera girl, and I would crowd around as he produced dresses, jewelry, and perfume for us to paw through. The fact that he was the size of a broad shouldered nine-year-old and had such a sad, lonely face made him irresistible to most of the girls. Nobody knew where his inventory came from. Nobody cared. More than once I saw a showgirl clutch Turk to her naked breast in appreciation of a good deal on a jeweled sweater, flashy rhinestone jewelry, or a designer knock-off dress. Turk, impassioned only by money, would wriggle free, muttering, "Twenty dollars, please. Twenty dollars, no tax."

The fact that, like a eunuch in a harem, he was unmoved

by all that bare flesh gave him a certain appeal. Even though the sign over Ciro's stage door proclaimed, "**Through these portals pass the most beautiful girls in the world**," Little Turk could not have cared less. I never felt that he was without a normal male libido; it was just that his passion for making money was so much stronger. All he wanted was to make some sales and quietly get out before Herman Hover, Ciro's owner, threw him out. So here he was, a survivor of the Strip's golden years, testing the waters of the 'sixties, like me. I hoped he was faring better than I was.

"So, what have you got, Turk? Rhinestone jewelry? Perfume from Paris?" I asked, eyeing the small case he carried.

He plunked the case down on the counter. "I'm not handling that stuff anymore. The showgirls are all in Vegas now. I've got a new customer base—girls like you, who're trying to make a buck. I've got something you can sell here at your concession. You can clean up with this little item. I can give you a deal at twenty bucks a dozen. You can get five bucks a pop easy."

I looked down at his serious young-old face wondering what he could have in his case that could turn that kind of profit. He opened the case and removed a small figure. It looked like a naked Barbie doll with long legs and high pointy breasts. Her hands were clasped behind her head and her legs spread apart.

"This little item is straight from Japan," Turk said. "I guarantee nobody else on the Strip has got one. I came to you first when I heard you was back in town, for old time's sake. Besides; she kind of looks like you, with the blond hair and all."

I gingerly took the small figure from him, not sure I was flattered by the comparison. I examined it and quickly discovered what the gimmick was. Embedded in the creature's genitals was a small wheel.

"Flick the wheel, flick the wheel," Turk implored. Holding the figure upside down I flicked. I gasped as a bright flame shot out from between the figure's legs. I dropped it on the counter and the flame went out.

"It's a lighter," Turk crowed with pride. "You can keep one on the tray and light guys' cigarettes with it. You know you'll get a good tip. Then you tell a guy that the little lady can be his for only five bucks. You can do real good with this little item. I don't know how long I can get 'em for you at this price, so you might want to pick up four or five dozen now."

"They're disgusting!" I said. "I'm not selling porno crap like this." I shoved the figure toward him. "Put it away."

"So what's with you?" Indignation gave an unusual animation to his usually stoical face. "This ain't Ciro's, you know. Chuck Landis is bringing in strippers next week. You gotta give the public what it wants and I think you're doin' that now wearing that costume. Besides, I saw the way you lit guys' cigarettes at Ciro's—holding a match close to your boobs so they get a good look while they're lightin' up."

I didn't feel like arguing the point. Years ago I had drawn a line about what was acceptable in this kind of work and what wasn't. So, maybe the line had shifted a little, but I still had remnants of my standards left. Sure, I could make money with this disgusting little lighter. It would appeal to the mostly male clientele of the Largo. For a moment the businesswoman in me calculated the profit I could make. Tempting? More than a little.

"I'm sorry, Turk," I said softly. "I really appreciate your thinking of me, but I can't sell these lighters. I've got trouble enough now with guys who think I'm up for sale. But it was really good to see you again." Surprisingly, I realized I meant it. Little Turk had given me a brief moment of nostalgia for the old days, those naïve, halcyon days when I believed in the magic of Hollywood, when the Strip was my Yellow Brick Road (before the time I found a little old man behind the curtain with his pants open).

Turk put the lighter back in the case, snapped it shut and looked at me with his sad, ancient eyes. He had wasted a trip, but he was used to it. He played the percentages. He would hit a couple of the Strip's go-go spots; and if he scored thirty percent of the time, he would feel he did alright. He knew his goals in life better than I knew mine. As he made his way to the door back onto the Strip, he didn't look back. I waved to him anyway.

⌒

Little Turk personified to me "the peddler" of history and nursery rhymes. Centuries ago, peddlers like Little Turk probably were sneaked under cover of nightclub-like dimness into the harems of sultans, where they enticed the odalisques with fragrant oils and potions. The peddler of old gained entrance into the women's quarters of Henry VIII's palace, disguised as a child. There he unveiled his inventory of spices from the East and brilliant baubles for the ladies to enhance their provocative *décolletages*.

Peddlers are not commissioned salesmen or factory representatives offering seven-business-day delivery. Their warehouse is probably a van parked down the street. They ask for cash, and all sales are final. (Ever have a guy in Times Square push up his sleeve and offer you a Rolex at a "steal" of a price?) The peddler does not sell his wares in storefronts or catalogs. He does not operate on a nine-to-five schedule or close shop on Sundays. He plies his trade where his prospective customers are, and he knows what they want. There are women peddlers in history too, but they are not so exotically ensconced. Eliza Doolittle's fishmongering and Mollie Malone's "Alive, alive-o" cockles and mussels do not have the mystique of Little Turk.

For some reason my heart always was and is with peddlers like Little Turk. He solicited his business cautiously in the places he knew would have customers. With his young-old eyes and small stature he elicited a sort of protective emotion in the women on whom he focused. They were the late night ladies—the showgirls, dancers, strippers and girls like me. It was all cash transactions and the money he received, after being carefully counted, disappeared into one of his tiny black boots.

I hoped that 20th Century technology would not cause peddlers like Little Turk to disappear or morph into Avon ladies.

⌒

The music from the show room caught my attention and startled me. They were playing "Cherry Pink and Apple Blossom White." Nostalgia struck again. This time I remembered lying on a lounge chair on the veranda of my old Hollywood Hills home, enjoying the warm summer night. Down the street Perez Prado was at home, playing that famous song of his on his trumpet. Did I not know then how brief and sweet those moments were?

I was jolted back to the present by a man who was approaching the counter with a familiar look on his flushed face. His eyes were fixed on the front of my costume. He was fiftyish, balding, and had a paunch that his polo shirt could not disguise. "I need a pack of Winston's, doll," he said to my chest. I walked the four or five steps to where my cigarette tray sat at the far corner of the counter. As I pulled a pack of Winston's out of the assortment in the tray, I asked, "Would you like me to open them for you?"

"Nah, just give 'em to me like they are," he replied.

"That's seventy-five cents, please."

"I've got a dollar here, but I could sure make it a five."

"Oh?" I questioned, pretty sure I knew the terms of the deal.

"I'd just like to tuck it down there where you keep your valuables. Know what I mean?" With that he produced a five from his other hand and made a quick, fumbling move to thrust it down the front of my costume.

I made a quick step backward and out of his reach. "Seventy-five cents," I repeated.

Just then Chuck Landis walked out of the show room and over to the checkroom. "Any problem here?" he asked.

"I just tried to give your little blond cigarette girl a five dollar bill for a pack of Winston's. She don't seem to want to take it," the man whined.

"Well, you know these Hollywood blondes. They don't come cheap," Chuck responded. "Offer her a fifty and she'll take you in the back room and screw your nuts off."

I bit my lip. This was not the first time I had heard Chuck brag that all the cocktail waitresses were hookers, but this was the first time he had suggested I was a whore. I grabbed my cigarette tray, slung the strap around my neck, and walked into the show room with as much dignity as I could muster after that insult. I made a slow circuit of the room doing my model's runway walk with a slight sway that was my tribute to Marilyn—shoulders back, chest out, hips undulating slightly, lips moist and apart.

I made stops at three tables. One table asked if I had any Russian *Sobranies*. Hah! Where did they think they were? Ciro's? I sold cigarettes at two other tables. One man asked me to light his Chesterfield. Remembering Turk's comment, I was careful to bend over as little as possible and to hold the match well away from my *décolletage*. I got a five-dollar tip anyway. But, unless the checkroom was going to get busy, it looked to be a lean night for me, everything considered. My cab fare home would take the five. For one crazy minute I thought about finding Little Turk and buying a couple dozen of his "porno" Barbies. Then I reminded myself that I wasn't that desperate. Not yet.

When I returned to the foyer, both Chuck and the creep were gone. A dollar bill lay on the counter. At least the jerk didn't stiff me. I put the bill in the cash compartment of the tray and unharnessed myself. Placing the tray on the counter, I smoothed my hair and hopped up on the stool that sat just outside the checkroom entrance. I crossed my legs and thought longingly about kicking off my high heels. I could, of course, place the stool back behind the counter and no one would know whether I had my shoes on or off. Since my legs were part of my credentials, I didn't give myself this luxury. At least not until maybe 1 a.m.

It was about time for the first show to begin. The new maitre d' had now taken up his post and put the rope across the entry. Anyone coming in now would be paying a cover charge. I smiled when he looked my way. His name was Carlo and he was northern Italian. I remembered Cole, my off- and-on boyfriend in the old days, telling me to never trust a blue-eyed Italian. Cole was a brown-eyed Italian. So far Carlo had not made any advances toward me, which both relieved and worried me. I didn't think he was gay. I could usually tell. I pegged Rock Hudson long before he started groping guys in a back booth at Ciro's.

I heard Buddy Lester starting his act. He did a pretty good show—hip enough for the Strip crowd and not totally over the heads of the out-of-towners. I shuddered when I thought about the next show featuring strippers. What was happening here anyway? Wasn't it just a few short years ago when stars like Cab Calloway, Sarah Vaughn, Sophie Tucker, Mel Tormé, Maurice Chevalier and Sammy Davis played this street, and the *Hollywood Reporter* called me the "Queen of the Sunset Strip"?

And what had happened to the blondes who were such a part of that golden era of the fifties? Doris Day's career was winding down, and I heard she was buying property in the Carmel Valley. Jayne Mansfield had become a caricature of herself and was reduced to playing mainly dinner theatres. Mamie Van Doren, who took roles Marilyn had rejected, was moving to Hawaii. Kim Novak's career had peaked with *Vertigo* and she was in a career skid. Sweet little Sandra Dee appeared to be on the same downward slide once she outgrew "Tammy."

Maybe if Marilyn were still alive things would be different, I thought. There might still be a demand for the sexy, sweet, man-pleasing blondes with their appealing vulnerability. These women were not bimbos. Rather, they were like blond geishas who a guy could introduce to his mom. Marilyn was our role model. She taught us to speak softly through pursed lips. But now, who was there to listen? Perhaps that's why women had a new icon, one who was elegant and educated and living in the White House. She was also a brunette with a chest as flat as yesterday's road kill.

Marilyn died in August of 1962, the same month I turned thirty. I know that it was a kind of death for me too. Or at least the woman I had tried to be. As I sat perched

Playboy Bunny-style on my stool, I drifted into what I called a "near-life" experience when the same reverie happened to me years ago. I seemed to float above my body and I saw myself in a not-too-distant future. My blond beehive hairdo was stiff with spray and my face was hard with cynicism. Like Little Turk, only money turned me on. Stuff a bill down the front of my dress? It had better be at least a ten. A part in a porno movie? Well, some say Marilyn got her start that way. A weekend in Acapulco with a wealthy man? Is he attractive and generous? Give a blowjob to a casting director? How good is the part?

I shocked myself back to the present. Could this ever be me? Was it already happening? Hollywood's effect on my moral standards? Years ago I had come down with an affliction named John Morrison. Hollywood was my cure, but now I was suffering the long-term side effects.

When I first came to Hollywood in the mid fifties I had tried to be Destiny Darwin (my stage name and sometimes alter-ego). For my auditions at the Player's Ring I wore my hair in a Grace Kelly French roll and paraded my University of Washington Drama School credentials and straight modeling jobs. But there were few jobs for Destiny. She was too classy. Too Seattle. The money I made was when I turned into a "bomblet." That's what sold in the "golden" era of the fifties. Now in the sixties there was little demand for this type—at least for things you could tell the folks back home about. I was on the dark side of thirty in Hollywood with not a whole lot of shopping days left.

"Could you check these please?" a male voice said. I hopped down off my stool, gave the man a dumb blonde smile and accepted a couple raincoats from him. He took the claim checks without a glance at my chest. *I hope he's gay,* I thought, *or my type is really finished.* As I started to hang up the coats I noticed that the shoulders were wet.

Rain! It had started to rain! Maybe there'd be more customers at the coat check counter!

But rain is also what had brought me to Hollywood in the first place.

This is my story.

Killing Me Softly With His Song
  Fox & Gimbel

2 The rain had started shortly after we left Tacoma and headed north to Seattle on Highway 99, the main highway before I-5 was built. It glistened on the dark pavement and gave a soft glow to the neon lights of the businesses that hugged both sides of the roadway.

It was Spring, 1955. Promises of beer, hamburgers and a good night's sleep drew cars on and off the highway, sometimes cutting across all four lanes of the rain-slicked ribbon that connected Tacoma and Seattle like a dark umbilical cord. The accident rate on this stretch had given it the nickname "Dieway 99." But I wasn't worried. We were traveling in a Buick Roadmaster, and my husband was a careful driver.

Rain, rain, go away, come again some other day. It's raining, it's pouring, the old man is snoring. I distracted myself by thinking of all the silly sayings I could think of about rain. *April showers bring May flowers.* A great second line popped into my head: *Mayflowers bring Pilgrims!* I turned to relay this piece of sophomoric wit to my husband. *Forget it,* I thought. *He no longer finds me amusing. Or attractive.*

I studied his pale, aristocratic profile. His long elegant nose, light gray eyes and long, thick lashes still made my temperature rise. His hands rested lightly on the steering wheel, a Camel held between his fingers. Those fingers! Those hands! More erotic than anything in the *Kama Sutra.* I thought back to the first time I had seen those hands.

I was a guest at a fraternity party at the Phi Kappa Psi house near the campus of the University of Washington and had wandered into the music room of the large, brick Tudor-style house. Lured by the sound of a Gershwin tune on the piano, I stood in the doorway. A tall, dark-haired young man was seated at the Steinway grand. I quietly walked up behind him and looked down at his hands as they moved confidently over the keyboard. Beautiful hands. Sensual hands. I could feel them moving over my body. As a warmth spread over me I sank down into a nearby chair, all thoughts of the date who brought me there forgotten. I was an entering freshman and still in awe of the great sprawling university. This was my first visit to Greek Row. To say that I was impressed with it all was an understatement. Mom had warned me about the punch, but she hadn't told me how intoxicating a moment like this could be.

The young man at the piano never acknowledged my presence, although I knew he was aware of me. The music between us was more intimate than a kiss. I knew if he stopped and spoke to me the magic would disappear. *Hi, I'm Karoline. Do you live on campus? What's your major? Do you know "April in Paris?"* I left the room as quietly as I had entered.

My date found me by the punch bowl. "Where've you been?" he asked.

"Looking for you," I lied. "I stopped by a room down the hall where some guy was playing the piano."

"That's gotta be Johnny Morrison. He's a friend of mine. We both came over from eastern Washington and both pledged Phi Psi. He's a pretty cool guy. You want to meet him?" he asked.

Did *I* want to meet him! A guy who made all his fraternity brothers look like Mickey Rooney after he'd run out of Clearasil? Yeah, I guessed I wanted to meet him. If John Morrison had looked like the Wolf Man in the light of a full moon, I still would have been smitten. But he didn't. He looked exactly the way I wanted him to: pale skin, tragic eyes, sensuous mouth. He may have been nineteen, but he was a man and I wanted him.

We went to the piano, followed by a bunch of the guys and their dates who asked him to play everything from "Elmer's Tune" to "Fur Elise." He obliged in a congenial manner. I left the room and stepped outside into the garden. Seating myself on a stone bench I let my fantasies loose. I recalled a movie I had seen a few years back. It was called *A Song to Remember* and starred Cornel Wilde and Merle Oberon. Early in the movie someone is playing the piano brilliantly in a darkened room in a mansion somewhere in Paris, or maybe Vienna. A woman enters the room slowly, carrying a lighted candelabrum. She approaches the piano and sets the candelabrum down. Everyone gasps in amazement. This was not Liszt playing—even though it was his house. But who else could perform all those arpeggios? It was Chopin! As the candles cast gentle flickering shadows on the handsome face of Chopin/Wilde, I knew that this was a man I could dedicate my life to. Now the torch I had carried for this 19th Century pianist-composer (or 20th Century actor) was finally extinguished. I had a new idol, and his name was John Morrison.

We went steady for two years. My dream role as

Chopin's lover George Sand turned out to be more of a Smiley Burnett to his Roy Rogers. I was not a patron or even a peer. I was a side-kick, always there, always loyal and always second banana. As time went by I knew John was spending less and less time pursuing his law degree and more time playing gigs around town. Could I blame him? No way. His versatility put him in demand, from accompanying strippers at stag parties to classical Japanese at the Buddhist Temple in Chinatown.

In his sophomore year John joined a group of other young jazz musicians in an organization called "Bumps Blackwell's Junior Band." They were an innovation in music, blending be-bop with jazz. Here he met Quincy Jones, who had a great influence on John. Jones was a serious musician and, though barely out of his teens, already had a hit on the jukeboxes—a be-bop tune called "Wino." Quincy may not have had the old Chopin/Wilde charisma, but I knew his was an awesome talent. I was proud that John was part of this cutting edge group. Everyone said there should be a moratorium on law degrees anyway.

My happiest moments were sitting in on the band's rehearsals, frequently held at John's parents' home. I was there to get Cokes out of the fridge and make sure everyone knew I was John's girlfriend. Once in a while I would ask them what they were playing. It seemed I always got the same answer—"How High the Moon." When I asked John why I never heard the melody, he explained that in this kind of jazz you play *around* the melody. I never understood this, but I accepted it.

Whether or not I understood the nuances of jazz or not, I knew I loved the scene. There was a glamour and excitement I quickly got addicted to. The private club parties, the hotel ballrooms, the jazz clubs in Chinatown—

this was heady stuff to a girl who had grown up on a small island in Puget Sound. Even though it was a prison island, the excitement of that was nothing like this. Gradually I, too, spent less and less time on my studies at the "U Dub's" School of Drama. After all, even though I had experienced some success as a child radio actress and done well in little theatre productions, there was no contest about who had the talent. My job, like Sand/Oberon was to hold up those candles.

One duty of a band's girlfriends was to carry the instruments into the dance hall or auditorium. While most of them carried relatively light burdens, such as clarinets and trombones, others were assigned more challenging instruments like the drummer's, which included several drums, hi-hats, and the base drum. The bass player's girlfriend had to be really smitten with him to struggle with that load. I was envied by all. Since the piano was already in place, all I had to carry was John's small briefcase of music.

When John played a solo piano gig he brought along something called a "fake book." Highly illegal, I was told, it was a large volume of hundreds of popular songs with lyrics and simple bars of notes. With this guide in hand, John could fulfill any request from a customer to play almost any standard tune that Irving Berlin or anyone else had ever written and published. If a patron wanted to hear "Melancholy Baby" (a frequent request), John could play it with all the flourishes of a concerto—and sing the words too, if necessary.

The camaraderie of the group was wonderful. They were not just a band. They were a team where there was no color line. If you were a good musician, that was all that mattered. Guys like Quincy Jones, Tommy Adams, and Ray Charles were important members of the brotherhood. Frequently

John would be the only white male in the group. No one noticed or cared, certainly not the girlfriends.

One evening I was out on the town with my cousin Elaine. We went to a well-known restaurant on Seattle's Fifth Avenue and sat in the lounge, where a member of our "brotherhood" had landed a job playing piano. I was curious to check out the swanky spot and the musician's performance, because there was a good chance that John would be the next featured musician to get a booking there.

Twenty minutes or so after Elmer Gill had launched a delightful sequence of Cole Porter tunes on the baby grand, a man at the next table leaned over to me and said, "Pretty good playing for a nigger, huh?"

I was so shocked I could think of only one response. "Sir," I blurted out, "before you say any more, there is one thing you should know. That talented musician is my husband!"

The man was appropriately mortified and so, unfortunately, was my cousin. I overrode her quiet protestations by elaborating on Elmer's wonderful and endearing qualities to the man next to us, while at the same time wondering how Elmer's wife would feel about my comments. It soon seemed wise to make our exit; so with a withering look at that man seated beside me, I walked over to the piano and gave Elmer a big warm hug.

I took my job as girlfriend very seriously.

You're in the Army now, sort of.
        ⌇ *Karoline Morrison*

3 One chilly March afternoon John and I were sitting in our favorite booth in a coffee shop on University Way, also called "The Ave." We were smoking and drinking coffee. In the two years that I'd known him, this was the first time I had seen him appear nervous and worried. I knew something was wrong, but I didn't want to ask. Instead I chattered on about gossip and rumors in the Drama Department, always a hotbed of intrigue. Finally, he took a deep breath and said, "I've been kicked out of school."

"Okay, so you've been kicked out," I said. "Is that such a big deal? You can transfer to another college, get your grade point back up, and then re-apply." Actually, I wasn't really surprised. I knew he had been on probation and had a lot of work to make up, but so what? He was bright and ambitious. He could recoup, and I could help him.

"No. I'm through with school. I never wanted to be a lawyer anyway. That was my dad's idea."

"So, what are you going to do?" I asked.

"I'm joining the Army."

23

I sat back in the booth and gripped the edge of the table. I couldn't believe what I was hearing. *The Army! My God,* I thought, *he'll be going to Korea. He'll be shot at!* My mind raced. Maybe I could join a USO troupe and go too. I could sing, be in skits. Sure I could. I would never let him be alone, facing danger.

As though reading my mind, he leaned forward looking deep into my eyes and said, "I want us to get married and then you can go with me." My heart did jumping jacks. Married! Of course, I had assumed that after graduation, when John was established in a good position as a lawyer or an entertainer we would get married. But now? Before we finish school?

"Yes, yes, yes, and yes!" I said. "We'll get married and I'll go to Korea with you. Pork Chop Hill, here I come!"

"I don't think I'll have to go to Korea. I spent all day yesterday at the recruitment office and they've promised I can be assigned to Special Services at Camp Roberts in California. That means I can serve out my enlistment in the states. After I'm discharged in two years, I can decide what I want to do next."

I was in a state of extreme intoxication. In the past couple of minutes I had learned that not only was I about to become Mrs. John Morrison, but I was going to California to boot. I finished spring quarter while John completed basic training. I worked evenings at the Seattle Yacht Club, and the money I saved went to buy a five-year-old Chrysler New Yorker and a lot of great clothes.

My folks were happy with the news and so were John's. I think his dad had long ago realized that John was more musician than attorney. My friends gave me showers and confided that I had made the catch of the decade. My mom worried a little about the fact that I was not at all proficient at cooking, bed making or dusting. (I was a somewhat spoiled only child.) I dismissed her worries by telling her that John would soon be making the kind of money that would easily pay for a housekeeper. My dad told me I had made a good choice. He said the two of us were headed for the kind of financial success he and my mom couldn't achieve when they married during the Great Depression.

We had a big traditional wedding. John looked tanned and fit, though thin, after his basic training ordeal. He confided to me before the ceremony that he had dug a ditch as part of his training. I loved him beyond words. In his beautifully tailored tuxedo he looked every bit as handsome as Chopin/Wilde. And he knew how to dig a ditch! No bride was ever prouder or happier than I.

After a brief honeymoon in Victoria, British Columbia, we headed south. John loved the Chrysler I had bought almost as much as the sexy nightgowns and underwear I paraded around in each evening. What a wonderful feeling it was to enjoy sex without guilt. After all we were married. Anything we did was legal. Just to be on the safe side I had brought our marriage certificate with us in case any hotel clerk was suspicious of our status. Registering as Mr. and Mrs. John Morrison was so gratifying. When I was addressed as Mrs. Morrison I swelled with a pride that eclipsed any ovation I had ever received on stage. I wished everybody would call me Mrs. Morrison and never use my first name—like in Victorian times when the first names of upper class women were seldom if ever heard, once they were married. Their identity was swallowed up in their husbands'. I thought that was wonderful, especially if your husband was handsome, charming and talented. Even Marie Curie who helped her husband discover radium was referred to as Madame Curie. She was part of a team, as I planned to be.

When we arrived in Paso Robles, where we planned to live, I was charmed by the little town with its quiet oak-lined streets and the famous inn with its little Spanish cottages nestled in a garden setting. That was where I wanted to stay. At least until we could find a house or apartment. My first disappointment was learning there was no room at that inn. Nor any other inn, motel, apartment or room in a private home. Nearby Camp Roberts had generated a bonanza of families looking for housing in a community ill prepared to handle the influx. For a while it looked as though we would spend the first night in our new town sleeping in the car, as many others were doing.

Late in the day we were having dinner in a café called the "Blue Moon" when we saw a soldier and several young women exiting a hotel next door. In spite of the fact that a "No Vacancy" sign was up, John jumped up from the table and said he'd be right back. Then minutes later he returned and asked me to close my eyes and put out my hand. The feel of that key was better than the feel of a diamond. He explained that there was no private bath, but that it looked clean and was run by an older English couple. There was one catch, however. Due to certain regulations, anyone staying more than a week qualified for a lower rate. Since the owners were loath to offer this when rooms were in such demand, everyone had to move out after seven days.

There was an answer to this curious problem, however. The little hotel across the street had the same rules, and everyone simply moved across the street for seven days when their time was up. It became a sort of game, since once in a while, someone would get left out—sort of like the slow, chubby kid in musical chairs. The three months we played this game were among the happiest of times in my life. I was one of many Army wives with time on our hands. We played Canasta, talked about our lives, and worried about our men being sent to Korea. Except for John. Everything the recruitment sergeant had promised had come true. John had been assigned to Special Services and soon was involved in putting together a show called "Basic Ballyhoo." It was a variety show written by a young private named Kenny Miller. Kenny was a talented guy who had just gotten started in Hollywood when he was drafted. When he found out about my background in acting, he put me in two of the skits. I also sang a couple of numbers with John. It was sheer heaven.

Soon John's talent brought him weekend jobs playing alone or with a group of other musicians at functions off the base. After awhile he was too busy to appear in "Basic Ballyhoo." I stayed in the show, and Kenny and I became good friends. He taught me the time step and told me stories about Hollywood. Fables, really. I didn't care. I loved hearing anything about Hollywood.

Things got better and better for John and me. He was assigned to the Officers Club. He worked with the manager during the day and on the weekends played with a combo he had put together. He was paid well for the weekend gig and could still work at other engagements when they came up. In other words, we were making money. We had moved from our hotel hopscotch situation to a little bungalow where I stretched my cooking skills. Kraft Dinners were behind me now. I had graduated to Swiss steak and tuna casseroles. John enjoyed whatever I made and even put a much needed five pounds on his slender frame. I was expanding my skills in other directions too. I got a part time job in an Army store in town where I worked three days a week. At the Paso Robles USO I got several of the other bored wives to help me put on a one-act play. I had directed a couple of plays in high school, but trying to motivate young women to rehearse a play in a sweltering community center when the temperature was hitting 100 degrees was the toughest task I had ever undertaken.

I lived for the nights. John would get home around five-thirty, shower and change, then eat my latest Betty Crocker special. Television had not yet made its way to the hinterlands of California. There were several small movie theatres in the area, and this was a very pleasant way to spend an evening in an air-conditioned setting. The true high points of my life, though, came when I was able to go along when John played special places. The best of these was The Hacienda on the Hunter-Liggett military reservation northwest of Camp Roberts. Here in the middle of nowhere William Randolph Hearst had built a Spanish hunting lodge.

It was absolutely beautiful. I didn't know why he needed the castle at San Simeon when he had this place. The courtyard fountain, the lush plantings and the huge elegant rooms made it an utter dream house. And the privacy! The privacy played an important role in the popularity of the lavish retreat for the Eighth Army brass. Usually, one weekend a month, the high ranking officers from the Presidio in San Francisco would fly in for R and R. Sometimes a U.S. Senator or cabinet member would be included for a couple of days' fun with plenty of wine, women and song. John brought in food and drink supplies from Camp Roberts. I don't know who provided the fancy ladies from San Francisco, but they were always on the menu. I was passed off as part of the band and John let me sing a blues number or two with the promise that I never mention anything I heard or saw.

I found myself both fascinated and repelled by the

women. They were well groomed and expensively dressed, not looking in the least like my idea of women who rented out their bodies. One night I chatted briefly with one of them in the powder room and learned she was completing her final year at Berkeley. She hoped to become a meteorologist! She said the job at The Hacienda was more fun than waiting tables, and the pay was a lot better.

When I made the weekly call home to my folks, I decided not to mention any of this. My dad was proud of how well we were doing, and my mom was just glad to know I was happy and eating properly. I had never lived away from home before and because I was their only offspring, they were very focused on my welfare. We seemed so young to them. They were ten years older than we were when they married. Although John was an only child too, his parents had a different attitude about him. He had enjoyed considerable independence for years. They felt he could take care of himself and me too. I knew they were right.

Then an incident occurred during our second year in Paso Robles that should have sounded a warning bell of things to come. I had gone with John to the base on Saturday evening. While he played his gig at the Officers Club, I went to a movie at one of the camp theatres. Then I returned to the Club to wait for him. But there was something different about this night. I sat at a table drinking a Coke and talking to people. Eventually there were only two of us at the table—me and a young captain who had just returned from Korea. He'd been telling me great war stories, which I loved, and bought me a whiskey, which I hated. Anyway, the next thing I knew, the Club was closing, and John was nowhere to be found.

In a panic I looked everywhere for him. I asked the bartender and the custodians. They all shook their heads. I went to where the car should have been parked, and it was gone. Slowly the realization swept over me that I was twenty miles from home with no car and no money. I looked for the Captain. He was gone too. The whole base was quiet and empty. I sat down on the wooden steps of the Club and tried to think what to do. We had no phone at our little cottage and somehow I knew that even if I were able to reach John, he wouldn't drive back to get me.

A voice from behind me gave me a start. "Somebody stand you up?"

I turned to see a man wearing a Major's insignia smiling down at me. "I guess I missed my ride," I said, too embarrassed to admit that my husband had left without me.

"Well, the night's still young. How about I take you home and you invite me in for a nightcap?" he asked in a smooth, oily voice.

Why don't you twirl your moustache while you say that line? the director in me thought. "Sounds like a good deal for both of us," I responded, knowing that if he knew he was taking me home to my husband, I'd not have a chance in hell to get home that night.

We got in his car and headed for the main gate. When we stopped there briefly for an exchange of salutes and a "Goodnight, Sir!" from the guard, I got a good look at him under the light. He was OLD. At least forty. Remembering the women at the Hacienda parties on the military reservation, I turned and smiled at him.

"I guess this is my lucky night." I murmured.

"Some people might say it's *my* lucky night," he said. "Where do you live?"

"In Paso Robles," I replied. "I'll direct you when we get there."

I kept up a line of chatter and the miles went by. I

told him I worked for the Bank of America in town and occasionally went to movies at the base with a friend who was in the service. He asked a few questions such as whether I had a "steady" date and so on. In the darkness of the car I palmed my wedding ring as I built on my character of a young woman on her own living in a small town and really thrilled to have a Major in the army taking her home.

While I rattled on, my mind was working at top speed. *Once we get to town, what do I do? I can't make a scene. Paso Robles was a ghost town after midnight and it was already 2 a.m. I couldn't do anything that would reflect negatively on John.* Then, suddenly, I had a simple, basic plan. Highway 101 became Oak Street at the city limits. All traffic lights went to amber during the night, except for one four-way stop two blocks away from our house. I had to endure the Major's hand on my knee for just six more blocks, I told myself, keeping my fingers crossed that he would obey the stop light, even at that hour. Sure enough, he slowed to a stop, I leaped out, said thanks a lot as I slammed the door and raced down a side street, cut through a yard and then hid behind a bush.

After what seemed like hours I decided he wasn't going to hunt me down. I came out from behind the bush and walked home cautiously. I opened the door to our cottage and found John sleeping soundly.

"Why did you leave me like that?" I asked, as I shook him awake.

"I was tired," he said, "and you were having a good time talking to that guy. Besides, I knew you'd find a way to get home."

An emotion filled me to the brim. Was it anger? No, it was pride. *Yes, I got home. I can take care of myself and John knows it. That's one of the reasons he married me. He never has to worry about me. I can manage.*

Our life together actually got even better after this incident. I had a new confidence in myself. Fortunately, I never ran into the Major again, and the incident was soon forgotten in the excitement of my life. John had been approached by a man named Jerry Nelson, who owned a small café in town. Mr. Nelson had an eighteen-year-old daughter with a classical singing voice. Her name was Donna, and she had been living in Hollywood each summer at her voice teacher's house. The plan was to have a radio show in San Luis Obispo sponsored by the restaurant. John would accompany Donna and also play a couple solos during the fifteen-minute show. We loved the idea, especially since it meant spending time at the Nelson's rehearsing. The Nelson family consisted of Jerry and Eunice and their children Donna and Bill. They were the most fun-loving, congenial family imaginable. They became our adopted family, and Donna became a close friend to me.

We didn't lack for friends. We met many people who had been thrown into a strange, though temporary, environment in a time of national crisis. This led to a kind of lifeboat bonding among all of us who hoped to survive and return one day to our real lives. John and I were popular, probably due to his charm and talent more than my attributes. We were the Tony Curtis and Janet Leigh of Paso Robles, and we knew it. We also knew how important the Nelson Family had become to us. As the end of John's two-year enlistment drew closer, we vowed to keep in touch with everyone who had been in the lifeboat with us. At the top of my list were song-and-dance man Kenny Miller and the then Donna Nelson.

When the big day came and John was officially discharged "under all honorable conditions," we headed home filled with hope and sadness. I was leaving our first home and so many memories: the shows we did and the friends we made; swimming in the little lagoon surrounded by oak trees dripping with Spanish moss; dancing in the moonlight at Nina's at Shell Beach; praying in the sanctuary of the Mission in San Miguel; Canasta tournaments in the lobby of the Antlers Hotel. These memories and the sheer happiness of being John's wife would haunt me and taunt me for the rest of my life.

4 When we returned to Seattle our welcome was no less than any battle weary veteran of war would have received. The fact that John had never endured the rigors of battle and had lived in a comfortable home furnished by Sears of San Luis, rather than a foxhole, did not change the equation. He was a conquering hero! He had served his country well. And so had I! Didn't somebody say, "They also serve who only stand and wait?" Well, the wait was over. Now we could get down to the serious business of John's career.

John's parents had found a delightful house near theirs on the Ship Canal, which cuts through Seattle and connects Puget Sound with Lake Washington. It had a glassed-in dining room and a large deck where we could watch the boat traffic. They gave us the down payment.

Within three weeks of leaving Camp Roberts, John had a job. He was hired to play six nights a week from nine to one a.m. at a lounge called "The Congo Room." It was a large space with faux jungle décor. Murals depicted a Hollywood-influenced jungle with black jaguars, leopards and a voluptuous woman wearing a strapless tiger skin. Seductive lounges and settees upholstered in velvet animal prints were grouped around the room. The bar stools were bamboo with zebra-patterned seats. In the center of this tropical extravaganza was a black grand piano with a black ceramic panther crouched on top. An overhead spotlight shown down on John and made the fake ruby studs in his tux shirt glitter. No wonder his tip glass overflowed! In deference to the theme of the room, I asked my mom to fashion some leopard and zebra cummerbunds and bow ties. He quickly became the talk of the town.

I would drop by two or three times a week to sit in a dark corner and listen. When he saw me he would play "Bésame Mucho" or "Malagueña." Most of the time, though, he played what the customers wanted, like "Three Coins in the Fountain" or "It Had To Be You." Once someone even requested "When Irish Eyes Are Smiling." Sometimes I wondered if Chopin/Wilde would have been happy playing music like that. I asked John how satisfying it was to play, night after night. He said that, although jazz, bop and even classical music can be satisfying to the musician, you have to play what the people want to hear. At the Congo Room they wanted mood music. And not too loud. It was a revelation to me that a great part of John's success was his ability to be a crowd pleaser. He had the musical talent to make even the most banal tune sound rich and melodic with his styling. His looks, charm and musical adaptability quickly made him one of Seattle's most popular entertainers.

Quincy Jones had left for L.A. while others from the old jazz scene were still hanging out in dives around town looking for more variations of "How High the Moon." For John it was enough to play watered down classical music interspersed with Top Ten hits in a place where tips, drinks, and adoring women were plentiful.

We separated less than a year after our glorious return to Seattle. It started with parties he was invited to without me. After all, at one-thirty in the morning I would be in bed, wouldn't I? Then there were nights he didn't make it home until late morning. "This agent came by, and offered me a gig in Reno at twice what I'm getting here. We went to a late night café to talk about it." Or, "A guy I went through Basic with came in. We went to Chinatown to talk old times." Then, "One of the waitresses couldn't get her car started, so I gave her a ride home." Next he came home with lipstick on his shirt and Chanel on his jacket. Some nights he didn't come home at all.

It was soon common knowledge that John was having an affair with a beautiful Japanese war bride who was recently widowed. His dad talked to him, telling him that Asian women look good when they're young, but turn into "squaws" after forty. My dad suggested it was okay to have a little fling, but do it quietly with discretion. I asked John what I could do to be a better wife. Change my hair style? Go to cooking school? I asked him to tell me what he wanted. The truth was he didn't know what he wanted, except that he didn't want to stop screwing Takiko.

I suffered. I lost weight. I lay awake at night wondering what had gone wrong. I was embarrassed and humiliated. My self-esteem was down around my ankles. This was not a role I was meant to play. *I* should be the "other woman." My friends stopped calling. I wasn't fun anymore. I spent hours sitting at the window looking out on the canal and hoping the nightmare would end and we'd have a good laugh when I told John about it the next day. But I never woke up from this bad dream.

Finally, at my request, John moved out of our house and in with one of the bartenders. As he piled his things into our Buick he told me not to worry. He still loved me. He just needed a little time to work things out. For more than four years he had been my whole life. My future. I

37

decided, all things considered, that I should give him some time. What other option did I have, anyway?

Three months later I got the call I'd been holding my breath for. John wanted to talk about moving back home. He heard a gasp of joy escape from me but quickly went on to explain that the bartender was leaving town and giving up his apartment. What John was proposing was that he move into the rec room in the basement of our house until he "worked things out" with Takiko. He said he couldn't just drop her because she was suicidal. "You know how Japanese women are," he explained. "Remember Madame Butterfly? I could see Taki doing something like that if I'm not careful about how I end our...our friendship."

I thought "Taki" was about as suicide-prone as a rhinoceros, but I said nothing. It wouldn't matter anyway, as I knew he had no intention of breaking things off with her. Moving into the basement sounded pretty flaky to me. Did it mean I would still fix him meals and do his laundry? Or would we be just casual housemates living separately under one roof? The idea revolted me, and yet I felt guilty about telling him no. After all, it was his parents who gave us the money for the down payment, and he was paying the household bills. Maybe I should move back with my parents. I could get my old job back at the Yacht Club and return to school and get my degree. But I didn't want to give up my home and retreat in the face of the enemy. It was Guadalcanal all over again, and I was prepared to fight for what I believed in—my husband!

With this in mind I suggested that John accompany me to Tacoma to my uncle's and aunt's silver wedding anniversary celebration. I felt that thrusting him into the bosom of my family to celebrate a happy marriage would remind him of the importance of wedding vows and a relationship of trust and respect.

The plan did not work as well as I had hoped. One by one my female relatives took me aside and gave me advice on how to keep a husband happy. The suggestions ranged from providing nightly massages with fragrant oils (Norwegians are as big on massages as Swedes) to being a better housekeeper to getting a lover myself. As I was receiving these tips, one of my cousins was flirting with John and expressing interest in some piano lessons during the day, while her husband was at the office. I had to plead a headache. I convinced John to take me home by promising to give him an answer on his proposal to move back in.

That's why I wasn't braced for sudden stops or swerves that rainy night on "Dieway 99." I had more critical things on my mind. As the wipers repeated an endless litany of "Should I, shouldn't I?" the decision was suddenly made for me. Out of the darkness in front of us a car appeared, skidding over into our lane. I had no time to scream or pray, as a galaxy of stars exploded in my head. The fear I had felt just before the crash was replaced with a sense of relief that I no longer had to worry about making choices that would gravely affect my life. My life was over, and I didn't mind much at all.

When I regained consciousness, I became aware of strong odors of perfume and gasoline. It was not an unpleasant combination of smells, I thought. I found myself curled up almost fetally under the dash surrounded by the spilled contents of my purse, like an Egyptian queen entombed along with possessions she would need in the afterlife. I was content to stay there breathing the effects of Chanel and Shell, but rough male hands were pulling at me. "We gotta get her out of here in case the car blows up," I heard a voice say. Someone else warned, "Watch how you move her in case her neck's broke."

Then, painfully, I was laid on the damp ground. I was dimly aware of some guy stripping off his tee-shirt and gently placing it under my head. The rain fell on me softly, and I pondered whether my polka dot tunic top was washable. A soft warm cloth was caressing my face. When my eyes were able to focus, I realized it was a large black dog, licking the blood off my face. My senses were overwhelmed with these smells: wet dog, blood, and male sweat from the tee shirt. Blood and sweat, my brain repeated, but where are the tears? I tried to move but couldn't. It was hard to breathe, and my chest felt like it was full of loose change. I was relieved my hair was down and flowing, since I was drawing quite a crowd of spectators.

Sirens were howling. On the way to another accident on this damned highway, I thought. Will people never learn? Why don't they take the train? Especially when it rains. I tried to find John's face in the crowd. Where was he? Dead or badly hurt, I thought. Otherwise he would be beside me, wiping the blood from my face instead of this big dog doing it. Then a new thought flashed through the twisted wires of my brain. *Had he tried to kill me? Yes, that was it! Just another highway on a rainy night. He didn't want me to drive, oh no. He wanted me in the suicide seat when he crashed the car into some obstruction. What a simple solution to his problems! With me out of the way he could move Takiko into our house and be free of financial obligations (once he had paid my funeral expenses.)* I also seemed to recall that he had just taken out a large insurance policy on my life. Then, as my brain slowly cleared, I remembered that was part of the plot of a TV movie I had seen last week. Besides, the man was found innocent anyway. I resolved not to die, partly out of spite.

The siren came nearer, and an ambulance approached

out of the darkness. I was lifted onto a gurney, wiggled my fingers in a wave to the dog, and then was stashed inside the waiting ambulance. It was good to be out of the rain at last. As we raced off into the night, I became aware that there was someone else strapped onto a gurney beside me. I couldn't see who it was, but a male voice kept mumbling, "Please don't die, lady. Please don't die." The slurred words, accompanied by the strong smell of whiskey, solved the mystery for me. I knew then that John Morrison was not the villain of the piece. It was Jack Daniels. I wondered idly where I was going. Back to Tacoma? On to Seattle? Maybe to the Mayo Clinic? What I never would have guessed is that I was on my way to Hollywood.

5 Two months later I sat in a chrome and green plastic chair in Dr. Green's waiting room. He had been treating me since my release from the hospital in Tacoma. It was to be my final check-up. Although my rib cage felt like cheap post-war construction that could collapse in a high wind, I knew that my recovery was nearly complete. My hair had grown out enough to hide the jagged scar where the back of my head had hit the windshield. My hair was cropped, but I still occasionally combed out tiny shards of glass that reminded me of the accident. As if I could ever forget!

Even the faint medicinal smell of the office brought back that terrible night when, for several hours, I was sedated, examined, X-rayed, and stitched up in the emergency room of Tacoma General Hospital. John finally came in. He had arrived in another ambulance and they had just sewed up a long cut along his jaw. Wouldn't you know it?! He ended up with a scar similar to those dueling mementos cherished by nineteenth century rakes. I ended up with the painful, unglamorous injuries of a punctured lung, broken ribs, and scalp laceration.

He walked over, looked down at me, and asked, "Do you come here often?" I looked up at him and said, "I can tell you're an Aries. Do you date Leos?" We both started laughing, and I guess it was that or the sedative that made me pass out. The next thing I knew I was in a bed, lying on a board, with a roommate who was ninety years old and spoke only Hungarian. I had a lot of time to think.

As the days passed, I wondered why John didn't visit me. Everybody else did. My mom and dad came with vital supplies like my toothbrush and makeup. My Tacoma relatives brought sympathy and magazines. Even John's dad came to see me, bringing flowers and a vague apology about John. Since our Buick had gone to meet its maker, John was driving an old car that belonged to some friend of his. His dad said John didn't feel comfortable taking it out on the highway. I could tell even my father-in-law thought it was a pretty lame excuse. He left, saying he hoped John and I would work out our differences soon.

Differences? *Oh, you mean like how he wants to have a wife AND a girlfriend?*, I wanted to ask. Of course, I was too polite to say anything beyond, "Thank you for the flowers and we'll have to have everybody over for pot roast soon." When he left I felt the old desperation returning. What was I going to do?

The day before my discharge from the hospital, my uncle came by to see me about a "serious matter." He warned me not to sign anything, especially if men with briefcases asked me to. I didn't pay much attention because this was the same uncle who gave my female cousins and me strong warnings about accepting funny cigarettes from strangers and told us how to protect ourselves from white slavers.

After ten days at Tacoma General Hospital I was ready to be released. The doctor needed to give me one last check-up, and I was instructed to have someone drive me home. I was set to stay at my aunt and uncle's Tacoma home. As I was packing my pitifully few belongings into a paper sack, I received a phone call from my cousin Elaine, who said she would be there at noon and that she had a surprise for me. Knowing my cousin, she was either going to introduce me to one of her former boyfriends (probably a hockey player) or she had a new boyfriend (probably a hockey player.) I remembered the last one, Andy, with few or no teeth. Andy's favorite good-bye was, "If I don't see you in the spring, I'll see you in the mattress."

Knowing my cousin would be very well dressed (she was a good-looking semi-natural blonde), I looked warily at my reflection in the brutally-lighted bathroom mirror. I felt a small shudder. Shortly after my arrival in the emergency room, I was told I had a serious lesion to the back of my head. I had suffered a brutal confrontation with the windshield of our car. Fortunately, when I saw the other car coming at us, I quickly turned my head away and saved my face; but the back of my head took a beating.

The doctor began by cutting off most of my blood-soaked hair, which revealed a large gash in the shape of a Z. As he put black sutures in it, he commented that I must have had a run-in with Zorro. I said that Zorro must have been a better swordsman than I. I pulled my remaining hair up into a meager top knot and secured it with a rubber band—not one of my favorite looks. The rest of me didn't look much better. The black pencil skirt I was wearing had survived the onslaught, but not the classic white pique top with puffy sleeves and ruffled peplum. Knowing my needs, my mom had sent me a blouse and "sensible" shoes with three-inch heels. I did my best to glamorize what was available. I put on the black, button-front blouse she had sent and tied it midriff-style at the waist. Of course, that revealed the unsexy rib belt that held my bones in place (visualize an ace bandage on steroids.) I put two little packets of sugar in each shoe which gave me maybe one-quarter inch more height. This was my best effort. When I finished I looked like a 1950's version of *The Bride of Frankenstein*, stitches and all.

My cousin arrived looking blond and gorgeous in an Anne Klein white sheath with patent leather belt. I felt like a street urchin beside her. She cheered me up by saying we were going to lunch at Johnny's Dock, an "in" spot on the Tacoma waterfront. That was her surprise. "Great!" I said. "If anybody asks me about my hairdo, I'll just say it's the rage in Europe. It's called The Zorro!"

After a short stay with my uncle and aunt, I went to my parents' home to finish recuperating. I put off my decision about John a little longer. It was comforting to be back in my old room with a hot water bottle greeting me after I turned off the TV and went to bed. My mom's kindness and thoughtfulness soothed my injured psyche as much or more than the doctor's attention to my battered body.

One afternoon a man with a briefcase came to call. He said the drunk who caused our accident was insured. Not only would my medical bills be paid but our car would be replaced, and I would receive "pain and suffering" compensation. My world suddenly became brighter. Actually, the pain from being dumped by John was much greater than the pain from the accident. But, like an actor getting a sympathy Oscar, I was pleased to accept it.

When I asked a relative, who was an accountant, whether I would owe income tax on my windfall, he replied, "No. Uncle Sam just considers that your body is worth that much less now." He went on to suggest some investment options that would give me security in my old age. My parents thought I should invest in a duplex where I could live in one unit and rent out the other. Neither of these options made my pulse race. And I still hadn't given up on saving my marriage!

So here I was, two months after the accident, waiting for the doctor to check my progress. I shifted my position in the hard waiting room chair and reached for a magazine, hoping to get my mind off everything. A picture of Marilyn Monroe stared up at me from the cover. Her red, moist lips seemed to be saying, "Go south, young woman. Go south." I had an epiphany! Everything was suddenly clear. I would go to Hollywood! Once settled in, I would establish contacts for John. I would act as his personal representative. When I had things in place he would leave Seattle (and Takiko) and join me. He would appreciate and respect me. We would recover the happiness we had in Paso Robles. We would live in a mansion in Beverly Hills with a pool in the back yard and send our kids to school in Switzerland (or maybe London). I'd work out the details later. The main thing was I knew what I had to do. Go to Hollywood!

When the nurse finally called my name, I knew I had come up with the right answers. What did it matter that my lack of ironing skills were the talk of the neighborhood? So what if I didn't have the most dust free house in town? I had a skill that in my mind was far more important. I could sell! And with John as my product, there would be no stopping me. I would make John a star, save my marriage, and make my dad proud of me too.

I followed the nurse into the doctor's office as if she was leading a conga line. The doctor was sitting behind his desk. He looked up at me over his glasses, and all I could see was Lionel Barrymore as Dr. Gillespie. "Well, you're looking pretty chipper today," he said.

"I can honestly say I never felt better," I answered.

"Well, let's see how I think you're doing," he said, as he

began his examination. He checked my ribs and listened to my lungs before examining the scar on the back of my head. "It's remarkable that this scar is on the back of your head instead of your face," he said, as he ran his finger over my Mark of Zorro. "Most people who are thrown into the windshield suffer facial lacerations."

I knew how it had happened. I had been sitting sideways on the bench seat looking at John when the crash occurred. My posture of adoration had spared me, much like those people who were spared in a tornado because they were kneeling in prayer.

"I think one of these days we'll see cars equipped with seatbelts like planes," Doctor Green said. "You would have been spared these injuries altogether if you'd been belted in." I nodded my head, but secretly thought that if I had been wearing a seatbelt I would not be going to Hollywood, so I'll take the lumps and the money, thank you very much!

"Your lungs sound fine and fortunately you didn't suffer any skull fracture. You're a very lucky young lady, you know."

"I know," I replied—thinking about the insurance money more than the fact that I had narrowly escaped death on ole Dieway 99. "Can I stop wearing this thing around my chest now?"

"The rib belt? I'm afraid you're going to have to wear support for your ribs for some time yet."

"But it's so ugly," I said. "And it itches. Isn't there something else I could wear instead?"

"Oh, I suppose if you had one of your grandmother's whalebone corsets around, that would do the trick. Of course, someone would have to lace it up for you, like Scarlett's mammy in *Gone with the Wind*."

"Wait a minute," I said. "You've just given me an idea.

Do you know what a Merry Widow is?" I was remembering a picture I'd just seen of Jayne Mansfield posing in one of them.

"I know what a waltz is, and an operetta," he answered, smiling. "Does that count?"

"One of the magazines in your waiting room has a picture of a movie star wearing one. It's like a strapless bra that goes down to your upper hips and makes your waist and midriff small," I explained.

"Hmm. The Journal of the American Medical Association rarely has information like that," he chuckled. "Anyway, go ahead and try one of these Merry Widows. If it gives you the support you need, that's all that matters."

"Thank you, doctor, thank you!" I said, thinking, *No, that's not all that matters. Wearing a sexy, strapless Merry Widow with lace garters is way better than an Ace Bandage.*

So it was under doctor's orders that I headed for the nearest department store's lingerie section to fill my prescription. The first garment I tried on was black lace with red bows for garters. I looked at myself in the mirror in total amazement. My waist was smaller than a baby wasp's, and my chest—well, imagine an hourglass with sand spilling out of the top. I loved it.

"Can you breathe?" asked the matronly saleswoman.

"Better than I've ever breathed before," I announced. "I'll take four in different colors."

Oddly enough, it was true. Whereas my body had felt fragile and vulnerable before, I now had protective armor that did a far better job than the drug store device. Furthermore, I would no longer have gouges in my shoulders from my bra straps. My one regret was that I had not been wearing a Merry Widow when the accident occurred. Not that it would have protected my ribs very much, but I would have looked sensational in the emergency room. Clutching my Merry Widows to my chest, I ran for the bus. I couldn't wait to get home and take my new measurements.

Wretched excess is just barely enough
⌒◝ Anonymous

John and I signed an insurance settlement for an amount that was surely far less than it would have been if we had hired an attorney. But I was eager to get on with my master plan, and John wanted to get another car. The fact that the drunk driver had insurance made me eternally grateful to him. If I had known his name I would have been tempted to name my first-born after him. He had given me a chance to redeem myself in the eyes of my husband, family, and friends.

I went from being an object of pity and scorn to someone who commanded the respect that a bank account and a new wardrobe deliver. It was like having a hunk of Tootsie-Roll in my mouth, knowing there'd be more sweetness once I really bit into it. I put most of the money in my parents' checking account. Then I took a fair amount of cash on a shopping trip downtown. The thrill of making slightly extravagant purchases did wonders for my aching rib cage. My first stop was I. Magnin. I had worked there behind the cosmetics counter as a student during many summer vacations. Now I could afford to shop there without waiting for special sales.

Before entering the store I stood in front of the Sixth and Pine window transfixed by the outfit the mannequin was wearing. How many times in my life had I stood like this admiring a dress that was totally out of my price range and promising myself, "Someday, someday." Now that "someday" had arrived. I took the elevator up to the salon floor and told the first saleswoman who approached me that I wanted to buy everything in the Sixth and Pine window; dress, jacket, shoes, long gold chain, short kid gloves—everything! If there had been a French poodle in the display I would have bought that too. The dress was a fitted black knit sheath with a tank top. Its long, matching jacket was made of quilted gold fabric with matching knit collar and cuffs. It was elegant and sexy. When I came out of the dressing room I drew a small crowd of admirers. It showed off my Merry Widow- shaped body to good advantage. The saleswomen who had known me as one of them now treated me with the respect a big spender always gets.

I spent the next two weeks doing this kind of therapy shopping. All my life I had had a passion for fashion and now at last I could indulge myself and feel no guilt. Not only had I paid in blood, but my new duds were an investment in my future. (And John's!) The Magnin's fling was a one-time event, however. After that, I looked for sales and stayed within a self-imposed budget. I was extravagant, but in a frugal sort of way. By the time I called a halt to my spending, I felt I had put together a sophisticated, trendy wardrobe that would wow them in L.A. I was my own Barbie doll.

I asked John to come over so I could outline my plan. I wore one of my new purchases. It was a full-skirted emerald green dress with a strapless top. The Merry Widow freed me from bra straps, and the dress showed off my twenty-two inch waist to full advantage. I was certain the way I looked would help me sell my plan.

John was enthusiastic. Being a part-time realist, I wasn't sure if he really wanted me to pave the way for his career in Hollywood or if he was just happy to have me out of the area and off his conscience for a while. No matter. He gave me Kenny Miller's Hollywood address as well as the addresses of a couple other guys from Army Special Service. I had kept in touch with Donna Nelson. She and her family had left Paso Robles just before the base closed and had opened a restaurant in Encino in the San Fernando Valley. In fact, the instant Donna heard my plan she invited me to come and stay with the family until I found a place in Hollywood. I was very grateful for the Nelsons' offer, as were my parents, who had a lot of concerns about their only child going off alone and unarmed into the Hollywood jungle. I assured them that I would be fine. After all, there were lots of nice people living in Hollywood—like Ozzie and Harriet!

John's parents thought our house should be rented out while we sorted out our future. We agreed. I really didn't care. I had spent too many long nights wandering around the house aimlessly, too many hours lying awake in the poster bed we had fallen in love with at the Sears store in San Luis. There had been too many days spent sitting at the front window waiting to see whether a big black Buick would pull into the driveway. I never intended to live there again, no matter what.

The night before I left on my great adventure, I looked at the pictures I had sent home to my parents from Paso Robles: John and I, stretched out on the sand at Pismo Beach; the two of us walking arm in arm down Powell Street on a weekend in San Francisco; a newspaper clipping showing us performing at Camp Roberts in "Basic Ballyhoo." So many good memories. Would I add to this happy collection with my present plan? Or was it an exercise in futility? I wasn't as confident on the inside as I tried to appear outwardly. But I told myself I was not a quitter and that if I wrote advice columnist Dorothy Dix about my situation she should surely say, "Fight for your man if he's worth fighting for." And he was. The thought of a future without him was unbearable.

It haunted me that I was not comfortable playing the rejected wife. If this were a play and I the director, I would cast myself as the other woman. So in a way, by leaving town and starting a new life I became the other woman. I liked this. Some writer once spoke of the "healing balm of action." I knew now what he meant.

John insisted on taking me to the airport and promised to be at my parents' home by nine in the morning. I sat waiting with my pile of luggage in the entrance hall. By ten thirty I knew he wasn't coming. I frantically called my dad at the U.S. Marshal's office where he was a deputy. He seemed to be expecting my call. Twenty minutes later a car with the U.S. Marshal's insignia on it roared up to the door. We piled my luggage inside and I gave my mom a tearful hug.

As we raced south toward Sea-Tac Airport, I wanted to ask my dad to slow down, since I was still suffering from highway nerves. But he was a long time law enforcement officer and did not take advice well—certainly not from me. Besides, I was so grateful he was getting me to my flight that I kept my mouth as tightly closed as my eyes. In spite of the fact that I always felt I had let him down by being born a girl, my dad was supportive of me and my activities. When I was fifteen I qualified for the special summer drama program at the University. He paid the tuition with money he had set aside for a new car. When he came to see me in any of my productions, he always clapped the loudest. Best of all, he never made me feel it was my fault that John had left me.

As we approached the airport and the traffic got worse, he switched on his siren. A highway cleared for us and we were soon in front of the terminal. In fact we made a rather spectacular arrival. A security guard came over and helped unload my collection of luggage. I was happy that I was wearing my new Magnin dress with the "sky-heeled" shoes. I waved to the onlookers as I rushed to the gate where my flight was being called. I hoped people would mistake me for some kind of political prisoner or important federal witness. I tried to look the part by turning up my jacket collar and looking furtively behind me as I rushed along.

As the plane roared off into the pale October sky, I sank back in my seat and kicked off my shoes. The overnight case I put under the seat contained my basic survival gear: makeup, toothbrush, hairspray, two changes of underwear, three changes of jewelry, a nightgown and two pairs of nylons. Folded into the toe of one stocking was a cashier's check representing the remains of my insurance money. I was ready, armed and dangerous. I would take Hollywood like Grant took Richmond. Also, the fact that John had not shown up to take me to the airport showed how necessary this move was. I had to get him out of Seattle and back to California where he belonged!

Excitement pulsed through my body. I thought, *Sherlock Holmes must have felt just like this when he said, "Watson, the game's afoot!"* I felt myself unconsciously trying to push my seat forward with body movements. The flight attendant noticed and whispered the location of the restroom. I got up and went there rather than admit to her that I was simply trying to make the plane fly faster.

Finally, the pilot announced that we'd be landing shortly, and the seat belt light went on. I checked my makeup in my purse mirror and put my shoes back on. The older lady sitting next to me had commented on the height of the heels and said she didn't understand how we girls could walk in them. I glanced down at her brown oxfords and felt I could ask her the same question. Instead I explained that I was wearing them under doctor's orders. She accepted this without further comment. I felt there was a measure of truth in my statement. Wasn't I wearing a black lace Merry Widow on advice from my doctor? Would he expect me to wear garments like that with crepe-soled gunboats? Please!

When I went to claim my baggage, I had to admit to myself that a change of shoes would be most welcomed. Perhaps to a pair of three inch heels? So, I had the first of many shocks yet to come when I learned that my luggage had not arrived with me in the Golden State. It had been sent to Atlanta, Georgia, by mistake. Well, wasn't that just peachy? After a frantic search, the airline promised to deliver my stuff to Encino within three to four days. I bit back the urge to ask whether they planned to send it west by covered wagon. *Better not antagonize them,* I decided. *I'll manage somehow.* But the sobering prospect of wearing the same outfit for four days, not to mention my hell-on-heels shoes, was quickly forgotten when Donna rushed over to my rescue. "You look fabulous," she cried. "You've lost weight! And I love your outfit!"

"Thanks, I'm glad you do," I said, "because you're gonna see a lot of it. Practically everything I own in on its way to Atlanta."

"Well that's better than if your stuff was here and you were on your way to Georgia. I'm really glad to see you. We've got a lot of catching up to do."

We chatted non-stop as she guided me toward the parking lot. I couldn't believe it when I saw the car she was driving—a baby blue Cadillac convertible! The California sunshine danced off the chrome trim on the fins.

"Are you kidding me?" I asked in amazement. "Is this car yours?"

"Well, actually it's my Dad's, but he lets me drive it anytime I want to," she said proudly. "And guess who it used to belong to? Elizabeth Taylor!"

"I can't believe that," I exclaimed. "Your dad must have struck it rich after you left Paso Robles."

"Hardly," Donna laughed. "He got a deal on it and, besides, he thinks it's good for business. When I'm not driving it he keeps it parked in front of the restaurant. It makes it look like a celebrity is inside having dinner."

"A shill car," I exclaimed. "I love it!"

As we headed out toward the freeway, I rested my head against the ivory leather seat and enjoyed the wind in my hair and the smog in my eyes. I knew without a doubt that I had done the right thing. I'd followed my star to Hollywood, and soon my real star, John, would be following me. Life would be perfect again.

7 As I sank back into the sensual embrace of the Cadillac, I realized my accident nerves were on hold. How could anything happen to me in this huge, elegant car? What driver, drunk or sober, would dare smash into us?

I expected to see other cars slowing down to gawk at us, but nobody did. After a few miles of observing the other cars around us, I understood why. At least half the other cars were convertibles, and Cadillacs were commonplace. What did you have to drive in this town to be noticed? Then I spotted a car the like of which I had never seen before. It was racy, flashy and dignified all at the same time. Donna said it was a Rolls Royce Corniche. Now it was clear why Liz had sold her Caddy.

We were headed directly to her family's restaurant in Encino, where Donna waited tables in the afternoons. She told me she was taking the next two or three days off to show me around. I was so grateful for her family's hospitality. Being on my own was a new experience, and I needed time to get used to it.

The wind unglued my hair spray. We were whipping down the freeway so fast that I put my foot to the floorboard in a futile braking effort. Conversation was impossible. Eventually we exited the freeway and made our way to

Ventura Boulevard. When our speed dropped to a serene 35 miles an hour, I was finally able to relax. We both lit cigarettes and started to talk.

"I can't believe you and John have split up," Donna said. "You two had that 'perfect couple' schtick down pat."

"Schtick?" I asked. "Is that another way to say the S word in L.A.?"

Donna laughed. "No, it's a Yiddish expression for routine. You know, a gimmick."

"Hey, you didn't use words like that in Paso. You're making me feel like a hick from the sticks."

I suddenly realized that Donna had changed from the nineteen-year-old kid I remembered. I was especially impressed with her eyeliner. It made her eyes look snaky and evil. I wondered if she would show me how she did it. "Anyway," I said. "I think maybe you're right. I've started to think that the two years in Paso Robles were not a marriage; they were a party! Now the party's over—at least for a while."

"What's this about John having a Japanese girlfriend? You mentioned that in one of your letters."

"Ah, so. *Takiko, The Yellow Peril, Strikes Again* by Karoline Morrison," I said, referring to an old Fu Manchu title. "Where's General MacArthur, now that I need him? Seriously, I think she's more a symptom than a problem. We got married too young, I guess. John hadn't had a chance to play around a little."

"What about you? Don't you need a chance to play around a little too? Maybe that's the real message in all this."

"Hardly. I just want him to be successful and happy. That's my goal. If he can be that without me, that's okay. I don't think so, though. He needs me, whether he knows it or not. Anyway, he's the one with the looks and the talent.

Women have always chased after him. I can handle that as long as I'm the most important woman in his life. I know I will be again, once I get him on the right track here in Hollywood. His success will be mine too."

I didn't want to talk about it anymore. Seeing Donna again reminded me of all the good times we used to have. I wanted to cry. Instead, I ground out my cigarette in the car's spacious ashtray and started checking out the street we were driving on. In some respects it reminded me of the Seattle-Tacoma highway where I had "hit the jackpot," so to speak. If "Dieway 99" could hit the jackpot with some renovation, it might look like this fabulous street. Huge impressive restaurants lined both sides of the road. Names like the Good Wife, the Ram's Horn and the Sportsman's Lodge flashed by. Valet parking? I wasn't sure I even knew what that was. These were not eat-here-and-get-gas establishments. Prestige and style were definitely on the menu.

"This is a great street. Where exactly are we?" I asked.

"Oh, this is nothing. This is just Ventura Boulevard, the Valley," Donna answered with a deprecating wave of her hand.

"Come on," I objected. This is great! Studio City, Sherman Oaks, I love the names. It's so trendy."

Donna shook her head. "You have no idea. The Valley is 'Squaresville.' I can't wait to get out of here. You've got to see restaurant row on La Cienega and Rodeo Drive in Beverly Hills. Of course, the hottest street there is the Sunset Strip!"

Although Donna was younger than I and had spent much of her life in a town much smaller than Seattle, I bowed to her superior hipness. If she said the Valley was square, who was I to dispute it?

When we arrived in Encino and pulled up in front of a small country-style café under a big oak tree, I breathed a sigh of relief. This looked so much like the Nelsons' former restaurant in Paso that I was instantly "at home." Donna parked the "shill" car in the prominent spot near the entrance. Her mother Eunice came rushing out to greet me. She was such an energetic, happy person, and her welcome to me was so sincere I could not believe my good fortune to have friends like this. She lent me her arm as I negotiated the gravel parking lot in my high heels. On hearing the news that my luggage was a continent away, she promptly offered me the loan of "waitress mocs" to wear until my own things came. I was instantly homesick for my own mother, even though I had left her only six hours before. As to the loan of the moccasins, I thanked Eunice, but thought privately that I would have to be pretty desperate to give up my Magnin stilettos for waitress shoes. Even the other shoes I had packed had heels nearly as high as the ones I was wearing. They were part of my image.

Donna showed me to the bedroom I would share with her. Having nothing to unpack, I wandered into the small living room. The back of the restaurant had been converted to living space consisting of three bedrooms, a bath and a common area that served as a casual eating space, TV room and conversation room. Cooking, of course, was done in the restaurant's kitchen. The sounds of the restaurant drifted back to the living area. I found it interesting and novel to live so close to a busy restaurant operation. When Donna came into the room I told her as much.

Donna looked at me with a fierceness in her kohl-lined eyes. "I hate it," she said. "I hate working in the restaurant, and I hate the Valley. I live for my weekly trips into Hollywood for my voice lessons. If it weren't for that, I'd go crazy." I was

shocked at the anger in her voice. In my mind s
lot of good stuff going for her—a great family, a beautiful
singing voice and a promising future. What more could she
want?

When I told her this she described how happy she was
when she was at her music teacher's home. She had spent
two summers living there while she was in high school
and now spent an hour there once a week. Apparently
that was not enough. She loved talking about her teacher,
Elena Peluso, who was a former opera singer now retired
and married to Thomas Peluso, conductor of the NBC
Symphony Orchestra. They lived in the Hollywood Hills
with their young son.

Donna went to the restaurant kitchen and came back
with a pot of coffee and cups. As we settled into easy chairs,
she began to talk about life at the Pelusos'. She described
their home as filled with music, laughter, and interesting
people. The food was wonderful northern Italian fare,
and there were always guests for dinner. She said that the
handsome Robert Alda and funny man Jerry Colonna were
regular drop-ins. She did funny imitations of the many
accents of the Pelusos' friends.

She told me about an elderly Hungarian gentleman who
asked the Pelusos' seven-year-old son what he wanted to be
when he grew up. The boy said he wanted to be Hoppy,
referring to the TV cowboy star Hopalong Cassidy. The
old man hugged him tightly and said, "And I hope you're
hoppy all your life." Donna said one night opera star Nina
Cochetts came to visit. She was coaching voice students
at the time and described how she constantly stressed the
importance of practice: "When you do not practice you are
not 'sheeting' on me, you are 'sheeting' on yourself!"

We talked and laughed for hours, eventually moving

to a booth in the restaurant for burgers and fries. When the café closed at nine o'clock, Donna's parents joined us and we talked and laughed into the night. I realized I was really "hoppy. " I had almost forgotten what that felt like. The old ache was still there, but I felt I had left my old, sad self behind. When John "sheeted" on me, he was actually "sheeting" on himself. With that gratifying thought I went to bed and slept soundly for the first time in months.

8 The next three days were full of conversation, laughs, and familiar camaraderie. I was fully accepted into the Nelson household. I even tried to help a little in the restaurant, but when I dumped some coffee dregs into a large plastic container, already filled with a dark brown substance, my kitchen duties came to an abrupt end. What I thought was a bucket of slop turned out to be a large commercial-sized container of maple syrup. So I resorted to sitting at the counter posing as a customer. When anyone sat down near me I took the opportunity to recommend one of the higher-priced lunch entrees. If Liz's car could work as a shill, why couldn't I?

When my "counter duty" got boring I ventured out into the neighborhood as far as my shoes would permit. I was eager to see how prices in the little clothing shops compared with Seattle's. The fact that I was wearing my Magnin scoop-necked, sleeveless dress jumper-style over a sweater and was roasting in the mild October weather definitely gave me an incentive to find something cooler to wear. I was tempted to wear the dress without anything under it, but decided it was far too theatrical for daytime Encino. Besides, I hadn't bought any clothes for a couple weeks and withdrawal symptoms were setting in.

I spotted a shop called Taffy's, showing some casual

fashions in the display window. Since it was within the limits of my high-heeled walking capacity, and the name was the same as a Cocker spaniel I owned as a child, I went in. Most of the garments on the racks were totally unacceptable, but I found a simple white silk tee shirt. It would be perfect under my dress, I thought, and later it would work with my black suit. Black and white had always been my favorite look, probably because of all the early Bogart movies I had seen.

When I took the shirt up to the register, the salesgirl immediately asked where I was from. I wanted to know how she guessed I was from out of town. She said that my clothes were so much more fashionable than anything in L.A. I was flattered and surprised. After all, I told her, L.A. was the western capital of the garment industry. She said that, except for San Francisco, most of California was very casual about clothes—especially in the Valley, where high heels were on the endangered species list.

I hobbled back to the restaurant buoyed up by this information. *People will notice me,* I thought, *and that will help me make contacts for John.* When I opened the door I found Donna on her break, sitting in a booth, drinking a Coke. I dropped like a rock on the other side of the booth, kicking off my shoes in one movement.

"Donna, I've got to start looking for a place to stay."

"So the Valley is getting to you too, huh?"

"No, of course not," I replied, thinking that actually it was, a little. "You guys have been so wonderful, and I'm having a ball. But that's not why I'm here. I have to get my plan in motion. I know you're going into Hollywood tomorrow for your lesson. Maybe I could ride in with you and check out a couple places."

"Sure. I would have suggested it myself, but I thought you were waiting for your suitcases and stuff. I really want you to meet the Pelusos. And we can drive down Hollywood Boulevard afterward. See all the characters."

I pulled the tee shirt out of my sack. "Look what I sprang for at Taffy's. I'll wear it tomorrow. How do you like it?"

"Ooh, very Grace Kelly—simple and restrained. I think your green sweater is more you, but you must be in sweat city by now. Of course you could have waited and bought something from Frederick's of Hollywood. Like a clingy blouse and a bra with the tips cut out of the cups."

"Oh yuck," I said. "I've seen their catalogues. Does anyone really wear that stuff? I mean out in public?"

Donna laughed, "Nobody I know, but then nobody I know has your figure either."

"I thank you on behalf of my Merry Widow," I said. "But, remember, I'm just a simple kid raised on McNeil Island. We didn't even have indoor plumbing."

"Hey, don't give me this country bumpkin routine," Donna said, as she set her empty glass down. "When I met you in Paso Robles I thought you were pretty hip and sophisticated. I was kind of in awe of you."

"No," I said. "That was John. I was just along for the ride."

"My God, what's he done to you? You were as popular as he was. I saw you in a couple of those camp shows. That comedy routine you did got a lot of laughs and applause."

"Donna, they just included me because of John. He may be a lousy husband at the moment, but you know he's got so much talent. My job is to market it here."

Donna threw up her hands. "Okay, okay. I've got to get back to work. Tomorrow we'll drive in to Hollywood and spend the day." With that she picked up her glass and went back behind the counter. I picked up my sack and went back to the living space where I heard canned laughter from the TV. Donna's brother Bill was stretched out on the couch with a sack of potato chips on his chest watching a Lucy re-run.

"Hi guy," I said, as I sat down on a big overstuffed chair next to the couch. "How's the job hunt going?"

"I think I'm in at Warner's," he said through a mouthful of chips. "The pay isn't really terrif, but the job's neat. I drive all these bozos from Kansas or somewhere around the lot in a bus and tell 'em what they're lookin' at. A friend of mine's been doing it. He says it's a gas. He says you can tell 'em anything and they'll believe it. . . .like those mountains you can see in the distance. You can tell 'em they're props. . . that Warner Brothers spent a pile of dough on special effects to make mountains for their westerns. I'm gonna have a ball with this job. No doubt about it."

"If I take the tour with you, you're not going to pull that stuff on me, are you?" I asked.

"As if you'd fall for stuff like mountains being props! You're a pretty sharp cookie."

"I hope so, but I don't feel so sharp lately."

"Hey, listen, I heard about you and John. That guy has got to be the El Boobo of the century. I thought you looked pretty okay back in Paso, but now, like wow! I mean you could be in Playboy."

"That's really nice of you to say, Billy, but I'm not looking for anything for myself. I just play Smiley Burnett to John's Roy Rogers."

"I think you're Gabby Hayes. I mean Roy Rogers' sidekick was Gabby Hayes. I don't mean you look like Gabby Hayes or anything," Bill stuttered.

"You mean the electrolysis on my beard was worth the money I spent, huh?" I joked.

Bill started to laugh too, and suddenly I realized he

was laughing far more than the subject called for. What was going on here? I stopped laughing and looked directly at him. Testosterone was emanating from every pore of his nineteen-year-old body. The lust in his eyes was startling and satisfying at the same time. I had a brief conversation with myself. *What the hell is going on with you?* I silently asked myself. *Do you realize you are sitting with your legs over the side of your chair and your dress hiked up above your knees? Do you realize that your back is arched so your chest is sticking out even farther than usual? Is it possible that you are flirting with this kid? Are you a slut or just desperate for male attention?* I pleaded guilty on all counts. As Bill's eyes traveled up and down my body I gave a small involuntary shudder. I noticed a definite bulge in his jeans that managed to kick my Presbyterian upbringing into action.

I stood up quickly, pulled down the skirt of my dress and said I thought I'd go lie down and read awhile. Mrs. Nelson had lent me an Agatha Christie novel I couldn't wait to start. Or so I told myself, not ready to accept the fact that I was getting turned on by turning on Donna's kid brother. If Bill was disappointed, he covered it well. He got up and said he needed to change the oil on his car and that he'd see me tomorrow.

I settled down with Agatha and hoped she would get the thoughts of my teenage seduction off my mind. She was not totally successful. My mind kept wandering down strange and erotic pathways, so it was a relief of sorts when Mrs. Nelson tapped on the door and told me there was a phone call while I was out shopping.

My heart stood still. It was John, for sure. He was worried about me and wanted me to come home. He had come to his senses and realized how much he needed me. The pounding of my pulse in my ears made it hard to make out at first what Mrs. Nelson was saying. It sounded like something about my mother. My mother called to say John was on his way down to L.A.? No, my mother was worried about me and hoped I was doing all right. Mrs. Nelson said she didn't tell her about my missing luggage since she didn't want to worry her further.

I muttered thanks for the message and tried to go back to my book or at least my sensual musings. I found I couldn't focus on anything but John. He wasn't missing me. He had Takiko. And who did I have? Some damn memories, that's all. Memories of a time so magical I was willing to do anything to get it back. Anything. If one day John would look at me the way Donna's brother had—seeing a Playboy centerfold that he loved and respected and would be faithful to—then whatever I had to do would be worth it.

9 The next morning I took a long, cool shower, then lifted my black lace panties from the towel bar where they had been drying overnight. I suddenly realized that Bill must have seen them, as he shared the bathroom with Donna. Again I felt that strange, tingling sensation I had the night before while displaying myself so casually in front of him. What was going on here? My father was the only male in our small household, and I never would have left my underwear hanging in the bathroom. He would have thought it was a sure sign I was on my way to utter debauchery.

Even after John and I were married I was always careful about casual nakedness, and I kept my personal things personal. I preferred undressing in the bathroom with the door locked. I was not a prude; I was just modest. So why did I feel a sense of pleasure now, thinking that Bill had seen my panties? Maybe touched them? Smelled them? I remembered something Oscar Wilde once said, "To be understood is to be found out." I decided not to think about it further.

When I picked up my beloved Magnin's dress I felt like throwing it in the restaurant dumpster. Day four! I had never in my life worn a dress for more than two days, and even that was rare. At least now I had a fresh new tee shirt to wear with it. I sniffed the deep neckline and the armholes. The smell of L'Aire du Temps overwhelmed me, but that was better than L'Aire du Sweat. I had heard that perfumes originated in France because French women bathed rarely, preferring the generous use of scent. *Vive la France!*

So feeling rather French, I ventured out into the restaurant and sat down to drink the cup of coffee Mrs. Nelson had poured for me. A few minutes later one of the regulars, whom the Nelsons had nicknamed "Short Stack," took the stool next to me. He called out his order to Mr. Nelson who was tending the grill. "Give me a short stack, will you Jerry?" he said. He turned to me. "Is that all you're having for breakfast, young lady? A cup of coffee? Why dontcha try the hotcakes here? That's what I have every morning and look at me. Healthy and fit. Betcha won't look like this when you're my age unless you change your breakfast habits."

"I'm sure you're right," I said, thinking, *You've just given me a good reason to stick to coffee and cigarettes. If it will keep me from having a gut flopping over my belt and more chins than a Chinese phonebook, I would eat fried weevils for breakfast.* Of course, I admitted to myself, it didn't really matter how much a man let himself go, there'd always be some woman grateful to wash his socks and keep him happy in bed.

Donna appeared in the doorway and put an end to my black thoughts. "Ready to go?" she asked brightly. "I've gassed up the car; and if we leave now, we'll have time to drive around a little before my lesson." I leaped up, eager to begin my mission. I was so happy I even turned to Short Stack and gave him a wink and a whiff of my generously applied cologne, saying "See you later, big boy," in my best Marilyn whisper. I exited to the sound of clucking from my robust counter partner.

We drove up into the Hollywood Hills, and I forgot my disenchantment with the Boulevard. Here were the bungalows and white stucco houses with red tile roofs that reeked of old Hollywood. Classic street lamps stood side by side with tall palm trees on the quiet winding streets. I loved it.

Donna pulled the car into the driveway of a lovely brick house with leaded glass windows and an arch-top front door with a huge iron knocker. As we stood waiting for someone to answer, I heard a cello and violin playing chamber music. At the same time I was overcome by the most extraordinary fragrance from a flowering shrub I had never seen before. I was falling under the spell of the Hollywood Hills.

We were welcomed into the house by Elena Peluso, a fair-haired woman of forty or so who seemed very much the diva. Her stance and her gestures spoke of years of training and stage experience, yet when she spoke, it was with a genuine friendliness and warmth. "I'm so glad to finally meet you, Karoline," she said as she grasped my hand with both of hers. "Donna has spoken of you so often I feel I know you already."

"Thank you. I feel the same about you. This is a great pleasure to me to meet you and see your home. I heard music a moment ago. Was that a recording, or live?"

"Ah, that is my husband and one of his old cronies who stopped by. Then Papa Hayden joined them. You know how it is when musicians get together. I understand your husband is a talented pianist."

"Yes, he is. That's why I'm here. To see what opportunities there might be for him."

"Why don't you come into the living room while Donna and I prepare for the lesson. My husband will be finished with his Hayden and friend soon, and perhaps the two of you can chat. He may be able to give you some suggestions."

Donna and Elena headed down the hall to the studio where the music had been coming from. I stepped into the living room and began to look it over. In front of the leaded corner windows stood a Steinway grand with a pile of music books on it. The piano dominated the book-lined room. There was a fireplace at the end of the room flanked by two overstuffed sofas. A French Impressionist painting hung over the mantel. Could it be a Matisse? The room gave off a sense of both comfort and culture. I hoped silently that someday John and I could have a home like this.

I heard two men saying goodbye to each other in the entryway and then a man walked into the room with his hand stretched out to me. He was slender and balding and slightly stooped, perhaps in his mid-fifties. "You must be Donna's friend, Karoline. I am Thomas Peluso," he said as he walked up to me and shook my hand. "Why don't we go to the kitchen and I will make you a café cappuccino?"

I had no idea what café cappuccino was, but I was more than ready to learn. He guided me to the rear of the house and into a small, cheery kitchen. He did not speak to me while preparing coffee in the elaborate espresso machine, I sat at a polished oak table and looked out into the pleasant back yard. I felt uncomfortable. Perhaps I was keeping him from some important work. After all, he was the conductor of the NBC Symphony Orchestra. He must have better things to do than make me whatever it was he was making me.

I could hear the sounds of Donna's warm-up exercises coming from the front of the house. "Everybody I know is here. Everybody I know is here," Donna sang over and over, as she progressed up the scales. I thought to myself, *No one I know is here; no one I know is here. How well do I even know Donna?* A wave of homesickness washed over me. I was a stranger in a strange land.

"So your husband and Donna performed together on radio in San Luis Obispo while he was at Camp Roberts?" Mr. Peluso said, as he placed a cup of blue-black coffee in front of me. "Donna has spoken much about your friendship and your husband's musicianship."

Now I was on familiar ground. I didn't even feel the need to ask for cream. "Yes. John is planning to join me here when his contract expires on his current engagement," I lied. John had no contract at the Congo Room. "I'm sure there are a lot of opportunities for a pianist here."

"A lot, no. Some, perhaps," said my host. "I am sure he would have no trouble finding work in one of the small lounges here, but I assume you have something larger in mind. Many people come to Hollywood looking for fame and fortune, but so few find it. Alas, it is not even necessarily those with the most talent who make it. It is so often a matter of luck, timing, who you know and many things other than talent. Perhaps for a musician it is a little better, as they have a talent that is easy to demonstrate. For actors it is not so easy. In the movies it is more important how the camera sees you than how gifted your acting ability is. Very few of the great stage actors become successful movie actors. But, I digress. We are speaking of musicians. Tell me a little about your husband."

This was an opportunity I had not expected. I was alone in the kitchen of an important man in the industry. His "many are called, but few are chosen" speech had not fazed me. I had heard it before from many drama coaches. My situation was different. John was already successful. At least in Seattle.

"I really appreciate getting your advice," I said. "My husband has played with bands, with small combos, and alone. I think he is at his best doing solo work, which is what he's doing now. Of course, the radio show with Donna was really popular."

"Ah, yes, radio. I think, my dear, we are seeing the end of the radio as we knew it. Of course, there will always be a demand for radio. What would we do without it in our cars? But radio is becoming a medium for news and recorded music. Dramatic entertainment is nearly over, along with the musical variety shows. People laugh when they remember tap dancing on radio, not to mention that well-known ventriloquist who didn't have to worry about moving his lips when he performed on radio. The future of entertainment is in television. Before the decade is over, television will have overtaken movies as the most popular form of entertainment in this country."

"But I love radio. It's so personal," I argued. "When I was away from home during John's army stint I would have been terribly lonely without Arthur Godfrey and the soaps to listen to. Not only that, but I'm a radio actress myself. Or was. While I was in school I appeared regularly on local radio shows. I'm even a member of AFRA," I said proudly.

"I love radio too, but did you know that AFRA is now AFTRA? The American Federation of Radio and TELEVISION Artists? For people like you, me and perhaps your husband, there will be little or no work in radio. All the big radio shows are going to TV: Jack Benny, Milton Berle, Bob Hope, Red Skelton. Milton was one of the first to go to TV, and he is much more popular than he ever was on radio. Lucille Ball and Desi Arnaz are much bigger stars from their TV show than they ever were in the movies. Their production company Desilu is making them very wealthy. Even the movie studios are now producing films just for television."

"Okay, I understand what you're saying, but there will always be a need for musicians, won't there?"

"Not as much. Few shows use live orchestra anymore. Background music is recorded and for the shows that use bands, they are not featured. For instance, Skitch Henderson, a fine musician, is wasted in what he does on the Steve Allen show. The recording industry will survive and grow, but the performer will need to establish himself in concerts or public appearances before he will be in demand as a recording artist. This, of course, is my opinion."

"But what about Liberace? He came out of nowhere and now he's a big hit on TV. He is known more for his flashy costumes than his musicianship. My husband is better-looking and plays better piano. He could be another Liberace."

"No, I don't think so. There is only room for one. Liberace is a novelty and that only happens once. Take this example. You have a friend who is a very attractive lady and also a terrific swimmer. Could she be another Esther Williams? No, there is room for only one. And after Esther retires? Still too late, as the public is tired of plots centered around a swimmer. Was there another Sonja Henie to move into her spotlight when she retired? Probably, but the public was tired of this plot line too. Now I'm sure your husband will be able to find work here. The nightclubs have house bands. Gerry Gallien has the band at Ciro's, and he is a fine pianist. Also, there is always a demand for personable pianists to play at piano bars and there is some work at the studios for off-screen musicians. Perhaps the future is rock'n'roll. As much as it pains me to say this, that is where music seems to be headed. Unless your husband decides to take up the electric guitar and gyrate his hips I don't see the opportunities much better here than in your home town."

This was not what I wanted to hear. This couldn't be right. "What about Quincy Jones?" I implored. "He's doing well and he doesn't...well, speaking frankly, he doesn't have John's looks and charm."

"Ah, but from what I understand, he has superb musicianship. He is a very talented composer and is starting to be in demand for scoring music for movies. That is a totally different matter."

Having added another blow to my hopes, Mr. Peluso got up from his chair and poured me another cup of his wicked brew. *That's right,* I thought, *ruin my day and then make sure I don't sleep a wink tonight either.* "But what about your plans for yourself?" he asked me. "I understand you studied drama in college and you say you have done professional radio acting? I would be happy to arrange an appointment with Phil Berle to see if there is something he can do for you personally. He is Milton's brother and vice-president at NBC. He is also a very nice man. There are still a number of dramatic radio shows on the air. You have a very distinctive voice. He may be able to get you some work. Please call me if you would like to meet with Phil. Also, I would be glad to meet with your husband when he arrives. It is always a pleasure to meet another musician."

I thanked him profusely for his kindness, even though I felt deeply disappointed by his remarks about John's Hollywood future. I thought his offer to have me meet with Phil Berle was merely a gesture to remove some of the sting of his earlier remarks. I had no intention of meeting with Milton Berle's brother. Not unless he could help me help John.

Our conversation moved to other topics that were less personal, like politics and smog. He was a stimulating conversationalist and I was actually disappointed when

Donna's lesson was over and she came to the kitchen to collect me. We said our goodbyes, and as we were leaving I was overcome with sadness. It wasn't the discouraging words I had listened to in the kitchen, but the sight of these two happy people standing side by side in the doorway waving goodbye to us. *Why do they have a happy marriage and I don't? It just isn't fair,* I said to myself.

Forty-five minutes later Donna and I were cruising down Hollywood Boulevard. I don't know what I was expecting, but this wasn't it. What I saw was a fairly typical main street of a small town lined with shoe stores, coffee shops and Thrifty Drug Stores. The only indication that it was not Peoria was the presence of several lavish movie palaces. The most notable, of course, was Grauman's Chinese Theater. Coffee Dan's and Aldo's had trendy signs, but it took only a glance to see that they were merely little hamburger joints. The Hollywood Roosevelt Hotel loomed tall on this street of mostly one-story buildings, but here again there was nothing to be impressed by. I caught a glimpse of the Broadway Hollywood department store at the famous corner of Hollywood and Vine—another yawner.

A little farther up Vine was the new Capitol Records Tower. It was round and a few stories high, but hardly a landmark. The only building of any interest was a rambling, bungalow style building that looked vaguely familiar. Donna said it was the old Hollywood Hotel, now closed and doomed to be torn down to make way for more boring stores like Karl's Shoes or the Thrifty Drug Store. What a loss, I thought. It had been the scene of many famous Hollywood parties and brawls in the heydays of the 1930's. It had been used in the background of many movies from that era also. I felt a sense of loss. How I wished I could have seen Hollywood then. No smog, no traffic, just orange groves and Rudolph Valentino.

But when we passed the intersection of Hollywood and Vine and I saw Schwab's Drug Store on the corner, I felt a surge of excitement. *This was it! Something of the Hollywood legend remains. Schwab's! Everybody has heard of Schwab's.*

"Stop the car," I pleaded with Donna. "I've got to see Schwab's. If only I had my camera I'd get you to take my picture sitting on a stool at the counter."

"Cool down," Donna replied. "This isn't THE Schwab's. This one doesn't even have a soda fountain. The Schwab's where Lana Turner was discovered is the one at Sunset and Laurel Canyon."

This was a serious letdown. Every teenager knew the story of the young Lana Turner. She was wearing her snug fitting sweater and sitting at the soda fountain in Schwab's when a talent scout or somebody spotted her and made her a star. It was part of the American Dream. Now I find out that this legendary event didn't even happen in Hollywood. It took place on Sunset Boulevard where the Strip starts. What will my next let-down be?

10 It was lunch time when we left the Pelusos'. I realized that all I'd had for breakfast was coffee and cigarettes. My mom's voice echoed in my head, *Breakfast is the most important meal of the day.* I never subscribed to this theory myself. Breakfast is anything you put in your mouth before lunch. It has no social connotations like lunch and dinner. You do not dress for breakfast. You do not even need to sit down. Lunch, now, can be an occasion that even eclipses dinner if it's eaten in the right places. With this thought in mind I said to Donna, "I don't know about you, but I'm starved. Let's have lunch. Pick someplace posh. And it's on my favorite drunk driver."

"Well, you can get a pretty good burger at the Carolina Pines, Jr." Donna replied.

"Hey, we can do better than a burger, can't we?" I said. "How about someplace where we might see celebrities, or at least interesting people. And remember, I'm spending my pain and suffering money, so let me splurge."

Donna laughed, "Well, since you put it that way, there's a place I've always wanted to try called Frascati's. It's probably pretty expensive, though."

"Sounds good to me. Is it in the Valley?"

"Hardly. It's way too hip for the Valley. It's at Sunset and

Laurel Canyon where the Strip starts."

"I love it already. Let's hit it."

A short time later we pulled into the parking lot of the very European looking restaurant. As we walked toward the entrance, I dawdled along admiring the expensive foreign cars that proliferated. They had to belong to people in "The Business," I thought. I hoped I would recognize somebody inside.

"Hurry up," Donna urged. "You've got to see the fountain. My dad said it's a copy of a famous one in Brussels."

Sure enough, as we approached the shrubbery-choked entrance we saw a statue of a little naked boy urinating endlessly into a basin. A terrace for outside dining overlooked a beautifully landscaped little garden with the fountain as its centerpiece. The simple architecture of the restaurant with its lush paintings contrasted sharply with the garishness of Hollywood Boulevard. I commented on this to Donna as we stood looking at the fountain.

"The saying goes that where Hollywood ends good taste begins. The Sunset Strip starts here and ends at the entrance to Beverly Hills," Donna explained.

"You mean the Strip is a kind of DMZ?" I asked, the terms of the Korean War still fresh in my mind.

"Actually, the Strip was kind of wild at one time," Donna said. "There was a kind of Mob war here a few years ago. In fact, Mickey Cohen, who took over the Bugsy Siegel mob after Bugsy was killed, was shot and wounded at Sherry's Bar just down the street."

"Now I'm really intrigued," I said. "Mickey Cohen did time in the prison on McNeil Island, my childhood home. Maybe I'll run into him and we can talk about his life as an inmate and my time now as an out-mate."

"Yeah, I'm sure he'd love that, especially if it was your

dad who locked him up. But, hey, we'd better go in and see if we can get a table without a reservation."

As we left the fountain I got to thinking how the Seattle City Council would react if a fountain like this were installed in front of a city restaurant. The whole town would be in an uproar. Churches would call for prayer vigils. PTAs would have emergency meetings. The Seattle Times would print an editorial with the words "Sodom and Gomorrah" appearing at least twice. No wonder Sir Thomas Beecham, who conducted the Seattle Symphony Orchestra for a few seasons back in the forties, referred to our city as a "cultural dustbin." Of course, he said that once he was safely back in London.

We lined up behind a group of well-dressed people in front of the reception desk. I thought that, like Sir Thomas, I was indeed fortunate to have moved away from the artistically constipated city that was Seattle. You couldn't even get a glass of wine or beer on Sundays! Barbaric! Still, I had to admit the statue was a trifle disgusting.

"That statue reminded me that I need to use the lady's room," Donna said. "Do you mind seeing if you can get us a table?"

"Of course not. Leave it to me," I replied, with fake confidence. I could see that most of the tables were taken, and those that were not had reserved signs on them.

"Good afternoon, Miss," said the tall impeccably dressed host. "The name on your reservation?"

Without missing a beat, I said, "It may be under my name, Karoline Morrison, or perhaps under Hughes. Howard Hughes. A table for two." He glanced at the reservation book, looked up at me, and then down at the book again.

"I would like a table out on the terrace, please. Mr. Hughes prefers to be seated outside whenever possible."

There was a five-second pause and then he sighed, picked up two menus and led me to a table on the terrace. He removed the reserved sign, put down the menus and said, "Enjoy your lunch, Ma'am." He knew he'd been had, but he couldn't take a chance. I felt instantly better about my ability to cope with the fast track, even if I was from a dustbin.

The tables on the terrace were shielded by canvas umbrellas advertising European mineral waters. *What a kick,* I thought. *Sitting outside, protected from the sun by umbrellas that spoke French. Not to mention the fact that it was mid-October.* The table was set with linen, silver and crystal. I had never eaten *al fresco* in such style. I was accustomed to paper plates and plastic forks. If there was a tablecloth, it was always red-checkered. I had no idea what the bill would be for this experience in Southern California up-scale dining, but I knew it would be worth it. A fleeting moment of guilt made me wish John were with me instead of Donna. But I told myself that without Donna and her family I would be very much alone.

I checked out the people seated around me. It was easy to tell the tourists from the natives. The tourists were the people who were looking at everybody else and whispering to each other. The natives were oblivious to everything and everybody, and they all wore sunglasses. I quickly whipped a pair of dark glasses out of my purse, grateful for the fact that I had picked up a pair during one of my shopping forays in Encino. I felt like Nanook of the North passing himself off as a hip Angelino. Actually, I thought I was doing a fairly good job. Hadn't I just locked down a table?

The waiter brought me a glass of wine of undetermined origin. I had asked him for something white, cold and not sweet. As I spoke these words I realized it sounded like a straight line, and half expected the waiter to answer something like, "Madam, you are speaking of my wife!" Fortunately he merely nodded and returned with the glass I was not about to sample. How wonderfully decadent it was to be drinking wine at 12:15 in the afternoon!

I placed the linen napkin in my lap thinking that it really didn't matter whether I spilled lunch on my dress or not. It would have to undergo serious cleaning anyway. If only I could have been wearing one of my new, high-fashion outfits! For an instant I had an extra-sensory flash in which I saw a Southern Belle wearing one of my dresses. And it was my favorite, the white lace number with the low cut bodice and full skirt enhanced by an enormous crinoline petticoat. It was a dress Scarlett would have killed for, sexy and virginal at the same time

"How did you get such a great table?" Donna said as she sat down. "I heard the host turning away people who didn't have reservations."

"You don't want to know. However, if anyone should ask, you're Howard Hughes' personal representative. He couldn't make our meeting."

"Lady, I have a feeling you're going to do okay here." With that, Donna picked up one of the huge menus and began a serious study of it.

I looked at the top of her head, which was all I could see of her from behind the menu. She was no longer the barely-out-of-high-school girl I had known in Paso Robles. In the year and a half since I had last seen her, her thick chestnut brown hair and fair skin had flourished. Weight had always been her bugaboo. I remembered her cursing the fact that she had inherited her aunt's ample hips and thighs instead of her mother's trim, athletic figure. Now with dieting and long full skirts, the heritage of Auntie Lou was scarcely visible.

"Donna you really look terrific," I said as she put down the menu. "I love how you're wearing your hair. You look like a young Susan Hayward."

She grinned at me in gratitude. "Seriously? I really tried to improve my appearance when we moved here. Partly, I guess, it was because my dad keeps telling me I can be a great opera star."

"So, tell me about your career plans," I said. "Is singing opera what you're shooting for?"

"Ask my dad," Donna sighed. "His lifelong dream is for me to be an opera singer. In fact he hates it when I help out in the restaurant. He says once a waitress, always a waitress. Anyway, I'm grateful for all the money he's spent over the years on my lessons, but I know I don't have what it takes for opera and I haven't got the nerve to tell him."

I signaled to our waiter and motioned for him to bring Donna a glass of wine like mine. This conversation was taking a turn for the serious, and we both needed fortification. "But you have such a beautiful voice," I said. "You can't just waste it."

"Even if I had the voice for opera, I don't have the stamina and the dedication. I'd love to do movie musicals, but they're on the way out. Thomas says that Shirley Jones is probably the last of the big musical stars who didn't come from Broadway."

"So why not try New York? I know there are so many musical theatres there, not just Broadway."

"I guess the real reason is that it just doesn't really excite me. If I could be any singer in the world, I'd like to be Lena Horne."

"I love Lena too, but she's black!"

"I think it's easier when you're black. I mean as far as

nightclubs and records are concerned. You don't have to be beautiful. Oh, sure, Lena and Dorothy Dandridge are knockouts, but Ella Fitzgerald, Sarah Vaughn, Billie Holliday, and Ethel Waters made it without being beautiful."

I didn't want to argue the point, but I thought about Marian Anderson not being allowed to perform for a women's group in Washington D.C. And the hotel that drained its swimming pool after pianist Hazel Scott took a dip in it. *No, it never could be easy to be a black performer.*

"Anyway," Donna continued. "The best I can hope for is to be a church soloist and one day give lessons."

Our conversation fell into old familiar patterns as we lunched. We observed the other patrons and created scenarios about them. One couple was in the midst of an affair, but the man was planning to dump her. (I was an expert in this area.) Notice how she has to light her own cigarette? He didn't even reach for his Ronson when she picked up her pack of Chesterfields. A sure sign. The older man so attentive to the young woman seated opposite him? Obviously his children's nanny. She had the look. He met her on a recent business trip to Europe and started an affair. Now he has brought her to his Beverly Hills mansion under the guise of an *au pair*. A few tables away a stocky, dark-haired man appeared to be reading the *L.A. Examiner*, but he actually was keeping a watchful eye on the man with the *au pair*. Definitely a private eye hired by the wife.

On and on we went. Even our waiter did not escape our speculation. His accent was unquestionably fake. He was working here hoping to be the next Louis Jourdan. When we ran out of people, we moved on to the little boy in the fountain. Donna referred to him as "Little Peter. " I pondered how he could be made acceptable in Seattle. Donna suggested a diaper or training pants. I said that no, even that was not enough. The water had to come from some other body opening, maybe dribbling down from his nose.

We kept laughing and sipping coffee as we leaned back in our chairs. I realized how much I enjoyed Donna's company and how much I had missed her. Even though I was married and a little older, we had so much in common, especially a zany sense of humor. Another plus was that Donna was the only female I knew who seemed to be immune to John's charms. She liked him and respected his talent, but there were no moon-eyed glances or flirtatious overtures that others always gave him.

"Okay," I said, reopening our earlier conversation. "So you don't know how to tell your dad that the life of a diva is not for you. Yet, you've got to do it sometime."

"I know. I've talked to Elena about it. I thought maybe she could say something to my dad, but she says it has to come from me. I feel so guilty about the money, too. My dad has worked hard all his life, but never with big financial rewards. He wants me to have the success he didn't have."

"Well," I said, "at least he has your brother. There's a line in Twelfth Night that I identify with. 'I am all the daughters of my father's house and all the brothers too.' I let my dad down by being born a girl. I'm always trying to make my dad proud of me. Even now. If I can help John be successful I'll be making three people happy—my dad, John and myself."

"You know, you sound like my mother in a way." Donna commented. "I mean, all she needs to be happy is for my father to be happy. He is her total life. I don't think I'd ever want to be like that. My parents are together morning, noon and night and yet they never get on each others nerves."

These words shocked me a little. Was I really like Mrs.

Nelson? Happy to be the traditional wife, mother, helpmate? No ambitions for myself? No separate identity? I had never thought of myself quite that way before. Actually Eva Peron was more my role model. She was an enormous help to her husband while at the same time she became a cultural icon that eventually eclipsed her husband's image. Not that I wanted that, but Eva's life seemed far more appealing to me than Mrs. Nelson's.

At this point in my reflections the waiter produced the bill. While I settled up, Donna excused herself to call home and say she would be home in plenty of time for the dinner shift. I looked at the bill wondering idly if the total was in francs or dollars because, written across the bottom, was *Merci beaucoup, Jacques*. I left a pile of bills and a generous tip. After all, Howard Hughes was a very wealthy man.

I went to the lady's room where Donna was just hanging up the phone. Since we still had time before she needed to be back, I suggested we drive down the fabled Strip. This, however, proved to be an idea for another day. Donna had unexpected news from home. Her mother reported that my long-awaited luggage had finally arrived—and so had John.

11 We drove back to Encino as fast as I could get Donna to go. My still jangled car nerves were temporarily on hold. Not once did I press my foot against the floor board in a futile effort to slow the car. I longed for my father's siren and flashing light. Donna knew very well that it was not my longing for fresh clothing that made me beg her to hurry. The main attraction was John, not low-heeled shoes.

I sat back watching the miles whiz past, puzzling over why John had arrived on the scene so soon. Did he miss me? Was he ready for a reconciliation? I had envisioned being alone for a couple of months, at least while I settled in and made my connections. Then he'd join me and together we'd examine our relationship and perhaps renew our wedding vows in some little chapel by the sea. Just the sort of thing Sand and Chopin might have done. Anyway, if he was ready now, why not? Maybe the past months were just a temporary aberration that we would one day look back on and laugh about. Whatever motivated him, I was breathless in anticipation to be with him again in California, where we'd once been so happy.

After what seemed like hours, we finally pulled up to the restaurant. A large white Lincoln with Washington plates was parked off to one side. *Could it be his? Even if he was*

*driving an old, pre-war Chevy, I wouldn't care. He was here
and that was all that mattered.*

I ran ahead of Donna, somehow managing not to turn
my ankle in the deep gravel of the parking lot. I entered
the restaurant, my eyes quickly sweeping over the small
dining room. He was in a corner booth, a cup of coffee in
front of him and a cigarette smoldering in an ashtray next
to it. He was wearing the brown leather bomber jacket that
I had given him for Christmas two years ago. With his two
days' growth of beard and bloodshot eyes, he was the most
beautiful sight I had ever seen. I slid into the booth beside him.

"Are you new in town, soldier?" I asked in my best, husky,
Lauren Bacall voice.

"As a matter of fact, I am. Think you could show me
some interesting sights?" he replied in his deep, rich John
Morrison voice.

"I can show you sights you've never dreamed of," I
murmured.

Donna walked over carrying a pot of coffee and a cup.
As she filled the cup she had placed in front of me and
gave John a warm up, she said, "That's the worst dialogue
I've heard since I watched an old Mae West movie on the
late, late show. Why don't you two finish your coffee and
then John can lie down and take a nap. Mom said you
drove straight through and you must be really beat. We've
given you guys Billy's room; that is, if you can take the smell
of old gym socks. Billy's going to spend a couple of nights
at a buddy's house. When you're ready for dinner just let
the maitre d' know. I'll warn you, though, Dad's trainee
cook is on tonight, so the house special will probably be
something like pot roast smothered in chili and topped
with Velveeta—his version of Tex-Mex."

"Well, as much as I hate to miss that, my plan was to

take the family out to dinner," John replied, snuffing out his cigarette. "You pick the place and make sure it's expensive. That's how we get our revenge on the drunk driver."

"Great idea," I echoed. "What a pleasure it'll be to treat your parents after all they've done for me." I felt a twinge of guilt that I hadn't done something like this already for the Nelsons; but when it came to charm, I was no match for John.

While John showered, I changed the linen on Billy's bed. My luggage had been piled outside in the hallway. I rummaged through one of the bags and pulled out a clingy, satin robe that wrapped and tied at the waist. While I was at it, I checked just to be sure that my ivory lace dress was there and showed no signs of use. In fact, all my luggage appeared to be there and in good shape, considering all the miles it had traveled.

I sat down on the bed after removing my "uniform," as I had come to think of my black knit dress. With the black satin robe thrown over my black lace merry widow I thought I must look pretty sexy. I remembered a famous picture of Rita Hayworth. Was it on the cover of *Life?* Anyway, she was posed in a nightgown, kneeling on a bed and looking up through her hair. I rejected trying to copy that, as my hair had not yet grown out enough to get the same effect. Then I remembered Marilyn's calendar sprawl. I tried that pose; but since Billy's bed had a decided sag in the middle, that wasn't workable either.

I was still practicing other poses when John appeared, shaved and showered and wearing only after-shave lotion and a towel. This was far sexier than anything I had thought of so far. The next couple hours were like our wedding night, only so much better. I realized how much more you appreciate something you believe you have lost, but then recover. When we later joined the family for our dinner outing, I felt like a newlywed again. Maybe, I thought, it was worth all the misery of the past months to experience such special happiness. And the icing on the cake was that John seemed as happy as I was.

All six of us piled into the spacious Lincoln—John, Donna and I in the front and the Nelsons and Billy in the back. We were all in a party mood. I loved the car. It might not have had the Elizabeth Taylor pedigree; but, to me, the fact that it belonged to John gave it even more distinction. Our destination was the famous Sportsman's Lodge. I was delighted with the choice. All through my teen years of reading *Movie Life* and *Photoplay* magazines, I saw famous Hollywood couples dining at the Sportsman's Lodge. Now we were joining that panoply of distinguished guests.

We had a wonderful evening. I was so happy and excited I couldn't recall afterward a thing I ate. To tell the truth, I would have been just as excited if we had gone to Bob's Big Boy in Burbank for a burger.

Mr. Nelson caught John up on what had happened in Paso Robles after Camp Roberts closed. Even though the permanent residents of Paso Robles had long resented the intrusion of the Army and the camp-follower wives, the departure of the thousands of personnel and families threw the little town into a general depression. Over a third of the businesses along Oak Street closed. The Nelsons had made enough money, however, to be able to get out of town and reestablish themselves in Encino. We all drank a toast to Paso Robles, the Seventh Armored Division, and the Koreans—both South and North. We had survived and actually prospered as a result of the conflict.

Only Billy was unusually quiet. He said little to John and never looked at me. At first I wondered if he resented having to give up his room to us. Maybe a little, but mostly I thought it was that I had been an unattached female, but now was clearly a wife. And not a poor discarded wife either, but one who inspired her husband to drive fifteen hundred miles nonstop to be with her.

After dinner we strolled around the beautiful grounds. Although we were well into autumn, the evening felt warm to my northern blood. The trout-filled ponds reflected little twinkling lights adorning the surrounding trees. A full harvest moon shone down on the lush landscaping. The scene reminded me of old sheet music covers propped up on my aunt's piano. But the title for this scene would have to be "Moon over the Valley" rather than "The Valley of the Moon," which was one of my aunt's favorites back in the thirties. Hey! Moon over the Valley? Moon Valley? Shine on Valley Moon? John could write the music and I could write the lyrics. We could be another Comden and Green. In Southern California, anything is possible.

I could have strolled the grounds for hours, holding John's arm and humming a nameless tune. John looked very much a celebrity in his white cashmere dinner jacket that we had purchased as an important investment for him a few months before. I was wearing my show-stopping ivory lace dress with its long matching stole trailing from my shoulders. I would have felt like a ballerina had I been wearing flat shoes. Instead, I felt like a bride.

After dropping Billy off at his friend's house, we returned to the darkened restaurant where we continued our reunion party in the family quarters. John played the old Baldwin grand and Donna sang. Mr. Nelson sat with his eyes closed, enraptured by his daughter's clear soprano voice. I felt a pang of sympathy for him as I remembered Donna's confession earlier in the day. Still, I thought that people should allow others to follow their own paths and not let their own ambitions affect someone else's life. I never for a moment thought that this applied to John and me. Mrs. Nelson brought out a fresh pot of coffee and said she and her husband would say goodnight, but encouraged us "kids" to stay up as late as we wanted. Donna did not have a breakfast shift to worry about.

Donna, John and I talked on for another hour or so, carefully avoiding any mention of the marital problems. I knew Donna was dying to know what had caused John to follow me down so quickly; but then, so was I. Had he ended his affair with Takiko? Had she ended it? Not likely. I felt I would know the answer soon enough. Tonight I wanted to savor the pleasure of the moment and the fact that he was here with me where he belonged

We finally called it a night and went to our, or rather, Billy's room. John told me as we started to undress that we should pack up and move into a hotel in Hollywood tomorrow. I started to object, thinking we weren't ready, that we needed more time. He said, "You've imposed on the Nelson's long enough. It's time we got off on our own."

Well, I thought, *since you put it that way!* So I agreed to an early start in the morning to look for a temporary place until we found a house or apartment. Fortunately, I had little packing to do, since my clothing was still in bags and suitcases. We curled up together in the hammocky intimacy imposed by Billy's bed and for the second time in a few hours explored the passion I thought I might never experience again.

The next morning Donna tapped on our door about ten a.m. with two steaming cups of coffee, asking if we were decent. "Barely," I replied. "But join us anyway." With Donna perched on a chair by Billy's desk and John and me gulping down the strong, delicious coffee, we told Donna that we were going to check out of the "Nelson Bed-Breakfast-Lunch-Dinner and Snacks" place. I could tell she was disappointed, but I assured her that I would call her frequently and that we should get together in Hollywood every week for lunch after her lesson. "We'll do a different place each week starting at the Beverly Hills Hotel and working our way down the Strip. I'll make reservations under various producers' names, so we'll always get the best tables," I joked.

"Well, there goes my diet," Donna replied. "If I end up looking like my Auntie Lou I'll know who to blame. Just keep me in mind when you guys hit the big time. Remember, I knew you when." With that, Donna went out and left us to ourselves.

I resisted John's amorous advances as I began to pile my makeup and nightgown into my overnight case. For me, mornings were a time to ease oneself into the reality of the day, not a time for sexual encounters. "Last one ready for breakfast's a rotten egg," I taunted as I escaped his lunge for my thigh when I headed for the bathroom down the hall.

Finally, packed and breakfasted we said goodbye and thanks to the Nelsons and were quickly underway. I looked back at the little restaurant under the big oak tree and knew how much I would miss that family. I'd even miss "Short Stack." As we headed down the highway toward Hollywood I discovered a sense of vulnerability I had not known before. I was leaving my home base for a second time. The Nelsons were surrogate parents and soon they would be almost as far away as my own parents, if not in distance, in guidance and protection. Even though John was by my side, I was unable to forget his rejection of me and all the pain he had allowed to enter my life.

I still didn't know where we were in our marriage. Last

night was a dream, a fantasy come true. I was able for a time to forget the loneliness I had endured. I could pretend there was no Takiko as we strolled in the moonlight. Our lovemaking was more intense, more passionate than ever. But now, in the cool, dim hours of the morning I found myself asking questions I dared not ask John. At least not now. Not yet.

12 As we made our way through traffic on Ventura Boulevard, I decided to tell John about my conversation with Thomas Peluso, leaving out the discouraging parts. I told him that Thomas would be happy to meet with him and give him some directions to pursue.

"That's great, sweetheart," John replied. "It sounds like you've made a terrific contact there. I'm anxious to meet him. We've got lots of time, though. Remember, I just got into town yesterday. Why don't we take a few days to relax and enjoy ourselves? You know, you're looking really sexy? I don't know what's been going on with you, but I get a hard-on just looking at you. Here feel this."

With that he took my hand and put it between his legs. No questions about it, he was aroused. I was pleased, but still a part of me asked what was going on. Why is he so hot for me now, when just a week ago I was as exciting as yesterday's mashed potatoes. I pulled my hand back and asked, "By the way, what happened to you the day I left? You had promised to take me to the airport."

"Oh, gosh, I'm sorry about that, baby. I stayed out a little too late the night before and overslept. Besides, I knew your dad would be happy to take you."

Sure, I thought, with the familiar taste of bitterness

in my mouth. *You probably went to the Wah Mee Club in Chinatown for some after-hours gambling. Takiko was with you, and you never gave me a second thought. Let my dad help me out? I'm his responsibility, not yours?* With a supreme effort I pushed these renegade thoughts back into the dark corners of my mind where they would starve to death. I refused to nourish them. John was here now, and my plan was ready to begin. That was all that mattered.

"Where do you think we should stay while we look for an apartment?" I asked, lighting cigarettes for both of us.

"A friend of mine in Seattle told me a good place in Hollywood is a hotel off the Boulevard in the residential area. The name of it is The Casbah."

"Oooh, 'Come weez me to ze Casbah,'" I said excitedly. "I'll bet it's very Moroccan. You know, white stucco, Moorish turrets, belly dancers as bellhops. It sounds like our kind of place!"

We got directions at the gas station on Sunset and found the Casbah. What a letdown! It was a large, grim building made of gray concrete. I would have thought we were in the wrong place if it were not for the sign over the entry that proclaimed "Casbah" in pseudo-Arabic script.

"Can this monstrosity be it? "I asked in amazement. "Other than the sign it's about as Moroccan as Alcatraz. In fact it looks like Alcatraz without the charm."

I was especially disappointed, since I had spotted so many wonderful examples of Spanish/Moorish architecture on my sightseeing trips with Donna. Whenever we drove along Sunset Boulevard, I would look up at the hillside at the twenties-era mansions of white stucco and red tile surrounded by exotic landscaping. It wasn't hard to imagine Norma Desmond inside one of those magnificent places— reclining on a satin chaise with a long, ivory cigarette holder to her lips and listening to tango music on a Victrola. Even the run-down Garden of Allah, where rumors said Errol Flynn kept a cottage hide-a-way, was beautiful in its decay. But this ugly place?

It had been built in the 'fifties, which I decided future generations would call the "Dark Ages of Architecture." Surely, the same man who did the prison at KGB headquarters in Moscow designed this one too. The no-nonsense palms that stood on either side of the entrance looked like prison guards. If I hadn't harbored so much nostalgia for my childhood on McNeil Island, I don't think I could have considered staying there. Actually, the penitentiary at McNeil with its soft hues and woodsy setting exuded much more warmth than this place.

John begged me to give it a chance. "Let's go ahead and check in," he said. "We can always move after a day or two. I'm still tired from the long drive down and I'd like to relax. Maybe it looks better from the inside, and there's supposed to be a pool. Why don't you go in and register while I park."

"Okay," I said, reluctantly. "But if I'm not back in ten minutes, call a good lawyer and try to spring me."

I entered the small lobby and approached the check-in desk, where a pale, slender young man greeted me. He didn't resemble either Charles Boyer or Tony Martin, who played the infamous Pepe le Moko in the two Casbah movies. But he was friendly. I told him I was looking for a room for my husband and myself. He quoted rates that sounded reasonable and added that if we stayed for seven days, we could have a weekly rate at 15% savings. My distaste for the hotel fought it out with my love of a bargain. Thriftiness won.

I signed the register; and, as I waited for the keys, I glanced toward the dining room and bar. Believe me, Rick from *Casablanca* would never allow his name to be attached to this bar. But if Sing Sing decided to add a cocktail lounge to their facility, this one could serve as a model—bare and institutional.

Carl, according to his name tag, handed me two keys and told me the rooms were "poolside." He told me he hoped we would enjoy our stay and to let him know if we needed anything more. I wanted to say, "Yes, Carl. I need mystery, intrigue and foreign atmosphere." But I said nothing, since I knew he meant "more towels."

I went back the way I came in and told John we were checked in and gave him the room number. I returned to the lobby and followed Carl's directions to our room. I opened the door that led to the inside of the hotel complex and found myself outside again. The chlorine fumes rising from a rectangular pool assailed my senses. A few unoccupied lounges and metal chairs were scattered haphazardly around. Although this was not the Beverly Hills Hotel, it did have a pool. How many motels in Seattle could make that statement? None, that's how many.

Trying to convince myself that we had made a good choice, I turned to look back at the building and begin the search for our room. My first reaction, as I saw the building from the back side was, "Help!" If the outside of the Casbah looked like a prison, the inside looked like a cellblock. This architect was really into his theme. All of the rooms above ground level opened onto the walkway with heavy metal bars and a security railing. The building was ell-shaped, and the walkways traversed both wings without a break. Access was from metal stairwells at the corners. Since our room was minimum security, I looked up again at the grim walkways. Where were the guards? At lunch? I had a wild urge to run along the walkways, pounding on doors and shouting, "Now's your chance. Escape while you can!" I found our room and entered cautiously. It may not have been as stark as a cell, but it was just as boring, with Danish style furniture and orange shag carpeting. On the wall opposite the bed hung a print of Gaugin's "Women of Tahiti." I wondered if the decorator thought these Polynesian women were Algerian. I tried the bed. Yup, hard as The Rock-Alcatraz. I heard John outside the door struggling with the luggage and ended my metaphor to help him. After all, most of the luggage was mine.

The grim surroundings that had so offended my sensibilities that first day developed a certain charm in the days that followed. For one thing, we were never there, except to sleep, make love, and change clothes. These were golden days followed by purple nights. We seemed never to get enough of each other's bodies. John's erotic inventiveness had risen to new heights, and I was borne along on a tide of unimaginable passion. If Takiko was in some way responsible for this, I didn't care. I was close to feeling gratitude.

In the everyday world I occasionally visited, I found time to take my Magnin's "uniform" to a nearby dry cleaners. I also deposited my insurance money in a Hollywood Boulevard branch of the Bank of America. Of course, I brought back a signature card for John to be a signer on the account. Even if it had not been required by law, I would have done it anyway. We were again an entity.

Our days were spent doing things like visiting Griffith Park and the zoo. We went to the planetarium and watched a group of teens there acting out the famous scene from *Rebel without a Cause*. All of the guys wanted to be James Dean. Nobody wanted to be Sal Mineo. We drove to the beach at Santa Monica to see the sea and see the action. We cruised on up to Malibu and wondered what the big deal was.

On our third day in Hollywood we reached Kenny Miller. He was delighted to hear from us and ready to be our guide to the hot spots on the Sunset Strip. We picked him up at his place in the Hollywood Hills and headed for action. We did the Mocambo and Ciro's. We enjoyed being insulted by Don Rickles at the Crescendo. The next night we picked up where we had left off: Fifi D'Orsay's, the Interlude, and then Stan Getz at the jazz club on the Boulevard. The fifth night of our stay we ventured out alone without Kenny as our guide and mentor. I wanted us to have dinner at Frascati's so John could see the infamous fountain. I relayed all of Donna's and my comments about the boy sculpture, and John added an idea of his own. He suggested that if such a fountain were ever proposed for Seattle, it would come about only after a contest was held. The boy who could pee the farthest would be forever immortalized in the centerpiece. I agreed. Seattle was truly a city that valued fairness above all else, and a contest would make the fountain politically correct.

After we left Frascati's, satiated with *haute cuisine,* we went across to Sherry's Bar. Here in this small, somewhat infamous bar John made his Hollywood debut. In the intimate room with tiny twinkling lights garlanding the room, John approached the pianist after a set and introduced himself. The next thing I knew he was asked to sit in while the pianist went on break. John began to play "Claire de Lune" accompanied by the bongo player, who apparently didn't need a break. It was the most beautiful music I had ever heard. Then he segued into "Malagueña," always a crowd pleaser, and the bongo player traveled right along. He ended with, what else, "How High the Moon." This time I heard the melody. Was I finally in the groove? I think it was the addition of the bongos that gave the piece a new identity. I even thought for a moment about the possibility of taking up bongos. Then John and I could perform together in a fashion similar to Mr. and Mrs. Nelson. Be that as it may, I left Sherry's very firm in my conviction that John was made for the Sunset Strip.

13 On the sixth day of our adventure in paradise, San Quentin-style, I decided to take advantage of the autumn heat wave and spend some time poolside. John had driven in to meet Brandy Brandon, who played piano at a club on Sunset. Apparently John knew him from someplace or other and said Brandy was going to get him together with his agent. Even though I was a little disappointed that I had not been involved in setting this up, I was happy to see John making some contacts himself.

I put on my new black, satiny one-piece suit and discovered how faded my Seattle tan had become. *Oh well,* I thought, *I'm a fast tan. An hour or so in the California sun should bring my skin back to that shade of golden brown.* As I stood checking myself out in the full-length door mirror, I suddenly felt weak and breathless. It was as though someone had removed a huge piece of my body. I realized I was having terrible Merry Widow withdrawal. So I put the little corselet under my swimsuit and instantly felt and looked better. I hadn't intended to take a dip in that chemically-laced pool anyway.

I stretched out on a lounge chair and put on my dark glasses, looking down at my left ankle. The night before, I had taken from my jewelry box a silver ankle bracelet John gave me when we started going steady back in our college days. The lock was heart-shaped with a small medallion on which were engraved the words "Property of John Morrison." I wondered whether I should remove it, so I wouldn't get a tan line there. Even though I hadn't worn it in years (thinking it pretty juvenile), I decided to leave it on. I remembered a line from a poem that said, "I am a slave, but I sing in my chains." I felt such a sense of happiness, I could scarcely contain myself. Things were working out just the way I had hoped. Maybe better. But just as happens so often in life, when you feel you have the world by the tail, you discover the tail is a hissing cobra that is about to strike you dead.

I returned to our room, tanned, rested, and ready for another exciting evening. My biggest concern was whether I should wear my green strapless cocktail dress or my long black Chinese style dress with the thigh-high slit up the side. I held up first one and then the other in front of the long mirror. Then John came in.

"Hi, sweetheart," I said. "Where shall we go tonight? Cugat and Abbe Lane are at The Coconut Grove. Or shall we go back to the Strip and catch Sheckie Green at the Crescendo? I really think, though, I'm in a Latin mood." I started to rumba with my long black dress while singing "Bésame Mucho". As I pivoted and dipped, I noticed that John was in the bathroom tossing his shaving stuff into a bag. Then he started taking his things out of the closet.

"What're you doing?" I asked with panic in my voice. "Are we being evicted? What?"

Without pausing in his hurried packing John said, "I've got to go back to Seattle for a while. Just temporarily. I'll be back soon, probably in a month or so. I'll call you as soon as I know."

"But I don't understand," I said, dropping down on the bed and still clutching my long black dress as though it were my shroud. "I thought Brandy Brandon was getting you an agent. What went wrong?"

"Oh, I cancelled that meeting because when I called Seattle I found out that Canlis wants me to play there for a few weeks. I always hoped I'd get a shot there. I can't pass that up."

Canlis was the most prestigious restaurant in Seattle. Located on a bluff adjacent to the Aurora Bridge, its wall of glass offered a panoramic view of the Lake Washington Ship Canal and the huge neon Grandma's Cookies sign. Playing Canlis was comparable to playing the Palace in the old vaudeville days.

"Canlis is terrific, but it's in Seattle! Look at the opportunities you have here in Hollywood. And what about me?" I asked plaintively.

"Why don't you stay right here? It's really not such a bad place. You and Donna can get together for lunch. You'll be fine. I want you to keep looking for jobs for me like you planned. I'll be back by Christmas for sure," he promised as he snapped his suitcase shut and put on his bomber jacket. "Oh, and by the way, I stopped by the bank and took a few hundred out of the account. I've got some bills in Seattle I have to take care of."

With that, he gave me a quick kiss and was almost out the door when he stopped and turned around. "I'm leaving the cashmere dinner jacket here. I'll be wearing my regular tux at Canlis. Take good care of it because I'll need it when I play the Sunset Strip." He gave me a wink and was gone.

I got up from the bed and went to the window. I watched him until he was out of sight. He didn't look back. I pulled the draperies closed, went to the bathroom and started to run a bath. I had to do something, and that seemed like a good start.

I was just about to take off my underclothes and step in when I heard a tap on the door. I rushed to open it without brothering to grab a robe. *It's John. I know it is. He couldn't leave me after all.* I threw open the door ready to fling my arms around him. It wasn't John. It was Carl.

"I'm sorry to disturb you, Mrs. Morrison," he said averting his eyes from my state of undress. "A message came for your husband about an hour ago. Is he here?"

"No, Carl, he just left. He had to go back to Seattle on business. Give me the message, and I'll read it to him when he calls."

When Carl handed me the folded slip of paper he looked at me strangely for a moment. What did I see in his soft, brown eyes? Not lust. No, it was more like pity. I thanked him and quickly shut the door. I put the note down on the desk and finished undressing. As I climbed into the soothing bathwater, my brain started to do damage control. *What was so bad about this anyway? He'll be back in a few weeks and have the job at Canlis on his résumé. And he left his beloved dinner jacket behind as a kind of earnest money. So what am I worrying about?*

I got out of the tub, toweled off and put on fresh underwear. I realized it was only five o'clock. For a moment the seeds of panic started to sprout in my stomach. Then I told myself I would spend a quiet relaxing evening— perhaps walk around the neighborhood, have dinner in the dining room, and then do my hair and nails while watching "Playhouse 90" on TV. It didn't sound too bad, I told myself.

Picking up my long black dress from the bed I took it to the closet, whispering softly to it, "It's OK. You're going to be going out on the town very soon. You know that old Chinese saying, 'A pleasure postponed is a pleasure enhanced,' or is that an old Scandinavian saying? Anyway, I'll be wearing you to some terrific place by Christmas."

I hung up the dress and noticed the white cashmere jacket shoved to the end of the rack. I decided to put it next to my black dress for company, but then on a sudden impulse, I put it on. The faint aroma of tobacco and lime after-shave brought John's presence back sharply. I hugged it close around me. Its white softness and familiar smell was as comforting as the 'blanky' I loved as a small child.

I caught sight of myself in the mirror over the desk and smiled at my image. The jacket hung down nearly to my knees and the sleeves hid all but the tips of my fingernails. As I stood there enjoying the ludicrous image, my eyes fell upon the half-forgotten note Carl had brought by. I picked it up and started to put it in the pocket of the jacket. I paused, wondering if I should read it. Even though I had been brought up to never, ever, read anyone else's mail, it occurred to me that this might be important. It might be from Brandy Brandon. Maybe he had a gig for John that would bring him back sooner than Christmas.

I unfolded it and started to read. Whoever had taken the message had printed it out in large block letters like a ransom note. At first my brain refused to process what my eyes were sending to it. It was like stubbing your toe. In the first split second you feel no pain, but you know it's coming. The message was from Takiko. It read, "So happy to hear from you. Can't wait to be with you. Good you got the money. Spend it on me. Love you, Taki."

A wrenching cry escaped from my throat like a sound from a mortally wounded animal. I sank to the floor at the foot of the bed. It had all been a fraud, and I fell for it. Reconciliation? No. Rip-off? Ooh, yes! Both emotionally and financially. How had I fallen for it so easily? Everything we had done over the past few days started playing over and over in my mind. Sitting on the floor with the soft jacket wrapped around me I shivered in misery. I couldn't cry. I didn't deserve that luxury.

Time passed without my awareness of it. The room became dark, but I did not turn on a light lest I see where I was. For the first time in my life I was totally alone without relatives or friends in the next room to call out to. A silent resignation swept over me. What I had feared and dreaded had come to pass. I had been placed in solitary confinement.

14 Hours passed. I lost all sense of time and space. My despair was like a drug that numbed me to everything around me. At some point I entered a fugue state that bordered on sleep and death. It was not unpleasant. My mind had shut down, and I drifted.

As I floated aimlessly in a vast space, I became aware of something up ahead, but it was not the light that people with near-death experiences see. Instead it was blackness—a huge black hole, and I was drifting toward it. How pleasant it would be to sink into this abyss. As I drew closer I recognized people standing near the edge. I recognized friends and family members who seemed to be waving me back. Donna was there in her Lizmobile. She was shouting something to me, but I couldn't make it out. I hovered over the abyss and looked down into it. It was full of weeping women! Bruised and battered, both physically and emotionally, they were clinging desperately to chains. The chains were held by men who were fathers, husbands, lovers, and bosses. Why didn't the women let go of their chains and climb out of the pit? Why were they accepting their roles as victims? Were they afraid?

I was jolted awake, my mind reeling with what I had seen. It was a near-life experience, like the ones of Ebenezer Scrooge; and, like Scrooge, I was getting a second chance. I got up from the floor, picking my way through ashtrays, papers and miscellaneous debris that had somehow accumulated around the spot where my body had been. I walked stiffly to the bathroom. I felt changed from my mental journey; yet, when I looked in the mirror I saw the same old me. No beauty, certainly. Takiko with her thick black hair, large almond eyes and skin like flawless ivory, had me beat by light years. I looked like most girls of Scandinavian ancestry: hair that had once been fair but was now a nondescript brown, matching brown eyes and strong teeth. Nothing there to be ashamed of, but "no cigar," so to speak. My body was my best asset, even without the Merry Widow's embrace.

So, I asked myself, *Why do I feel so dependent on John? Do I believe I can't attract another guy? At least of his caliber? I had a lot of boyfriends in college before I settled on John. Quite possibly I could have married any one of them. Would my life have been different if I had married a doctor, an architect or an Army officer? I think so. I did, after all, marry a guy in a high-risk profession. I wanted the glitz and the glamour. I wanted John Morrison, and I realized with a sigh of resignation that I still did. But from now on, it's got to be on my terms. I will not be a willing victim. I want a peer marriage, and the only way to achieve that is to make something of myself, I vowed.* I looked down at the ankle bracelet, snatched it off, and threw it into the waste basket. It was a start.

After showering and washing my hair, I returned to the bedroom and was startled to see that it was morning. I had been totally out of it for nearly eighteen hours! As I started to pick up the mess on the floor, I saw a sheet of paper covered with my writing. I vaguely remembered writing something during the night. I looked more closely at it and saw that it was a poem. When I was a child and had suffered loss or disappointment, like when my dog was hit by a car, my mom would tell me to write a poem about it and that would help. I began to read what I had written.

Lightly,
The blossom floats upon the lake
Softly,
With only fragrance in its wake
Lonely,
No longer needed by the tree
Dying,
From the moment it was free.

I crumpled up the paper and threw it across the room. *That may have been me yesterday, but not today. I am no Madame Butterfly! I'm a fighter, not a whiner. Besides, what would my father think of me? What am I doing,* I chastised myself again. *I'm worried about what some man thinks of me. From now on I will look for approval only from myself.* I told myself that I was young, healthy, and had money in the bank. Not as much as I had before, but still enough to tide me over until I found a niche for myself. *Besides,* I thought, *John will find the new independent, successful me much more attractive.* I was not snuffing out candles in the old candelabrum, mind you; I was just going to try to get a little glow on myself.

Fresh with new resolve, I made my plans. Although I had not slept or eaten anything in ages, I felt ready and able to leap into action. First, I had to find another place to stay. While John was there the place had a certain tacky charm, but now I saw it as a sleazy, poorly built refuge for losers. I had to get out of there AND SOON.

I dressed in a white shirt and black slacks and the lowest heeled shoes I owned. I grabbed a cup of coffee and Danish in the hotel coffee shop. With the surge of energy that only coffee can give a Norwegian, I started out to scour the neighborhood on foot.

The morning was warm, and I began my search for vacancy signs with high hopes. After walking four or five blocks I finally spotted a vacancy sign. It was the most impressive vacancy sign I had ever seen. It was made of polished brass and the lettering was in script. Of course, considering the building it was attached to, it could not have been less. The tall building was as elegant as any I had seen on Park Avenue. *This is it,* I thought. *This will be perfect.*

I entered the marbled lobby and found myself lost among potted palms and small settees. Finally, I spotted a reception desk. A dark-haired man with a small neat mustache looked up and asked in a bored manner, "Something I can do for you?" He sounded exactly like the stuck-up floorwalker on the Jack Benny Show. Could it be? Maybe the actor moonlights here.

"I'm looking for a one bedroom apartment and I happened to see your sign," I said. "Is the vacancy you have furnished?"

"As a matter of fact it is," he replied in his snobbish voice, "However, there may be one slight problem. You must be over sixty to live here."

"You mean this is an old people's home?"

"We prefer to call it a retirement residence," he answered smugly.

"Well, why doesn't your sign say so?" I retorted. "Anyway, by the time I'm sixty I'll be living in a mansion in BelAir!"

"Of course you will, my dear," he said. "Now, if you'll excuse me?" He returned to reading his racing form, or whatever it was.

I quickly exited through the ornate brass doors. *What's wrong with this town?* I thought. *None of the apartments have vacancies except this one, and it's for old people.* Then, suddenly, my lack of sleep caught up with me. The hard bed at the Casbah beckoned. After all, I still had a couple of nights paid for there.

I returned to my room with a copy of the *Hollywood Star* under my arm, determined to take a short nap and then go out again. I awoke at 7 p.m. starving to death. This would be my first night to eat alone, and I debated with myself where to go. The simplest answer was to eat in the hotel dining room. I was still recovering from my near-life experience, and I thought I could eat while checking apartment ads, so I could get an early start in the morning.

After repairing my makeup, I pulled on a tight black skirt and red turtle neck sweater. Pawing through my jewelry box I selected long, gold colored drop earrings and a snake bracelet. As I closed the box I was startled to see the silver slave ankle bracelet lying innocently with the other chains and bracelets. *What does this mean?* I wondered. I distinctly remembered throwing it in the waste basket. *Was it an omen? Or was it simply that a maid had spotted it when she did up the room while I was out and put it in my jewelry box?* I thought about trying to throw it away again, but I was afraid it might return again. *Better to just leave it where it is,* I decided. *After all it's not as though I'm going to wear it.* I looked down at my gold wedding band. *Should I toss that into limbo too? No,* I decided, *I wasn't quite ready for that.*

In the four-inch heels I thought I might never subject my feet to again, I made my way to the dining room. The host greeted me as though we were old friends and then seated me in the back corner of the room. Women eating alone were like a plague to any restaurant, and I was isolated as if I were contagious. I looked around at the other diners. They were mostly middle-aged couples, probably hoping to catch sight of a celebrity. I saw some of them look at me and then whisper to each other. *Do they think I'm "someone,"* I wondered. *Well, then I'll be "someone." I'll be Destiny Darwin, my stage persona.*

Destiny was born one rainy afternoon in an off-campus coffee shop in Seattle. Several of us drama majors at the University of Washington were drinking endless cups of coffee and discussing stage names. Names like Tondelaya Jones, Montana Copperfield, and Ima Horre were tossed into the ring, mostly for laughs.

If at that moment I had been a character in a comic strip, a light bulb would have appeared over my head as I jumped to my feet and exclaimed, "Destiny Darwin! I want to be Destiny Darwin!"

Everyone around the table was suddenly quiet. Then Fluffy Chorlton, star of many a campus production, tossed back her mane of red hair and said, "I think it's fab. Just fab."

"I love it too. It's really darb," echoed Pat French, Fluffy's second in command.

Now that it had been officially sanctioned by our upper-class women leaders, everyone wanted to know how I came up with it. I really had no idea, but that didn't stop me from coming up with an off-the-cuff explanation. "Well," I expounded. "First of all I was born in Tacoma, known to all as the City of Destiny. Then at an early age I read Darwin's *Origin of Species.*" This produced a few lady-like catcalls from the gang, but I continued. "Anyway, Destiny Darwin is my idea of a new type of mid-century woman. I will strive to live up to the name."

All of the girls raised their Coke glasses and toasted the

arrival of Destiny Darwin, woman of the fifties.

So ever since then I occasionally thought of myself as this concocted persona. Destiny was strong and confident. She bore some passing resemblance to Nancy Drew, Girl Detective, except sexier and better dressed. She could have solved crimes if she really wanted to, but what I liked about her was that she was master of her fate and captain of her soul.

I hadn't been Destiny in a long time and I thought that this was the perfect time for a Destiny moment. I slowly took a tortoise shell cigarette holder from my purse. I don't think it was real tortoise, but it was from Magnin's. I slowly inserted a king size Pall Mall into it. Without removing my black gloves I held the cigarette expectantly until a waiter appeared with a light. I really didn't like to smoke before dinner, but this was too good an opportunity to miss. I had the attention of the entire room.

Before I had a chance to study the menu fully, a waiter appeared with a glass of champagne on a silver tray. "From an admirer in the bar," he explained. I accepted the glass graciously.

"I hope it's French and not one of those little California labels," I said, playing Destiny to the hilt.

"No, ma'am. It's Dom Perignon."

"Please thank the gentleman for me," I said. I wasn't sure who or what Dom Perignon was, but it sounded expensive. Suddenly the old Casbah didn't seem as deadly grim as I had thought. Of course, I wished John was there to see me now, but then I realized that if he were, I would never have been sent a glass of Dom Perignon.

I checked the menu and found it fairly routine with pasta dishes, steaks and turkey dinners. Perhaps because I was a little homesick for my mom, I decided on the turkey with dressing and mashed potatoes. And, after all, it was November. I knew Destiny would never have ordered something as mundane as turkey, but I felt the need for comfort food.

As I enjoyed my home-style dinner, the waiter brought me two more glasses from my unknown admirer. He was still intriguingly anonymous. I felt sure that he would make an appearance before long. Meanwhile, it was obvious that I was making an impression on the other diners. Some of them never took their eyes off me. And many of them were women! I felt I was on stage and I loved it. With my third glass of champagne I felt the knot of agony over John's infidelity diminished to a small discomfort, like a headache after the third aspirin. Part of the painkiller was the fact that even though my husband had deserted me, there were others who found me attractive.

After signing the bill I returned to my room. My secret admirer had not made his identity known, and I was grateful. All I wanted to do was wash my hair, do my nails and then watch "Playhouse 90." I now felt that, with the champagne and turkey under my belt, I was capable of enduring solitary confinement for another night.

While I dried my hair I flipped through the TV Channels. L.A. had so many more than Seattle. I found one station showing "How to Marry a Millionaire." I decided to watch it. When it ended at eleven I shut off the set and settled into my hard and unforgiving bed. I thought about the movie and its message. *Marry a millionaire? Is that the goal for most women? Not me. My goal is to make a man a millionaire.*

With a sudden sinking feeling I realized that I had not lost just my husband, I had lost my product. Oh, well. Like Scarlett, I would think about it tomorrow. I fell asleep instantly, only to be awakened twenty minutes later by the phone. I was wide awake instantly. *It's got to be John. He's calling to say he's on his way back and he's really, really sorry.* I scrambled to the phone, knocking over my travel clock on the way.

The person on the phone was not John. Not even close. It was Huntz Hall! He was the unknown admirer at dinner. I was stunned. At first I thought it was some kind of weird joke, but then I recognized his voice. I slammed down the phone.

Back when I was a kid I used to enjoy the Dead End Kids of the Bowery Boys movies. Leo Gorcey was the star, and his sappy sidekick was Huntz Hall. Neither of them was any threat to Cary Grant, but Huntz was really a drip. He had a long, horsy face with protruding eyes and wore a nondescript baseball cap to complete the image. In my college sorority he was the code name for the date from hell. And he was my champagne benefactor!

Shortly after telling him I was not interested in meeting him in the bar or inviting him to visit my room, I noticed I was feeling queasy. *Well, Huntz Hall would make any girl feel sick,* I thought, as I fought back waves of nausea. A few minutes later I was throwing up violently in the bathroom. The phone kept ringing and I kept throwing up. On and on through the night. I didn't know which was worse, the terrible nausea or Huntz' terrible pick up lines.

By four a.m. I thought of calling my mom in Seattle to see if she could fly down and take care of me. A little of Destiny was still in my system, so instead, I called the desk and got Carl. I told him I either had been poisoned by the turkey or Huntz Hall's incessant phone calls. I asked if he could please help me.

A few minutes later I heard a tap on the door. Thank God it was Carl. He brought a large bottle of 7-Up and a lot of sympathy. I welcomed him without a thought of how

I must look or how the room must smell. Carl stayed with me until the paroxysms of my vomiting abated. He held my head, wiped my face with a soft cloth, gave me sips of 7-Up and, best of all, he stopped the calls from Huntz Hall. Around five-thirty a.m. I finally fell asleep. I was vaguely aware of Carl covering me up and quietly leaving. As I slept I knew I had been taken care of by a guardian angel. There were moments when I thought it was my mother. Sometimes I thought it was Chopin. I never thought it was John.

When I awoke at noon I had a sore stomach and a slight headache, but otherwise felt ready and able to get on with my plan to find a place to live.

As I showered and put on my makeup, I remembered how Carl had taken care of me the night before. With a sigh of resignation I accepted the fact that even if John had been with me during my night of misery, he would not have provided the tender care that I got from Carl. He would not have told me at one point in the night that he was an ex-prisoner of the North Koreans and he knew about suffering. Why couldn't John have been given less talent and more compassion? While I asked myself this question, I felt an answer forming that I didn't like: if he were more like Carl, would you be so crazy about him?

"And den?"
⌒⌒ Mrs. Peusa

15 John had vanished and the bubble had burst. I started thinking about my childhood and the people in it who taught me valuable lessons.

When we moved from my beloved island paradise, we were assisted by Rain-in-the-Face, the prison trusty who had become a good friend and a model of kindness. (Trusties were inmates who helped discipline other inmates or were given special assignments). He helped my mother and me settle in with my grandmother on Trafton Street in South Tacoma. Dad had gone back to lumberjacking in the northern part of Washington State. We saw him every other weekend. He always brought me a present paid for by his poker winnings. One was a deep violet hat and muff that made me feel elegant in my worn cotton dress and gave me an idea of how rich girls lived. (Or so I thought.) At any rate, Father was away a lot.

A special new experience awaited me in Grandmother's house. While my mother maintained her position as chief cook, I was assigned to do the shopping in the store down the hill on Railroad Avenue. The store was owned by Mrs.

Peusa, a middle-aged Polish lady and her son Oxley. She had short brown hair with bangs. Her brown eyes were kind and they crinkled when she smiled, making up for the fact that she was missing her upper teeth. She pulled items from the shelves as requested by customers, bagged them and ran the cash register. Oxley ran the butcher shop in the back. Mrs. Peusa always dressed the same—baggy brown sweater and skirt covered by a generally pristine white bib apron. I rarely saw her lower half, but I believe she wore dark "service weight" stockings and oxfords.

The first thing I did when I walked up to the counter was proudly produce my list. I felt great responsibility holding this list. On the island my dad had bought our food from the prison commissary. There were no stores of any kind there. I guess he too had a list from my mom; but, being a man, he could make any changes he wanted. When my mom asked for a pound of bacon, he might come home with five pounds, which he then consumed in two days.

I would pull the list out of my pocket and stick to it. I would read off the first item, "a quart of milk." Mrs. Peusa would go to the chiller case and return with a bottle of milk. She would look at me and ask "And den?" I would read off the next item, "box of Wheaties." Mrs. Peusa would bring that item and again say, "And den?" Thus, working as a team, she posed the questions and I had the answers with the help of my list.

This routine was repeated two or three times a week without failure until one day, after the third "And den?" I had no answer. The last item on my list was hard to read. Perhaps a raindrop had spoiled my mom's precise school teacher cursive. The illegible word started with a "t" and ended with an "a." I showed it to Mrs. Peusa and she too was baffled. Even though I was smart enough to skip the second grade I could not think of any word starting with "t" and ending with "a" that my mom needed for dinner.

I trudged my way home up the hill, overcome with a great sense of failure. It was not my own but a failure of those lists that had been my paradigm, my guide, my roadmap to life in the city.

My mom laughed when I arrived without having completed my job. "What did you want that ends in "a" and starts with "t?" I asked, very close to tears. "Oh, that's tapioca," she explained, "I thought I would try and see if you liked it for dessert tonight."

I learned a lesson from this. It's good to have a list, to know what you want next; but even a well-prepared list can fail when you are asked, "And den?" and you can't see the answer. I call it the "tapioca effect." It is the X factor, the unknown entity. It's door #1 on "Let's Make a Deal." Perhaps one day as I lie dying, I will hear Mrs. Peusa's voice asking the eternal question "And den?" And my answer will be "tapioca."

16 Even though the weather was warm, I dressed in a black wool skirt and sweater and slung my white leather jacket over my shoulders. I walked through the lobby and noticed that many of the residents were in shorts and tee shirts. *Well, so what! I was from Seattle where we respect the change of seasons. November calls for wool and leather. In dark colors. Period.*

I had decided to check out a couple of ads for apartments off Wilshire, having given up hope of finding anything in the area around the Casbah. I had a bus schedule and knew where to transfer. After all, I had been taking busses in Seattle for years. I should have no problems here.

I found a pleasant bench at the bus stop with an advertisement for a local mortuary on the backrest. *This is something we should do at home*, I thought. Seattle had no bus benches, and surely the ads would pay for their construction. *Hmmm. Maybe this would be something I could make money at back home.* Then I dismissed the thought. *I am here. I am not going back. I will find work for myself and then, eventually, for John. Still*, I thought, *these mortuary bus benches are not a bad idea. Maybe someday.* At this point I realized how long I had been sitting there. I remembered Bob Hope in one of his monologues saying that when there is a bus strike in LA, it's at least three weeks before anybody notices.

I looked up Sunset Boulevard. What a beautiful street, I thought, even before it becomes the Strip. It is the Street of Dreams, the Yellow Brick Road, the....Hello! The Yellow Brick Road! Maybe I am a Toto-less Dorothy. I'm on a journey, a quest. An innocent girl alone in an exotic place. My mind, which is quick to dramatize things even in ordinary situations, leaped to this analogy. Is Donna "Glinda the Good?" No, she's too young. It's her sweet mother. Carl is definitely the Scarecrow with this warm heart, but not an especially huge brain. All these people are helping me on my journey.

I was so lost in my Ozian fantasy that I didn't notice the young man who had seated himself next to me. "Hi," he said. "Do you mind if I sit here for a minute?"

He was a handsome, dark-haired young man probably in his late teens with a small, compact build. I noticed his left arm was withered and he held it across his body.

"Be my guest," I replied. "Or maybe I should say, the guest of Forest Lawn." He smiled at that and I noticed what great teeth he had. I felt a wave of sympathy about his arm, but he seemed unconcerned about it.

"Could I talk to you for a minute?" he asked rather shyly.

My mind reeled with the feeling that here was my Tin Woodsman. His crippled arm was like the Woodsman's before Dorothy oiled him. "Sure. Go ahead," I replied, as I glanced over my shoulder just in case a Cowardly Lion was nearby.

"My name is Morgan Lee. Pinky Lee, the comedian, is my dad."

"Oh, sure. I know who Pinky Lee is. I've seen him in lots of movies. He's really funny," I lied. Pinky Lee was no Jack Benny or Milton Berle. His shtick was speaking in a kind of juicy way. He was sort of a human version of Daffy Duck. But still, a star is a star. "Are you planning to be a comedian too?" I asked

128

"No, thanks. One in the family is enough. My dad has his own show on NBC now. It's a kids' show, but it's getting good ratings. Anyway, I'm working on a show for NBC, and that's what I wanted to talk to you about."

"Joo eenterest me strengly, joong man," I said in a cornball Russian accent.

"Hey, I liked that. I just knew you were an actress when I saw you sitting here, and I could tell you would be perfect for my new show."

"Really? Seriously? I *am* an actress, you know, from Seattle."

"Perfect. Just what I'm looking for. My show is going to be called *Dollars for Scholars*. Students from all over the country will compete for scholarships from universities. It will be like Quiz Kids, only for high school students. What do you think of it?"

"Wow, it sounds great. But what do you need with an actress on a quiz show?"

"On radio we wouldn't, but TV has changed everything. Even a quiz show needs sex appeal. You would be the 'Presenter Girl.' You know, those girls who carry the Oscars up to the podium on the Academy Awards? That's what we want. You would wear a sexy costume and point to the prizes and then present the scholarship award to the winner."

"I could handle that. Do I need to provide my own costumes?"

"No, a designer would provide the clothes to get the publicity. Just like the mortuary and their bus bench."

I wasn't sure I was crazy about the comparison, but when Morgan suggested we go a nearby coffee shop to discuss it further, I accepted eagerly. If Lana Turner could be discovered on a drug store stool, why couldn't I be discovered on a bus bench advertising mortuaries?

We got into his Oldsmobile convertible—*Did everyone in LA drive a convertible?*—and drove to a near-by Coffee Dan's where Morgan said he had a "special" booth. I had no apprehensions about getting in his car with this total stranger. He was not much taller than I was, he had a crippled arm and he was the son of a TV star. What gave me the most confidence in him was my belief that he was my Tin Woodsman who was going to help me find the Wizard.

We parked right in front of the coffee shop, just like in the movies; and when we entered, one of the waitresses called out, "Hi, Morgan! Be right with you." I was totally charmed with the small-town atmosphere I sensed in Hollywood. It really IS Ozzie and Harrietville. *I'm probably much safer alone here than I would be in Seattle,* I thought. Even Huntz Hall was more of a nuisance than a threat.

I told Morgan my real name, resisting the temptation to be Destiny. Somehow, I knew this was not a job for her. I filled him in on my background with the emphasis on my work in Seattle radio and at the UW. I told him my husband was a pianist who had returned to Seattle on business. Morgan seemed a little disappointed that I had a husband. I would have been disappointed if he hadn't been.

We sat in a back booth at Coffee Dan's for hours. Morgan told me how difficult it is to be the child of a celebrity. He said he knew the Crosby boys, and they too shared the blessing/curse of a well-known father. Even though Pinky Lee was not in the same category as Bing Crosby, I understood what he meant. The name opens some doors but you still have to prove yourself.

With all the candor Morgan showed I found myself telling him more about myself than I intended—about my U.S. Marshal father with his expectations of me and about my husband, with his rejections of me. I could not have had a more sympathetic listener. He did not try to hide his pleasure that I was *de facto* separated from my husband. I did not try to deny to myself that Morgan was developing a crush on me.

When dinner time rolled around we ordered cheeseburgers and fries. I found this familiar food a welcome panacea after my turkey bout of the previous night. By six thirty we pretty much knew each others' life histories. I empathized with his desire to find a niche in "The Business" while his dad wanted him to be an investment banker. He understood how hard I had tried to make up to my dad for not being a boy and how I was now trying to prove myself to my husband. We hadn't really talked about *Dollars for Scholars*. Our need to talk about personal matters seemed more important.

It wasn't until Morgan paid the bill and we stepped out into the neon-lit evening that I realized the day was gone and so was my plan to find an apartment. As we drove back to the Casbah, Morgan said, "I know exactly what I want us to do tomorrow. Drive to Malibu for lunch. There's a place you'll love and I want to show it to you."

"Malibu! I've heard about Malibu and I'd love to see it, but I've got to find a place to live. That's what I was starting out to do when you saw me on the bus bench."

"Hey, wait a minute," Morgan practically shouted. "I've got the perfect place for you. A friend of mine who's a model has just taken an apartment up on Beachwood Drive. She's looking for a roommate and you would be perfect together. Why don't I pick you up tomorrow and you can meet Jackie and check it out. Maybe we'll still have time for lunch."

"Morgan, you're too good to be true. This sounds wonderful. You are so kind to me, and I'll never forget it." I got out of the car at the forbidding entrance to the Casbah, cheered by the thought that my sentence may be up soon. Maybe tomorrow. Morgan reached over and kissed me on my cheek, saying, "Just remember, you hold this boy's heart in your hands."

I pondered that remark as I walked to my cell. I liked the fact that his reference to his heart in my hands went sort of along with his Tin Woodsman persona. Still, could he be expecting some kind of romantic relationship here? He's just a kid. I'm a married woman, more or less. *Well,* I thought, *I like him; and even if his quiz show goes nowhere, at least he may have found me a place to stay.*

When I unlocked my door and stepped into my room I saw a note had been slipped under the door. It was from Carl. He said he hoped I was feeling okay and asked if I would meet him in the bar when he finished his shift at eleven.

I kicked off my shoes and sat down on the bed thinking about what a sweet guy Carl was and how much I was in his debt. He had seen me at my absolute ickiest. No makeup, sweat-soaked hair, and smelling of L'eau du barf. And he still wants to meet with me.

I watched "G.E. Theatre," imagining myself in the ingénue role. I was totally convinced I could have done a better job as the soundwoman who suspected her husband of trying to kill her. At 10:55 I turned up the volume while I stood in front of the bathroom mirror brushing my hair and renewing my lipstick. Just as I expected, the husband of the woman in the drama totally vindicated himself in the end, and the nice next-door neighbor was taken away in handcuffs. Sure.

After giving myself a liberal dousing of "My Sin" cologne (in case any traces of last night were seeping through my pores), I added a wide jeweled belt to my dark skirt and sweater to emphasize my twenty-two inch waist. I hoped this would erase Carl's last image of me in a stained, smelly baby-doll nightie.

I went to the bar and looked around. Thankfully, Huntz Hall was not in sight, but I saw Carl seated in a booth with a beer in front of him. When he saw me he stood up and gave me a small wave. I slipped into the booth opposite him and asked if I could have a Coke.

"I guess you've had enough 7-Up for awhile," he said with a smile.

"Honestly, Carl," I said, I really don't know how I would have made it last night without you."

"Hey, it wasn't your fault you got sick. I try to eat in this place as seldom as possible. That turkey had probably been around since last Thanksgiving."

"Well, let me at least buy you a beer," I insisted.

"Oh, I'll just nurse this one for awhile. Anyway, the other thing I wanted to explain to you was about that guy calling your room all night. He didn't get your room number from me. He got it from the switchboard gal, and I've had a talk with her. It won't happen again. You know it's kind of pathetic, guys like Huntz. They're still trying to cash in on a career that's been over for years. There's a lot of guys like him hanging out in Hollywood bars, and I'm sure you'll be hit on by some more of them.

"But that's not the main reason I wanted to talk to you. Now, I know that your husband left you kind of sudden. I took that message from your husband's lady friend. It made me sick that you had to see it, and I blame myself for not giving it to him directly. Or throwing it away. Anyway, I know you're looking for a place to live and you're probably a little short on cash. I just want you to know that if you want to stay here for awhile till you get work, I can fix it so it won't cost you anything."

Tilting my head to one side, I looked at Carl quizzically. "You mean you can cook the books so it looks like I'm paying for my room, but I'm not?"

"Well, no, I couldn't do that, but I get a room here as part of my pay. It has twin beds and all. You'd be under no obligation to me to….well, you know. Anyway, I could look out for you and no Huntz Hall or anybody else would be bothering you."

I was stunned, and a little disappointed. If I could have had my room with no charge for another week or so I could have put up with the San Quentin ambience. But as for sharing a room with Carl, that was unthinkable. Even if I was attracted to him, which I wasn't and never would be, there was just no way. Yet I was very touched by his kindness.

"I really appreciate your offer, honestly. It's so kind and generous, but I think I'm okay. A friend of mine has an acquaintance who's a model and she's looking for a roommate to share her new apartment. I'm checking into it tomorrow." I felt it was not wise to mention that the "friend" was a guy I just met while I was waiting for a bus.

"I just want you to know that with you being down here alone and young and pretty you need someone to look after you. Last night was just a sample. And I don't mean the turkey. Now I know it's not my business, but I think that husband of yours has rocks in his head to take off and leave you alone like this. It's just not right."

I smiled at him and touched his arm. "I'm going to be fine. I've got friends who live out in the valley and a friend from my Paso Robles days who lives right here in Hollywood. And I've got you too, Carl." I squeezed his arm lightly. "I'm so grateful for your coming to my rescue last night, and especially for getting Huntz to stop calling me for a date. If he had seen me like you did, he would have run off pretty fast."

"OK, then," Carl said with a sigh. "But just remember there are a lot of creeps in this town and I don't want you bothered by any of them. If you need me, you know where I am. If I'm not on duty, just leave a message and I'll be there right away."

I didn't know what to think. Here is a guy who barely knows me and he's ready to love, honor and protect. And I believe he would. Why couldn't I have married someone like him? I knew the answer. *He doesn't make my heart pound when he looks up at me across a grand piano. He doesn't have beautiful hands that make wild music when they touch me in the dark. I think I'm cursed with a disease for which there is no cure.*

We sat and talked for an hour or so. I asked him about his prisoner of war experience in North Korea to which he had alluded the night before. He told me just a little. It was enough to make me ache with pity for him and the other men who endured this fate. At the same time I was also grateful that John's talent had spared him from going through a hell like Carl did.

He walked me back to my room where we said goodnight outside my door. He promised for the second time that there would be no further calls to disturb me and wished me a good night's sleep. As I shut the door and heard his footsteps fade away, I was sad for a brief moment. I knew that I probably would never see him again. However, my mood lifted when I reminded myself that Morgan was coming to get me tomorrow and I would be moving in with a Hollywood model and have lunch in Malibu!

17 True to his word, Morgan showed up promptly at ten the next morning. Fortunately, it was raining, so I had an excuse to wear my white vinyl raincoat with tiny rhinestones on the collar points and on the belt. If I was going to meet a model, I definitely didn't want her to think I was fashion-impaired.

Morgan complained about the rain, mainly because he had to put the top up on his car. He did say that I more than made up for that inconvenience by wearing my stylish raincoat with its matching umbrella.

We drove up Beachwood Drive and into the Hollywood Hills. I noticed, gratefully, that there were bus stops all along Beachwood, though I never saw a bus. Small charming houses lined the street, reminding me of the Peluso home.

Just as I was beginning to visualize the Spanish style building with red tile roof that I'd be living in, Morgan pulled up in front of a close cousin to the Casbah! The color was what I think of as goose-dropping beige with that hint of green. Ugh! There were large windows with no shutters, the roof was warehouse plain, and the landscaping was as exciting as the grass around a trailer home. "So, what do you think? Isn't it great? It's a brand new building, just barely finished," Morgan said proudly.

I resisted the temptation to say it wouldn't be finished

until the construction crew came back and added trim, balconies, eaves, palm trees, grill work, ANYTHING! Instead, I said, "It looks really well built, Morgan. I'm sure it would hold up well in an earthquake." *Hah!* I thought. *A nice big earthquake would give it a little distinction--like a dueling scar on sweet Van Johnson's face.*

Our knock at the door was answered by my roommate-to-be, Jackie Benoit (pronounced BenWAH). She was a cool blonde who, whether by accident or design, resembled Grace Kelly. The apartment she showed us was furnished in a style that matched the exterior. My first thought was that this was the perfect place to recover from a nervous breakdown. There was nothing to stir the senses in any way. The furniture was simple and basic—a sofa, two chairs, a coffee table, lamp table and desk in the living room. In the dining area there was a chrome table with four chrome and vinyl chairs. The bedroom had twin beds, a night stand and a dresser with a mirror over it. The wood was pale oak, the carpeting was pale beige. There were no pictures on the walls and there was no TV.

"It comes furnished," Jackie explained. "Personal touches can be added later."

Yeah, I thought, *a bullfighter painted on velvet would help a lot. What is happening to Hollywood, anyway? This is awful.*

As Jackie showed me the laundry room and other exciting amenities like the storage lockers, I had a chance to check her out. She was dressed in a simple beige dress and wore a simple pair of gold hoops in her ears. If she had sat down on the sand colored upholstered sofa she would have disappeared. One thing about her impressed me no end, however. She was wearing nylons with seams up the back! In Seattle I took a modeling class when I was seventeen and was told that a lady always wears nylons with seams; seamless stockings are just for casual situations. The fact that Jackie wore any kind of stocking in this bare-legged L.A. was amazing!

"I'll take it," I informed her without even finding out what my half of the rent would be. The apartment might have been dull and boring decor-wise, but it was the Palace of Versailles compared to the Casbah. We agreed that I would move in the next day, and Morgan offered to help.

As we drove off I thought about my decision. The apartment might not be quite what I expected, but it was a start. I was on my own and on the bus line. So what if Jackie seemed as bland as her apartment. I wasn't looking for a girlfriend. I had Donna. Even though Donna didn't wear nylons with seams, she was my very good buddy. And I couldn't wait to call her and give her all my news.

Because it was raining, Morgan decided we should stay in town and have lunch at the Brown Derby. We didn't go to the REAL Brown Derby that was shaped like a hat; we went to the one on Vine Street. There was an autographed picture of Pinky Lee on the wall near our table. Morgan was greeted by name when the waiter arrived. He obviously loved it and so did I. Unlike the waitress at Coffee Dan's, the waiter here called him Mr. Lee.

I looked around the room and spotted several familiar faces. Since this Brown Derby was near CBS and NBC, a lot of stars had lunch at the Derby. I saw Steve Allen and then Art Linkletter. Morgan pointed out Army Archerd who wrote a column in the *Hollywood Reporter.*

"Army has spotted us. Maybe we'll be an item in his column next week," Morgan whispered. "What would you think of that?"

I said, "The item would say something like 'Morgan Lee,

talented son of NBC star Pinky Lee, was seen lunching with some unknown out-of-towner at the Brown Derby last week.' That's what he'd say."

"Wrong," Morgan replied. "He'd say, '. . . .lunching with the young woman who will be appearing in the new NBC quiz show *Dollars for Scholars*.' And that brings me to something I want to talk to you about. Your hair."

"My hair?" I asked touching it to see if it was still in place. "I know the length is still kind of uneven since my accident, but..."

"No. No, the style's okay, it's the color. I want you to become a blonde!"

"A blonde? I don't know. Maybe. I used to have blond hair when I was a kid. I even tried blond streaks when I was seventeen."

"I want you to be a light, light blonde."

"You mean like Marilyn?"

"Exactly. You've got the figure and the personality. You'll be great as a blonde. And in this town blondes are in demand. I want you to see a color specialist I know. He's got a salon on Wilshire. His name is Mister Larry. I'd like you to make an appointment tomorrow."

"Tomorrow? But I'm moving in with Jackie tomorrow."

"Why don't you move in this afternoon? That will give you plenty of time tomorrow to meet with Mister Larry and get your hair done."

"Morgan, this is all moving pretty fast. What's the big rush?"

"It's the show. I need to have pictures to submit to NBC. The way you look is really important in getting our pilot shot."

"Well, then, I guess I'll move in today, if it's alright with Jackie," I replied. I really was not looking forward to another night in my Casbah cell. And even though things were happening pretty fast, I reminded myself that this was Hollywood where miracles happen everyday. I'd better get used to it.

Morgan called Jackie who said it was fine to move in right away. We went back to the Casbah and I started to pack. Morgan helped. I tried not to worry too much that he was taking over my life and making decisions for me. After all, isn't that what agents and managers do? I had nearly all my things together when Morgan spotted the white cashmere dinner jacket John had left behind.

"This is a really beautiful jacket. Is it your husband's?"

"Do you mind if I try it on?" he asked, as he took off his lightweight windbreaker. He put it on and stood before the mirror. It was, of course, far too big. His hands disappeared in the sleeves and the shoulders extended far beyond his own. I remembered the first time I saw John wearing it. He looked handsome beyond belief, and I was so proud of my elegant husband in his new dinner jacket.

"Take it," I said. "It's yours. I'm sure you know a good tailor who can make some adjustments on it. It really becomes you Morgan, and I want you to have it."

Morgan was as pleased as a kid with a new bike on Christmas morning. I was not oblivious to the fact that it was in some way symbolic to him. He thought he was replacing John in my life.

Blondes may have more fun, but becoming a blonde is not fun
    ⌒ *Karoline Morrison*

18 The next morning Morgan dropped me off at Mister Larry's Salon with the promise to return to see the finished product in three hours. I was nervous with apprehension. It seemed so much was riding on this bleach job—my future, Morgan's future, and NBC's future.

I was ushered into a private booth, given a cup of coffee, and then awaited the arrival of Monsieur Larry himself. I had never had my hair done by a man, and I didn't know what to expect.

A few minutes later a slender man of about thirty entered the cubicle. My first thought was that I would kill for his outfit. He was wearing tight black leather pants and a white silk poet's shirt open halfway to the waist and exposing his tanned, hairless chest. His hair waved gracefully about his face in a longish style reminiscent of Lord Byron. He was carrying a white toy poodle. The pet crushed his Lord Byron image. So did his Bronx accent!

"Fifi, this is Karoline, Morgan's friend. I want you to be a good girl and not bother us while we talk colors." I wasn't sure whether I should try to shake hands with Fifi, who jumped down and went off to a corner to clean herself. I smiled at Larry and said, "What do you think about turning me into a blonde?"

He tapped his teeth with a rattail comb and narrowed his eyes as he looked at me. "Yes. Morgan is right. You are meant to be a blonde. I need to know what kind. There are cute blondes, hot blondes and cool blondes. Marilyn and Jane are hot. Grace and Lana are cool. Kim is coolish; Doris and Sandra Dee are cute. You are somewhere between hot and cute."

"What does that mean, as far as shading goes?" I asked, trying to show my disappointment in not having achieved a rating of cool.

"It means a soft pale gold," Mr. Larry said. "I'll use Roux gold and tone it a little with Clairol drabber. First we bleach the color out and then we tone the right color in. Let's get started."

Whoever that was who said blondes have more fun was not talking about the process involved. First my hair was sectioned off, then a mixture that made my eyes burn was applied to my hair. A timer clicked away while Mister Larry paced, I smoked, and Fifi licked. A strand of hair was checked. The verdict: a little more time. Then I was ready to be shampooed. But was I through? Hardly. After my hair was partly dried, a toner was applied and the timer re-set. Ten minutes later I was shampooed again. My scalp begged for mercy, and I was developing a deep hatred for Mr. Larry and possibly even Morgan.

It was impossible to tell what miracles were taking place since my hair was plastered flat to my head with a foul smelling concoction. The smell was as toxic as the fumes from the Casbah swimming pool. It was just as well that

I wasn't facing the mirror most of the time as Mr. Larry inspected his handiwork with a furrowed brow. Whatever he felt about the process he kept to himself. When the timer beeped for the last time, I was cooked, basted and now done. Larry confirmed this as he stripped off his gloves and tossed them in a basket. Fifi knew it too. She stopped licking and stood up expectantly.

"My assistant will take over now, and I'll see you for the final inspection," Mr. Larry announced, as he made his exit from the cubicle with Fifi in his arms.

An assistant? I thought. *Of course! There is an Igor for every Doctor Frankenstein, someone to attend to the little details that are beneath the master's concern. Once the creature has been given life, the great doctor surely doesn't stick around to see to the little details, such as parting the hair, making sure the boot laces are properly tied and, most importantly, that the monster's fly is buttoned up.*

"Hi, I'm Michele," declared a plump middle-aged woman, as she popped into the laboratory (pronounced laBORatory). I was a little sorry for such a mundane ending to my little fantasy, but at least Michele looked capable of giving me a little TLC. "I'm going to rinse and set you," she said.

"My head's pretty sore, Michele. Couldn't you just wash the goop off and dry it. I can set it later, myself," I pleaded.

"Oh, no. Mister Larry wouldn't want one of his customers leaving the salon without looking their best. What would the ladies in the waiting room think?"

She wheeled me assertively to the shampoo sink and started hosing me off while I fumed. *Whose hair was this anyway? And what about Morgan? That kid who's putting me through all this just so I can walk out on a studio stage and hand some other kid a piece of paper. Now if I were going to present the students with diplomas and maybe make a few comments such as, "The future of our country is in your hands," that would be different. Or better yet, if I were going to drive out on stage in a new two-seater, Thunderbird convertible, this all might be worth it.*

I tried to distract myself while Michele set my hair with huge metal sci-fi looking curlers. *Klaatu barada nikto,* I said under my breath.

"I beg your pardon?" she asked looking at me strangely.

"Those are the words you have to say if you ever run into the robot Gort. It's from *The Day the Earth Stood Still*," I said. *Jeez, she doesn't know what everybody else on the planet knows? And she's from L.A.?*

"You must be an actress. Are you up for a role where you need to be a blonde?" I forgave Michele for her lack of sci-fi lore. "As a matter of fact, I am. There's a new quiz show coming on NBC. I need to be a blonde for my role in it."

"Well I hope you let all your fans know that Mr. Larry is your hair stylist."

Although somewhat mollified by Michele's mention of my fans, I still fumed inwardly as I sat under the dryer reading about Rock Hudson's latest hot romance with a young Fox starlet. In the past three days I had been dumped by my husband, got food poisoning, and had my scalp massacred by unknown chemicals. On top of all that, I rubbed my nose and realized it was sun burnt!

Two *Movie Lifes*, one *Look Magazine*, and a *Photoplay* magazine later I was pronounced "dry." An alcoholic coming out of treatment could not have welcomed the word more. Michele whisked my chair back to the comb-out table and summoned Mr. Larry. He appeared *sans* Fifi (could she be having her nails done?) and he began to remove the rollers and turn me into an earthling again. I barely watched

146

the procedure. All I could think of was escaping from this torture chamber and having an enormous cheeseburger with extra fries

But burgers and fries went off my radar screen when I saw what was emerging in the mirror. Mr. Larry proved to be a 20th Century alchemist. He had taken the dung brown substance that had been my hair and transformed it into spun gold. Not only was there a major change in my hair, but my eyes appeared larger and browner and my skin pinker (that, of course, may have been a result of my time under the dryer). Still, I looked fab, and Mr. Larry accepted my accolades graciously.

When Morgan arrived he joined in the celebration of this born-again blonde. He tried to pay the bill, but I wouldn't let him. After all, there was a limit to how much I wanted to be obligated to him.

"Well, where shall we go for dinner?" Morgan asked, as we emerged into the evening air, lights winking on all along the Miracle Mile. "There are some terrific places here on Wilshire."

"You know what really appeals to me?" I said. "I'd love to go to that big drive-in on Sunset, where the carhops wear roller-skates, and I'd like to order a burger and a malt."

"You mean Tiny Naylor's? Sure, why not. Even Marlon Brando goes there. I'll put my top down so I can watch people stare at you and wonder who you are."

And so it seemed that my immediate problems were behind me. I had a new friend, a TV job coming up, an apartment I'd be sharing with a model, and—most exciting of all—tomorrow morning I would wake up as a Hollywood blonde!

19 If I had set out to find a roomie in Hollywood, Jackie Benoit would not have been at the bottom of my list but certainly nowhere near the top either. She made Grace Kelly look like a disheveled, dissolute barfly. She used industrial-strength hairspray so generously that, if I entered the bathroom right after her exit, I needed a respirator. I peeked into her underwear drawer and was impressed. . . not with the contents, because I had some pretty fancy stuff myself, but because I didn't know Chanel made drawer liners.

Would her Radcliffe accent rub off on me? When I was little, my mom could tell which friend I'd been playing with because I would come home speaking just like they did. A talent Jackie had that really did impress me was her ability to recognize the sound of a Cadillac door closing. Whenever Donna drove over to pick me up, I never had to watch for her when Jackie was at home. One faint slamming sound from half a block away and Jackie would announce, "Your friend is here."

I spent several days in Jackie's boring-beige-modern Beachwood Drive apartment waiting to hear from John, NBC, Donna, a crank caller—anybody!! Then she mentioned that the agency she was with was looking for models to work "Market Week" in downtown L.A. Market Week was a seasonal event where the reps of clothing manufacturers showed their current lines to retail store buyers. The idea appealed to me because, hey, the pay wasn't much but it was a glamorous-sounding job and something to do while I waited to hear from NBC and John.

As so often happens, reality is not quite what you had expected. First there was the forty-minute ride by bus to tacky downtown L.A. Then the negative ambience of the garment district. Worst of all, there were the men! I was hired by a company that manufactured medium-priced junior fashions. I had dreamed of Oleg Cassini, Dior or Valentino, but had to settle for a line featuring blouses with Peter Pan collars and peasant skirts with eyelet trim. My measurements were not really junior, but the little man who hired me didn't seem to care. He told me he could make some quick alterations to the fashions I'd be showing. This involved much groping, which he referred to as "taking measurements." At one point I asked him whether we wouldn't be more comfortable in the back seat of a car! He cackled at that and kept on measuring. First he needed to know the length from my crotch to my knees while sitting, then standing, then bending over, and finally while dancing the cha cha. Then we moved on to my bust measurements.

Why does life hand you a platter of sawdust when you're expecting *petits fours*? Or at least Oreos? I had envisioned myself walking down a runway while elegantly dressed people sat in little gold chairs taking notes. The reality was that I remained in Sol's cramped, dingy rooms putting on a series of boring little outfits while men asked me to raise my arms, stand with my legs wide apart, bend over from the waist, and submit to their disgusting little tape measures!

Three days later I called it quits. When I picked up

my check from Sol's sweaty and oh, so familiar hand, he asked if I would be interested in a full time job as a fitting model. He explained that, since my measurements were not standard, he would have to make special clothing cut just for me and I would be allowed to keep it after the showings. I grudgingly admitted to myself that, had he been Cassini or Valentino, I might have wavered, taking the possible first step to whoredom. Luckily, Sol's company made clothing more suited to Gidget than to me.

I was waiting for the elevator when I noticed an expensively dressed man nearby carrying a monogrammed brief case—quite a contrast to the grubby reps I had been fending off for three days. I smiled when he spoke to me.

"You look as though you've had a tough day."

"My first and last Market Week," I replied. "Are you in the clothing business?"

He smiled back. "Not directly, but a client of mine is. I'm an attorney."

The thought of suing a couple of the more lecherous reps flashed through my mind as the elevator arrived and we stepped inside. When he pressed the lobby button I noticed his manicured and ringless hand. Perhaps catching my glance he asked, "Would you be offended if I asked if you have dinner plans this evening?" I had planned on stopping at Coffee Dan's on Hollywood Boulevard before transferring to the bus that took me up the hill to home. Not a very exciting end to a dreary day.

"Actually, I do," I said with a sigh. "But it's with my agent and I was thinking of postponing. I'm exhausted." That part certainly was true. In a way Jackie was my agent, at least for what was probably my last modeling gig.

Twenty minutes later I found myself seated in a soft leather booth in a mahogany-paneled bar just off the dining room in a beautiful hotel. So much for Coffee Dan's. Not being an experienced drinker, I ordered a martini. I hated the taste, but I loved the look of holding the glass with the stem cradled between my fingers. If I ever owned a boat I would call it "Dry Martini," I decided. My new acquaintance ordered scotch on the rocks. Great drink for a man, but not good for a woman or a boat.

Our conversation rolled along smoothly, maybe because it was mostly about me, a subject I was almost an expert on. I told him I was an actress from Seattle with a husband who was a musician and would be joining me as soon as he finished his current engagement. I felt this version of the truth was far better than saying I had recently been dumped by my husband for Tokyo Rose and only by the grace of a drunk driver was I here with a great wardrobe, living in the Hills with Grace Kelly's twin.

I tried to find out something about Alan Woodward besides what I could see for myself. He was thirtyish, Harvard grad-looking, medium height, and I'd have bet major bucks that he was not carrying a tape measure. He didn't seem to want to talk much about himself. In fact, he was more interested in keeping his drinks coming and talking about me and my future. He explained that he had a lot of contacts in "the industry" (that's what people here called the movie business). He offered to find me a good agent and also to represent me in any future contract negotiations. I was so impressed with this I forgot how hungry and tired I was. *Sure, Morgan Lee was helping me, but this guy was a successful L.A. attorney!*

While I played with my martini olive, Alan downed three scotches. I was grateful when the maitre d' came to our table and asked if we were ready to be seated. I accepted for both of us, as my hunger pangs screamed for attention, and

I could see that Alan needed something besides scotch on his stomach. With my consent Alan ordered for both of us. I tried to remember what it was he ordered for me so I could impress Donna, but it was beyond my high school French. The bottle of wine the steward suggested was a Chateau Rothschild and must have cost more than I had earned in my three days of tape measure torture. It all seemed too good to be true. I sipped my wine and thought about how this all had come about. . . my own personal Yellow Brick Road, starting with the accident on Dieway 99 and now here I was waiting to see where the road would lead next.

Suddenly there was a crash and a spray of water flew into my lap. Alan had knocked over his water goblet. The waiter came over quickly and took care of the spill, also removing the empty wine bottle. In a slurred voice Alan ordered after dinner drinks.

"I really should think about getting home soon," I said. You probably should too. Do you live far?" I had hoped he would drive me home, but now I wanted to be put in a cab.

"I'm not goin' home. Keep a room here," he muttered. "C'mon. I'll show it to you." With that, he scrawled his name on the check that had suddenly appeared and grabbed my arm, pulling me from my chair. I went along without a struggle, thinking that when we got into the lobby I would get away. He pulled me toward a waiting elevator. There was no operator and no one in that part of the lobby. My survival instincts kicked in. I tried to remember my dad's judo instructions, but my torturous high heeled shoes came to my rescue. As he tried to shove me into the elevator, holding both of my arms in a vise-like grip, I brought one of my stiletto heels down on his foot with all my might. It seemed I could hear his yowls of pain all the way to my bus stop.

On the bus I leaned my head against the cool window,

wondering for the first time if I really knew what I was doing with my great plan. John had wiped out most of my bank account and gone back to Seattle. Everybody I met wanted to be my mentor, agent, or attorney. *Maybe I should pack up and go home,* I thought. *John will eventually come to his senses and we'll settle down and raise a family. I could get a job in a department store and, if necessary, date some guy who works at Boeing.* The minute I fleshed out this scenario, I rejected it. Maybe for some girls it would work, but I wanted excitement in my life and, let's face it, tonight was pretty exciting. Maybe there would be some bumps in the Yellow Brick Road, but then, who ever knows for sure what lies around the next bend?

20 My wish that a new adventure would happen soon came true the very next day. As soon as I had settled into the apartment on Beachwood, I called John's old army buddy Kenny Miller and gave him my number. He had promised we would get together soon. When he called back he invited me to a party to celebrate his landing the role of Danny Kaye as a young man in the story of Hans Christian Anderson. To say I was excited was a vast understatement. I was ecstatic! My first Hollywood party! He told me to ask Donna to come along too. He had gotten to know her during our Paso Robles days and said it would be a reunion as well as a celebration.

Kenny was living in a duplex in the Hills with two other guys, both would-be actors. He said that he had told them all about me, which is something I always hate to hear. (Would they want to meet me anyway?) The party was two days off, barely giving me time to decide what to wear.

When at last the party day arrived I sat wearing a classic sexy dress (visualize Marilyn Monroe in a dress borrowed from Grace Kelly. At least that was how I hoped I looked.) Being a blonde was something that took a little getting used to. I tried my hair in a French roll. Too Kim Novak. Pony tail? Sandra Dee, not me. Hanging loose? Well. . .a Marilyn wannabe. No, I decided to do my "Jayne Mansfield after being sent to an expensive finishing school" look.

Jackie arrived home in time to give her Cadillac door alert. She checked me over like a sergeant inspecting a new recruit. I hoped she wouldn't get too close and notice I had used a little of her Chanel No.5 cologne.

"Big date?" she asked. "No, just a party with a few actor friends of mine," I said. "I think Danny Kaye is going to be there." I had to throw that in, just in case he did show up. I snatched up my white poodle cloth stole and headed for the door. "See you tomorrow," I said over my shoulder, hoping she got the message that I would be very, very late.

Donna and I complimented each other's outfits as we settled ourselves into Liz's baby blue Caddy. She was wearing a very full blue cotton skirt which hid her overly generous hips and an off-the-shoulder peasant blouse. I thought she looked great. With me in my long, tight black sheath with a slit in the back and long strands of pearls, we looked like Heidi meets Mata Hari.

We drove down Hollywood Boulevard toward Highland. Unfortunately, we had the top up to protect our hairdos, so we did not get the stares I was sure we would have otherwise. As directed by Kenny, we turned up Highland and drove to the first light above Franklin which was Camrose Drive. Amazingly, it was not a real street but a beautiful walkway lined with lush plants and flowering trees. We parked as near as we could and started toward the duplex, where the sounds of a party were underway. Donna pointed out a structure nearby that looked like the Washington Monument. She explained it was called "High Tower" and contained an elevator that took you up to two levels of lanes with charming houses scattered on the hillside. Clinging to the hillside nearest the tower was a modern building with curved glass walls. It was a triplex, and Russ Tamblyn lived in the largest unit. My sense of being in the Land of Oz got stronger and stronger.

Kenny met us at the door with hugs and compliments. He immediately took us through the living room filled with people talking, smoking and drinking to seek out his two housemates. I resisted the impulse to clutch at Donna and ask if she was seeing what I was seeing. In front of us were two of the handsomest guys I had ever laid eyes on. First we met Zollan. He was muscular and tanned with dark wavy hair and strong white teeth. If that weren't enough, he had kind eyes. Nearby, talking to a tall, bored-looking female with waaaay too much hair spray on was Cole. Like Zollan he had dark, wavy hair, but it was set off by creamy pale skin and intense dark eyes under arched eyebrows. When we were introduced he smiled, and I saw flawless blue-white teeth behind Michelangelo lips. Whoa! Nobody in Seattle looked like this! I wondered if they were gay. I suspected Kenny was, so maybe so. Anyway, it was a pleasure just to look at them.

The duplex, from what I could see of it through the throngs of people, seemed to be a spacious two-bedroom apartment with a homey living room complete with fireplace, large dining room, kitchen with built-in nook, two bedrooms with a bathroom, easily located by the women who were already lined up to use it. The large living room window overlooked downtown Hollywood, and I could see Grauman's Chinese Theatre blazing with lights below. Kenny explained that the guy who got the bedroom with the double bed also got kitchen clean-up duty, while the two who shared the twin beds cleaned the rest of the apartment. Zollan had the private bedroom, either because he was better in the kitchen or needed privacy. I guessed maybe both. The furniture was similar to what most of our

157

parents owned: pre-war comfortable, and slightly shabby pieces, undoubtedly furnished by the building's owner.

As we did our tour I caught snatches of conversation over the lush sounds of Sarah Vaughn coming from the stereo. I heard references to Kaz, Tony-Jan, and "Ten." I figured out Kaz was Elia Kazan and Tony-Jan were Tony Curtis and Janet Leigh (top of the social A-List). But Ten?

I asked Kenny how he had met Zollan and Cole. He said that, after getting out of the service he enrolled in an acting school in Hollywood under the G.I. Bill. Zollan and Cole were also Korean vets and were doing the same thing. The school was run by Dan O'Herlihy who had won a best actor Oscar for Robinson Crusoe. Kenny said that even though he considered himself a song and dance man, he was getting some small acting roles and thought this would be a great opportunity to study with a fine actor like O'Herlihy—the Lee Strasberg of Hollywood, as he put it.

At that point he excused himself to greet a newcomer (no sign of Danny Kaye yet) and left me with Phil Dixon, a comedy writer. Phil was mid-thirtyish, dark-haired and balding. Kenny had said he could answer any and all questions about Hollywood and its denizens. When I asked him who "Ten' was, I thought I might have stumped him.

"Ten . . .Ten," he mused, stroking his clipped beard. Then he broke into a grin. "I've got it! Did you hear it from that Rock Hudson look-alike over there? He's pretending to have a thing going with Tennessee Williams, because no one else calls him Ten." It was part of the game of being hipper than everyone else. Phil took me under his wing so we could circle the room and he could point out who was phony, who was real, and who was a little of both.

"Am I real or phony?" I asked with a smile.

"Well, let me see," he answered. "Tell me who you've met

since you came to Hollywood. I mean, drop some names on me."

"Okay. While I was sitting on a bus bench I met Pinky Lee's son Morgan. He's getting ready to do a TV show for NBC and he introduced me to Phil Berle, Milton's brother. Then when I was having lunch at the counter of Dupar's on Vine I met Benny Gray whose brother Bill Gray is a comedian who owns Billy Gray's Bandbox, a pretty nice nightclub. How's that?"

"You've met everybody's relatives. That's good. That's not phony, because nobody cares about relatives. For instance, I live up the street, and do you know who my paper boy is? Rita Hayworth's brother, Ed Cansino. Do I brag about that? No. But if I referred to 'talking to Joan Collins last week and that we were getting pretty friendly,' that's semi-phony. The translation probably would be, 'I parked her car at Ciro's last week and I told her to enjoy the show.' By the way, the Bandbox is nothing much in the way of nightclubs. Ciro's, Mocambo, Interlude, Coconut Grove—namedrop those, kid."

"You work at Ciro's? I thought you were a comedy writer."

"I am. I just finished some stuff for Buddy Hackett, but when I'm between jobs, I park cars. By the way, if someone tells you they're going down to pick up a check at 'U.I.,' they're not talking about Universal International. It's unemployment insurance they're talking about. This town is full of phonies. You'll find out."

With that, Phil walked away leaving me slightly confused. What does this mean? Nobody cares about celebrities' relatives? What about Phil Berle? He's a vice-president at NBC. Certainly he can help me. Then there's Morgan and *Dollars for Scholars*. I thought I was doing pretty well, even with my recent modeling fiasco.

I went looking for Donna and found her talking to Zollan. I didn't want to interrupt, so I found Kenny. "This is really exciting that you landed a role in a Danny Kaye movie! You're on your way!"

"Thanks, but you never know. It's not a very big part, and there's always the old cutting room floor. My agent has a couple of other things I may be best for. So, where's John? I thought he'd be in Hollywood too."

"Oh, he will be," I replied, "but he had a chance to play at the best restaurant in Seattle. So we thought he should do that while I settled down here." I didn't want to tell Kenny the whole sordid story, so instead I said, "I like your friends. Phil is a kick and I see Donna is entertaining Zollan, or vice versa."

"If Cole could break away from his old girl friends, I'd like for you two to get acquainted. I know you'll like him."

I felt a strange sense of relief. *So he's not gay.* Then I wondered why I cared. *I'm not looking for a romance, am I?* When I left Seattle my friends predicted I'd start an affair right away, if for no other reason than to show John I could. *Ridiculous!* But then there was something about Cole that was strangely appealing. Not sexy, exactly, but as if I'd known him in another time and place. Suddenly he looked over at me and I felt something like goose bumps. He got up and started toward me, and I had to sit down.

"So this is Karoline, star of 'Basic Ballyhoo.' See, I know a lot about you," he said, in a deep, husky, cigarette voice. "That's a great dress, by the way. You must have bought it in Seattle because this town is too casual for real style."

"Thank you. I did get it in Seattle. I haven't had time to look around the stores here very much. Where do you think I should shop?"

"You look like Magnin's to me. There's a Magnin's in Beverly Hills, but meanwhile, are you doing anything tomorrow night that might be more interesting than what I'm doing?"

"Talk about a loaded question," I countered. "What if you're going to wrestle alligators and I'm going to a fashion awareness session for Masai tribal leaders taught by Zsa Zsa Gabor?"

"Fair enough," he chuckled. "Zollan and I are going to a little party at Ray Harryhausen's. He's the special effects guy who just finished *Jason and the Argonauts*. I thought you might like to see his place and meet him."

"Wow and wow! I'd cancel a night of debauchery for that," I said. "Harryhausen is a legend, even in Seattle."

"Okay, give Zollan your address and we'll pick you up at eight. Wear one of your Seattle dresses. Maybe he'll use you as a model for one of his mythological creatures."

"I'll be sure to wear my Medusa party dress with dress-up snakes," I said breathlessly. "Good," he replied, "just as long as it's not the couture from the Black Lagoon."

We laughed together heartily, and I walked away with the happiest feeling I'd had in months. I dragged Donna away from Zollan reminding her that she had to drive back to Encino. I didn't mention my plans for the next night, partly because she wasn't invited and partly because it almost sounded like a date and I wasn't ready to think about that yet. Maybe the best part was that, unlike all the other men I had met so far, Cole wasn't asking to be my mentor, agent, manager, or companion. He just seemed to like me. He never once looked down at my chest. Perhaps that's why I decided that tomorrow night I'd wear my white cashmere sweater over my most uplifting Merry Widow. Couldn't hurt!

21 The next night Cole picked me up and we headed for the party at Ray Harryhausen's.

The first thing I noticed in the room was a large Godzilla-type monster on the main table, surrounded by trays of hors d'oeuvres. If the purpose of the monster was to discourage guests from helping themselves, it wasn't working. They were consuming liberally, as were the guests at the drinks table that was guarded by a two-headed creature. Someone had placed a cigar in the clenched teeth of one of the heads. Cole said it made the monster resemble his landlord. I laughed and slipped a wine glass into the flexible claws of the poor fellow.

"I see you're having fun with my children," a voice behind us said. Turning around I saw a tall, slender, fortyish man. Cole introduced me to our host. Ray was not what I expected. No Dr. Hyde was he, but rather a professor-of-ancient-studies kind of guy. "I can't have fun if they're not having fun," I said. "Besides, I want to be on their good side."

As we chatted about his latest monster movie, I couldn't take my eyes off what appeared to be a human ear in a shadow box frame at the front door. Now this gave me the creeps. I asked if it was real, and Ray said indeed it was. *An original Van Gogh?* I wondered, but something in our host's manner told me not to pursue it. Besides, a little mystery is the way all things should be left.

Cole had been cornered by an old friend, so I wandered around the room looking for more oddities. Suddenly a drink was placed in my hand by a man with a decided East Coast look—medium build, thinning dark hair, and expensive-looking sport coat. "My name is Bob Kane. May I know yours?"

"Karoline. Karoline Morrison," I replied, adding, "Your name is so familiar, yet I can't connect it."

"Happens a lot," he said. "You might be more acquainted with my alter ego, Batman."

"Of course! Batman! My favorite superhero. Wow, what a thrill!" I gushed, trying to hide my disappointment that he didn't look even remotely like Batman. Not that he would, of course.

We sat down and had an interesting conversation. He was newly divorced and was looking into some TV possibilities in L.A. He told me he didn't have to be present in his New York studio to draw the pictures for upcoming issues. He had a file of Batman in various poses, so his assistant would, for example, look in "Drawer C" for Batman rescuing a child or whacking a villain and so on. It really sounded like a heck of a deal to me. The comic strip produced itself, so to speak. No wonder he was looking for new avenues for Batman and his many villains. We spent some time discussing why Batman was sexier than Superman. He really seemed to want my opinion. So I gave it to him.

"First of all, Superman's suit is, well, garish. Bright blue with red trim and then that big S! And don't get me started on that cowlick! Now Batman's costume is tasteful. There are shades of dark with a small color-coordinated bat in the center. The cap is very trendy with its sharp scallops.

The boots are low key (not bright red, like you know who's) and the headpiece lends an air of mystery. No one would guess he was Bruce Wayne, if they didn't know about the Bat Cave in Wayne Manor. As for Superman, who does he think he's fooling, just taking off his glasses and changing clothes? Come on!"

Anyway, when I felt I needed to get up and move around the room, Bob asked if I would mind giving him my phone number. He said he might be able to suggest a few contacts for me. I had told him that I was looking for acting or modeling jobs. I said nothing about John. Actually, for a while, I had forgotten about my real reason for being in Hollywood. I gave him my roommate Jackie's number and said I would look forward to hearing from him.

When we left the party, I was very excited. Wait till I tell Donna! Guess who will be calling me soon? Batman! Well, sort of. A few days after the party at Ray's I found a message from Jackie on my pillow. "Some guy called for you, said his name is Bob Kane, and he has a job offer for you."

First thing in the morning I called Bob's number. It went to an answering service, so I left my name and said I'd be around all day. An hour or so later he returned my call. We exchanged a few pleasantries, and then he told me what he was proposing. He had an offer from Playboy Magazine to do some work for them, just while he was waiting for his TV show to start. He really needed a Playboy-type model, so he thought of me. He explained that the work would take place at his apartment in Hollywood, and probably he would want to work outside around the pool.

I appreciated the fact that he was calming any fears I might have that this was just a ploy to get me alone in his apartment. *Hey,* I thought, *this is Batman, kind of, sort of, so what the heck, I'll do it. Besides, after my recent experience with the drunken attorney, I think I can take care of myself.*

Thus began some pleasant afternoons beside the pool at a classy neo-Hispanic apartment building. I don't think anyone knew who he was. Jackie didn't. He sketched while we talked and exchanged stories. I knew he didn't need a model. He had reams of sketches of voluptuous women in a drawer at his east coast office. I usually brought a two-piece swimsuit or wore short shorts and a halter. There was a small cabana near the pool where I changed.

Only once did I go into his apartment and that was because it started to rain. The first thing I noticed were several photographs of Marilyn Monroe hanging on the walls of the small living room. There were also some sketches he had done of her. Unlike the ones he was doing of me, these were exquisitely done—the work of an artist rather than a cartoonist. Seeing my obvious interest in his work he smiled. "As you can see, I am an admirer of Marilyn. I was able to meet her and spend a little time with her now and then." I thought to myself, *admire her? I would say smitten with her.* He began putting away his sketching materials and said, "Look, I think we may as well call it a day. How about next week? Surely the rain will have stopped by then." He handed me fifty dollars, the usual amount, which I tried to refuse. He placed the bills in my hand and closed my fist. "Karoline, it's worth it just to have you here for a few minutes and brighten up a rainy day in L.A." Sitting on the bus going back to my apartment I started to wonder if I might be getting into a situation more involved than I expected or wanted.

The next day the sun was out and I got a call from Morgan Lee. He invited me to a picnic in what he described as "a very unusual place." He said he would get some sandwiches from Canter's Deli and pick me up at noon. I realized I was looking forward to an afternoon with Morgan. He was young, cute, and non-threatening. Maybe best of all, he had connections. I put on a bright blue and white halter-topped dress. It looked enough like a picnic tablecloth to be suitable. I added my snake-proof straw wedgies to the ensemble, and I was ready!

The day was sunny and warm, so we drove with the top down. Instead of heading toward the beach, we drove up into the hills. We wound round and round and finally turned into the driveway of a house that appeared to be under construction. I was flabbergasted. "Have a picnic in an unfinished house? Come on!" This is the way I was talking to Morgan as we got out of the car. He told me just to wait and see. We walked around to the back side of the house where a spectacular view spread out before us. We could see the ocean in the far distance. Only after oohing over the magnificent vista did I see where we were headed. On the brink of the hillside was a finished swimming pool and in the middle of it was a small island with a live palm tree growing in the center of it. It was crazy and beautiful at the same time.

"That's where we're having our picnic," he said. "We'll pretend that we're shipwrecked, like in those cartoons."

"But how are we going to get there without getting wet?" I asked nervously.

"Just wait here a minute," he said, as he walked to a small shed nearby. When he returned he was carrying a small inflated boat that would barely hold two people. There were a couple paddles inside.

"Normally, we keep this on our boat, but I brought it up here just for us." He launched it into the pool and put the deli sack and wine bottle in the bow. Next he took off his shoes and suggested I do the same. He got in, gave me his good hand, and I managed to clamber aboard. He grabbed the mini oars and seven seconds later we made landfall. Morgan secured the "boatlet" to the small cleat embedded in the cement foundation of the island. We disembarked and unloaded our cargo. As I looked for a suitable picnic spot on the twelve-by-twelve-foot island, Morgan announced he would be right back. He hopped aboard our craft and came back carrying a portable radio.

We found a spot on the "far" side of the island. The ground had been planted with some sort of dense green growth. (At least it wasn't indoor/outdoor carpeting, which had just come into vogue). We sat down, opened the bottle of wine, and took two plastic glasses out of the deli bag. Two glasses later it was clearly time to have lunch. The large deli bag contained sandwiches, napkins, potato salad, and forks, but no tablecloth!

"We don't have a tablecloth," I complained.

"Do we need one?"

"Of course we do. We may be marooned on an island, but we still have our standards. Would there be something in the house?"

"Nothing I can think of. Maybe some tar paper."

"I will not eat lunch off tar paper," I said, and two minutes later I was spreading my dress on the ground with the food arranged on the full skirt and the forks and napkins tucked into the halter top. I was spooning out potato salad and baked beans, being careful not to spill on my dress-tablecloth. Certainly Hugh Hefner would approve of my hostess attire: low cut, white lace Merry Widow with matching lace panties.

Later, when I was leaning against the palm tree (I had named it General Lee), I felt I had "gone Hollywood." And if I had, so be it! Listening to Sinatra on a fake island, looking good in my underwear, and knowing John couldn't be having this much fun, I felt my life was on the upswing!

Shine glorious sun, filling all with hope and cheer
Banish paleness forever! Your tan is here!
      Parody of an old song

22 I have always cultivated a summer tan, even though life in Seattle limits tanning days to afternoons from late July to mid-September. During these times I would grab my tube top and short shorts to sprawl on a blanket in the back yard. If it appeared we were going to be blessed with a full day of sunshine, I'd go with a girlfriend to nearby Green Lake or Golden Gardens, a beach on Puget Sound. I had been told that a better tan is achieved near a body of water. More importantly, the public beaches were the place to see and be seen by boys. This was the basic Seattle formula for getting a tan.

In Hollywood one warm summer evening, I was waiting for Donna in the bar of Sherry's on Sunset Boulevard. I noticed two muscular guys in tee-shirts sitting at a nearby table. Each of them had one arm stretched across the table. *Aha!* I thought, *I am about to see an arm wrestling match.* I put my money mentally on the one who had rolled up his sleeves to shoulder height. Very Brando! I waited and waited, and nothing happened. Suddenly I realized they were not about to arm wrestle at all; they were comparing tans! Unbelievable! Is a tan a measure of macho? While I didn't get to see an arm wrestle, I was satisfied that my favorite contestant was the obvious winner with a deep bronze tan that extended way up under his jaw. No farmer's tan there.

The next day I described this incident to Cole. He laughed and explained that getting the perfect L.A. tan was very serious business. He said he was prepared to give me instructions in a master class. The requirements were tanning lotion (without sun screen), two walnut shells, minimal swimsuit and an egg timer. A portable radio was optional. Of all these items the egg timer was the most critical. It would be set to go off at fifteen-minute intervals. That buzzing indicated it was time for a quarter turn. Starting face up with walnut shells firmly in place over the eyes, by the time an hour passed, every part of one's exposed body would be equally exposed to the sun. This precise program was to be repeated twice a day every day and would guarantee an even, contest-winning tan.

A week later, comedy writer Phil Dixon told me where to see the best tans in town. He invited me to accompany him to pick up his check at "U.I."—the Hollywood unemployment insurance office. "The people in line there have the best tans in town," he said.

23 I threw myself into the hurly-burly world of actors (working ones and hopeful ones), comedy writers, and groupies. Cole, Kenny, and Zollan's place was a sitcom come to life. The talk was all about who was up for which part, who was sleeping with whom to get a part, or who had been cast in something. If it was a movie role, that was a major coup. A TV appearance was great, if it was for a hit series. A modeling job was commendable, if it was for a TV spot. Residuals—the gift that keeps on giving? Or to be on the cover of an album? Eh!

Advice started coming at me from all directions. "The Player's Ring is auditioning for 'Voice of the Turtle,' and all the studio casting directors come opening night." "NBC has a variety show in the works. They want girls with figures like yours!" "To do what?" "Oh, just stand around, I guess, but lots of people are discovered that way." "I have a friend at MGM. You've got to meet him. He can see that you meet the right people!" "What does he do at MGM?" "Oh, he works the commissary, but he waits on all the big stars."

Such was the chatter about what the studios were looking for. There was also constant agent talk. Who's gotten an agent, finally! (You can't get a part without an agent. And you can't get an agent unless you have or have had a part.) I was respected by the gang for belonging to

AFRA, which was now AFTRA, as Thomas Peluso had pointed out to me. I assumed I was grandfathered into the TV membership category, along with Jack Benny and Bob Hope, even though I had not done any work in TV at that point. In the Seattle market women on TV usually did only weather reports or dressed like clowns to entertain children.

The only person in our group who was actually making a living from acting was Kenny Miller, our old Army buddy. He had a part in *The Search for Bridey Murphy*, a movie based on the book about a woman who, via hypnosis, was taken back through time. She revealed the many lives she had lived. Kenny played her brother. It was a dull role, and he had leg cramps from the three-inch lifts he had to wear in his shoes. For some reason the director wanted him taller than his own five feet seven inches. No one knew why or cared. It was a part with screen credit—that's all that mattered. But it gave me the idea of having a "Who were you?" party. Someone in the group knew a hypnotist who agreed to help us carry it off. That is how I learned about parties in Hollywood. In Hollywood, you'd invite ten or fewer people to a party, and you'd get twenty. In Seattle, if you wanted twenty people to attend, you had to invite forty.

The hypnotist, Don, a slender, pale, balding guy in his late thirties, agreed to hypnotize three people. The night of the party we drew straws. They all went to women. One guy drew a winning straw but passed, saying he had a nervous bowel condition and didn't want to take any chances. This was greeted with heartfelt applause.

We were packed tight in the living room and dining room with a single chair in the center. There was only one lamp on, and the effect was a tad eerie. The first subject, a thin blond girl who worked at Coffee Dan's, seemed to slip easily into a trance after a few standard words from

174

Don. "You are relaxed. You are getting drowsy." I expected her to go back in time in stages, but she immediately jumped back 2,000 years. She said she was the daughter of an Egyptian pharaoh and her name was Selkit. We all gasped and giggled. A guy next to me whispered that he was sure that her mother had worked as an extra in "The Ten Commandments." She woke up the minute Don snapped his fingers and said she had no idea what had happened. We told her.

The next two, not to be outdone, had equally famous, previous lives. One was a Viking princess. In a voice that was slightly Nordic sounding she told of sailing with Leif Erikson to the New World, where she died a noble death fighting off the natives. It seemed an unlikely story, but she was a robust, blue-eyed blond, so who could say?

The third person was a tall, stunning girl with glossy black hair and coppery skin. Once into her trance she began to speak a strange, guttural language, then English, but very softly. She said she was lying on a sacrificial stone slab atop a pyramid. As a virgin daughter of a Mayan chief, she was about to be sacrificed in an ancient ritual. Her heart would be cut out with an obsidian knife. The room was deathly still. No one moved. Suddenly she opened her eyes wide and with a soul-shattering scream fell off the chair onto the floor. The crowd erupted. Several people left the apartment. Others brought water and cold cloths and said comforting words. Don, paler than ever, kept saying over and over, "I've never had this happen before." The young woman assured us she was okay and didn't want to talk about it. The guy who brought her found her jacket and said he'd take her home.

After they left, opinions flew all over the place. Most of the questions were asked of Don, who avoided them and excused himself. Kenny ended the speculation by saying, "Well, I hope that last one was faked, because she could really have a future in Universal's horror pictures." At that point Zollan brightened the mood by announcing the next party. He had just gotten a part in an episode of "Ramar of the Jungle." Since he was to play an East Indian, he was required to completely shave his entire body. "Here's my invitation," he said. "I'll supply razors, shaving cream, beer and wine. You do the rest. Meet Saturday."

The next morning I got a call as I was getting out of the tub. Hoping it was John telling me he was on his way down from Seattle, I said hello with puppy-like eagerness. But it was just Jim, a guy I had met at the Bridey party. Jim said he had a part in a Western at Warner's and he needed to get really good at using a foot-long bull whip. He said he practiced up in the hills near the Hollywood sign. Would I like to come along and watch, tomorrow? I consulted my calendar and said tomorrow would be fine. He suggested I wear boots, since sometimes there were rattlesnakes around. I said I didn't have any boots, but I had three-inch wedges with ankle straps. He said that sounded fine.

The next day he picked me up wearing chino pants tucked into army boots topped off with a short cowhide jacket. I was wearing tight pink cotton Capri pants with a pink and white polka-dotted jacket. My outfit went well with my snake-proof wedgies. We looked like we were from two different movies—Betty Gable meets Lash LaRue. The whip was long and black and very mean-looking. He wore it coiled around his left shoulder as we walked up into the hills. I wished John could see me.

Jim uncoiled the whip and grasped the braided handle. Stepping back a few steps, he raised his arm up and back. The whip rippled out, making a satisfying crack. "Wow, that was great," I said. "Just getting warmed up," he answered. He continued the exercise, and the crack got louder and sharper. I wondered briefly if I could try it, but decided it didn't really go with my look of the day. Now, had I been wearing my black leather pants and vest, I could have been enticed.

As he practiced, he moved steadily away from me. When he was about thirty feet away he suddenly yelled, "Don't move, whatever you do, don't move!" I didn't, and the whip lashed out near me. Dropping the whip he ran over and bent down on the brush next to me. When he straightened up, he was holding a headless snake that still seemed to be writhing. "Look at what was ready to kiss those pretty ankles." He tossed it as far as he could into the brush. "I think I just saved your life," he said.

"I need to sit down," I said. He coiled the whip, held my arm, and we both walked out alive—me barely.

The next day I realized what a great adventure I had had. It was a new version of *The Perils of Pauline*. I couldn't wait to rush over to tell Cole, Zollan and Kenny what had happened. Grabbing a cup of killer coffee from the bottomless pot in their apartment, I started to tell my tale of high adventure in the famous and deadly Hollywood Hills. When I got to the end, Cole looked at me over his coffee cup and asked, "Did he hit on you after you got to the car?"

"Well, maybe, sorta. I mean he said now we have this bond. And in China, when someone saves your life you belong to that person spiritually."

"So, did you go to bed with him?"

"Of course not. I hardly know him!"

"But he saved your life!"

"So? A mailman once warned me about a vicious dog in

177

our neighborhood, but I didn't go to bed with him."

Cole laughed, "Good for you. Now tell me, did you get a close-up look at that snake?"

"Yuck! I didn't want to look at that thing."

"I think you might have been surprised if you had. Jim has pulled this before. He puts a rubber snake with the head cut off in his boot. When he looks like he is getting it out of the bushes, he is really pulling it from his boot. He's probably got a drawer full of headless rubber snakes."

That night I thought a lot about life in Hollywood, land of make believe. What is real? Was the girl in the trance real or was it great acting? Are there any real snakes in Hollywood? At least one for sure, and I never wanted to see him again. As I was falling asleep in my lonely little room, I wondered, what if that had been John with the bullwhip and a snake? I would have gone to bed with him, even if I knew it was a fake snake.

It is myself that I remake
⌐─⌐ *Yeats*

24 Among my friends there was not a single nine-to-fiver in the bunch. Sometimes one of us would have an early morning appointment for an audition or a small part in a movie or TV show. In that case, any complaint about getting up early was far outweighed by the gloating. Our real jobs tended to be in nightclubs or dinner houses, or something similar, as we waited to be discovered.

Left with time on our hands during the day, we frequently gathered in one of the coffee shops, such as Coffee Dan's or Aldo's, that thrived along Hollywood Boulevard. These were cheap gathering places for the would-be famous. After all, wasn't Lana Turner discovered at that counter in Schwab's drug store? We would find a prominent booth near the entrance where we drank endless cups of coffee, gossiped, and critiqued everyone between the ages of sixteen and thirty who came in the door.

"Here's a Natalie Wood-be who needs a nose job," someone might say. A curvy blonde would elicit something like, "Here comes a Jayne Mansfield with knock-off knockers wearing a 40D bra on 32A boobs. No centerfold for her!" A handsome, slender guy might get "Are those Queen-size cigarettes in his back pocket?" A stocky sunburned teen might elicit, "Too ugly even for Rock Hudson." We showed no mercy, and we loved it!

If business was slow, we sometimes amused ourselves with a contest called "How Far Would You Go to Get That Part?" Screwing the old and ugly gossip columnist was mentioned so often we put her in the "Hollywood Hall of Horrors."

As the only female in the group, my ideas were always eagerly awaited. I had no trouble with the concept. I always came up with Bob Hope's agent. He was an older man with the complexion of an anorexic corpse, thin wet lips, and an apathetic comb-over of thin strands of gray hair. Just helping him into his raincoat would be way too intimate. Kissing him on the cheek would require extreme stamina. The thought of going to bed with him was such a scary thought you'd want to sleep with the light on. When I said this to the group they accused me of not being properly career-motivated. Besides, how else do blondes get parts?

There were times I wondered just how far I really would go to get a break. I would stop thinking about it by telling myself that if it ever came up, I would decide then. Naïve me lamented that sex seemed to be the bartering tool in Hollywood. In Seattle it was a girl's typing speed that got her the job . . . wasn't it?

One afternoon, while waiting at Aldo's for Donna to get off work, I sat at the bar and caught myself in the mirror. I liked what I saw. I was wearing a brown soft jersey that clung deliciously to my body all the way to my knees, where it flared out. The sales girl at Nancy's across the street called it a trumpet dress. *Yes*, I thought, *but not blowing taps— more like reveille*. The look was sexy in an elegant kind of way. It was a look seldom seen in Hollywood since Grace Kelly left town.

Suddenly a wave of memory washed over me. In my youth I had been the subject of intense physical scrutiny, just like the ridicule my buddies and I were dishing out at the coffee shops.

I was ten years old when my parents and I left our beloved prison island home and moved to Tacoma, Washington. My dad could no longer endure the rigors of being a guard in a large federal penitentiary. He actually didn't mind handling the toughest of the men and frequently came home bruised and battered. When we exclaimed in horror, he would say, "You oughta see the other guy." In fact he was chosen to head the team of guards transporting the worst of the worst to be relocated at Alcatraz. It was the lonely hours of tower duty that really got to him. No reading, no one to talk to. Just hours of staring endlessly at the penitentiary grounds. Even though he appreciated McNeil Island after experiencing the grim and forbidding bareness of Alcatraz, he felt he had to go.

I had loved my little two-room school on McNeil. It was presided over by two German sisters. One taught first through fourth grades (my room), and her sister (the kinder, gentler one) had the fifth through eighth grades. After graduation from eighth grade the students would take the prison launch to the mainland, then transfer to a bus that took them to Clover Park High. I had been looking forward to going to high school in that adventurous fashion. I loved the sometimes stormy trip to the mainland and would laugh at those who got seasick.

My favorite *trusty*, Rain-In-The-Face, an Alaskan Indian, frequently piloted the boat without even a guard aboard. He was a trusty with a capital T. My mom told me he was in prison for killing his wife; but that was not considered a serious crime by the authorities, since it was not a crime in tribal law. His wife was guilty of having an affair with another man. I think my mom secretly felt the wife got what she deserved. Rain-In-The-Face was short and stocky with a kind, dark face. When he carried me as a baby I could smell the woods after a rainfall in his prison jacket. I remember the roughness of his hands. He was always my dad's choice when we needed help at our house and was the one who helped us move away. I cried when we said good-bye.

My mother was worried about Dad not having a job in the midst of the Depression. I was worried about leaving our beloved beachfront cottage, which my father had described once as "three rooms and a path." Even the thought of having an indoor bathroom like my cousins on the mainland didn't make up for leaving my island paradise.

My first day at Edison School in Tacoma was awful. The building was a large, cold, brick structure not unlike the prison on McNeil. There were thirty-two kids in my room, the same number in the whole school on the island, where each grade was seated in one row. I didn't mind the classes. I didn't chew gum or whisper, so I never got in trouble. On my letter of grade transfer from my old school, it said I was a very bright student and had skipped second grade. I got a certain amount of respect from my new teachers because of this. I did not get it on the playground.

Recess was the hardest part of the day. Back on the island, recess was a time for hopscotch on a grid drawn in the dirt with a stick, or playing in the nearby woods (unless there had been an escape; then, of course there was no school at all). At my new school, hopscotch was played on a painted grid without the challenging irregularities of one that was stick-drawn. When I was on the playground, the large building looked more and more like a prison where I was serving out a life sentence. While the other girls played games or stood in groups talking and laughing, I stood silently on the sidelines. I was out of place. Even my clothes were different. On the island everybody dressed pretty much the same. All of us had fathers working for the prison and earning about the same amount of money. Shopping was limited to occasional trips to the mainland. In other words, we were innocents in the world of fashion.

One winter, at my new school, the Cummins sisters showed up wearing long black stockings. They were both upper graders and treated us lower graders with the traditional disrespect. I was shocked by this strange new garment of theirs, but also felt a kind of pity for them that was unfamiliar to me. The rest of us girls were wearing the standard long, oatmeal-colored stockings hooked to our elastic garter belts. It was the traditional look every girl had until Easter, when we joyously changed to ankle socks.

To my amazement, the curious pity I felt the first day changed to a certain kind of envy as the days went by. It was similar to the impact of those American women who came back from Paris wearing sheer nylon stockings while everyone else still wore dull rayon with crooked seams up the back. The black stockings of the Cummins sisters were a fashion innovation! Part of the secret was the way the Cummins sisters wore them. With total confidence! Pride even. I simply had to have a pair. Soon all the girls were begging their moms to go to the nearest Penney's and bring home a pair. My fashion consciousness was born!

The girls on the playground wore skirts and sweaters mostly and sometimes blouses. One day, when the weather had warmed up I looked down at my faded strapless cotton dress with its pathetic little flower design and realized that my anklets did not match my dress in any way. This made me especially hesitant to go through the playground entrance to the girls' basement—normally a place of refuge that was dimly lit. To get to the basement one had to pass by two upper grade girls who had stationed themselves on either side of the stairway. Like my Hollywood friends and I, they had anointed themselves fashion and good looks arbitrators. Every girl who passed beneath their critical gaze was given an instant assessment: "cute" or "ugly." That was it. No in-between. They were even harsher than we were from our judges' table in the coffee shop. At least we Hollywooders would occasionally give murmured advice like, "Lose the nose and forty pounds." At my new school, "cute or ugly" was it. There was whispering but no verdict. Hung jury.

After Christmas vacation, I was wearing a gift from my Aunt Hannah. It was a blue sailor dress with a large white collar. In addition, it came with a bright red tie, knotted navy style for the front of the dress. I was sure I had seen a picture of Shirley Temple in a similar dress. It was the best Christmas gift ever. On the island I would have wanted a basket for my bicycle or a copy of a good book. Not now, maybe never again. Clothes were IT!!

When recess time came I approached the guardians of the basement with a confidence I had only experienced when taking a test at school or being asked to read aloud. I held my head high, shoulders back and marched forward like a sailor going off to meet the enemy. I was like a Cummins girl. I looked good, and I knew it. When I got the long awaited "cute" designation, I didn't even care. The lesson I had learned was that if you believe in yourself, walk with an air of confidence, and have the right clothes, you can achieve almost anything you ever wanted.

25 As the days drifted by, I began to believe I was truly in the Land of the Lotus Eaters. I had left the apartment on Beachwood Drive and moved into a small ground floor apartment on Broadview Terrace next door to Cole, Kenny and Zollan. The owner of the house was a recently widowed woman who welcomed having a young woman downstairs. Unfortunately for her, I was never there. I spent most of my time with the guys. For one thing, there was no bathtub in my new digs, only a primitive and temperamental shower. I was a frequent sight on that strange little "no-street" going back and forth through the tropical foliage that separates the two properties. My usual attire was a short, short terrycloth robe, high-heeled mules and a bath towel draped across my shoulders. Phil Dixon said that his friends asked to be allowed to come and see this example of Hollywood's loose but clean living.

However entertaining the parade of out-of-work actors was, my old, traditional work ethic was kicking in. I was brought to my senses watching Phil, who wrote freelance comedy for Buddy Hackett, and others run down each week to pick up their checks at "U.I." I knew I had to break the spell I was under and find a job.

A few days earlier I had seen an ad in the *Hollywood Star* for a model photographer. I didn't know whether it was for someone to photograph models or for a photographer with impeccable, exemplary standards. I called and found out they wanted a female who would take pictures of patrons and also appear in pictures with them. It sounded perfect for me. The location was a bar on Hollywood Boulevard called the "Seven Seas."

I went to the interview in my best Destiny Darwin look. Designer dress, black velvet hat, pearls, hair in a French roll. I out-Graced Grace Kelly.

The man I met with was a dentist by day, but by night had the camera concession at the Seven Seas. He developed the pictures in a darkroom at the back of the building. The theme of the Seven Seas was the South Seas. There were three shows a night featuring hula dancers, firewalkers, ukulele players and anything else that evoked the South Pacific. The room had the usual bamboo and rattan furniture with bright flowered upholstery. The part I loved was that the entire room, except for the stage area, was densely planted with tropical foliage. Every twenty minutes, except during show time, it rained. Not just rained, it poured down on the surrounding jungle. It was Seattle in the tropics! I was to wear a sarong, flower in my hair, and not only take pictures of patrons learning to hula on stage, but be available to have my picture taken with them. At those times George, the dentist, would come out and take the photo himself. He was hoping to get a brunette for the job (too late; I was already a blonde). It didn't pay much, but he said the tips would be good, even though I didn't have brown hair.

I took the job, of course. I even offered to provide my own sarong. (If I could make a tablecloth out of a dress, I could make a sarong out of a tablecloth!) He said he provided sarongs and could I start that night. And I did.

The sarong was tight and low. My chest ranneth over as the saying goes, so the tipping was good and a lot of guys from "East Podunk" wanted to have a picture taken with me. I was frequently asked to autograph it "Love, Jayne." Some guys felt sure they could tell the folks back home I was Jayne Mansfield, since many of the pictures showed me putting a lei around a man's neck. One night George shocked me with his latest "brainstorm." He wanted to take some of the folders in which the photos were placed and have them inscribed "I got lei-d by Jayne" or "Jayne gives a good lei." That was when I decided it was time to take my show back on the road.

The very next day, Zollan gave me a lead that knocked me off my feet. He told me the cigarette girl at Ciro's was looking for an assistant and would I be interested. Would I?! Ciro's was my Shangri La, my El Dorado, my Emerald City!

I went to Ciro's that evening. I met Lynn, who had the concession for hat check and cigarettes. She was a thin, pale, wispy young woman more like a high fashion model than a cigarette girl. She asked me to try on the costume, a short strapless outfit to be worn with long, black mesh stockings. I looked into a mirror. *Yup,* I thought, *that's a cigarette girl. But is it me? Who am I now anyway? Doesn't matter,* I quickly decided, *this is a part of my master plan. I will get John a job here playing before show time. He will be discovered, then tour, sign a recording contract, replace Liberace on TV and give up other women.* I turned to face Lynn. "I'll take the job," I said.

"Don't you want to know what it pays?" she asked. "Oh, of course I do," I said. Little did she know I would have been willing to pay the last of my accident money for a chance to work at Ciro's. She told me the pay rate and said I was to turn in all tips, because they went to overhead and to her.

But she added that any tip of five dollars or more I could keep because "Then they are tipping the girl, not the job." "Sounds fair to me," I said. "When do I start?"

"Could you start tomorrow night?" she asked. "You should be here before eight to put on the costume and fill the cigarette tray. I'll leave a change bank of ones in it. Cigarettes are fifty cents a pack, cigars one dollar, except for the ones in the metal cases. Those are three dollars. If they hand you a five, say you're out of ones. The coat hooks are all numbered. Keep the checks here at the counter. Hats go on the shelf, put the check number in the brim. Oh, if it's a celebrity, never give them a check. It insults them. Just remember who it belongs to. Put their name on the peg if you think you can't remember. When you're not busy, put cigarettes on the tray and stroll through the show room. We do not call out, 'Cigars, cigarettes.' That's just in the movies or at low-class places. If someone wants cigarettes they tell the waiter who tells the maitre d' and he will give you the table number. You can leave after closing. I'll come by to pick up the money and lock up the checkroom."

"You mean you won't be here during the evening? " I asked, trying to keep the panic out of my voice. The answer was "No, why do you think I have an assistant?"

That first night at Ciro's was a blur of sights, sounds and the scents of expensive perfumes and good whiskey. I met the maitre d', Farrell, a Swede who was one of the biggest snobs I had ever met. When he had that velvet rope up, it was intended to exclude everyone he thought did not meet the Ciro's code of acceptability. One evening I heard him remark to Manuel, his handsome Aztec, god-like assistant, "Is this a farm now? Look, they are letting the animals in." This kind of remark was made about a hapless looking family from the Mid-west who just wanted a bite to eat and a peek at the stars.

On the other hand, Manuel was one of the sweetest men I had ever met. He helped me through that first evening and seemed to be happy to do so. The headliner that night was Nejla Atesh, a Turkish belly dancer, who had become a huge hit on Broadway the past season for her appearance in the musical *Fanny*. Since Maurice Chevalier, the star of *Fanny*, had fairly recently appeared at Ciro's, the word was that he had somehow convinced Ciro's owner, Herman Hover, and George Schlatter, Hover's show producer, to book Miss Atesh. Although she put on an amazing show, I don't think it was the "smasheroo" that had been anticipated. I found her performance fascinating but disturbing. I had seen belly dancers before. They were mostly suburban housewives who had taken lessons either to lose weight or to return passion to their marriages. What Nejla did was, well, creepy. Although she was a very attractive young woman in a beautiful costume, she danced like someone in the throes of a difficult childbirth. Her stomach heaved, contracted, swelled hugely, then contracted again, this time in circular movements. Someone near me whispered that they had been trained since childhood to control, not let go of, their abdominal muscles. I thought Nejla belonged at a gynecologists' convention, but I loved the music.

The big celebrities did not exactly rush in to see Nejla, except for poor Sonny Tufts. He was one of the very few male movie actors who had not joined the army during the war, so he had snagged roles in a few movies. He would come to Ciro's often, I was told, to sit at the bar and tell people who he was or used to be.

Since business was not booming that night, Manuel and I had a chance to talk about the history of Ciro's and its owner, Herman Hover.

Hover was a short, burly, dark haired man of Jewish

heritage who had led his family out to Hollywood in the thirties to get into the entertainment business. He had operated Ciro's since 1942 and then purchased it in 1946. The rumors were that Ciro's became popular during the war years because Herman had a connection to a meat packer. He was able to get expensive cuts of meat at a time when meat was rationed and fine steaks were rare. The building was large and loomed rather awkwardly up against the barren hills that looked down on the Sunset Strip. The name "Ciro's" was outlined in white neon script. The "C" was huge. Below the neon sign was a marquee carrying the name of the current show or entertainer. A sign over the stage door facing the street proclaimed, "Through These Portals Pass The Most Beautiful Girls in the World." Hover claimed to have coined this motto for Earl Carroll's Broadway and Hollywood theaters when he worked for Carroll as a publicity man in the 1930s. Carroll's Hollywood theater, bearing this sign, was sold in 1948 after Carroll's untimely death in an airplane crash.

To enter Ciro's was to enter a world smelling of expensive perfumes, good cigars and the best whiskey and women money could buy.

There was a semi-circular driveway where cars pulled up to have the passenger door opened by a well-dressed doorman. At the same time a valet opened the driver's door, quickly displacing the driver and whipping out into the Strip traffic. This was frequently a wild left turn to go to the huge parking lot a block and a half east, where he would make another left turn accompanied by much honking of other cars. If the arriving customer was a star, royalty, mogul or mobster, he or she had the privilege of parking in the small area next to the building. The drivers of these cars never got a claim ticket. That was for the peons.

The entrance to Ciro's was through double, opaque, wavy-glassed doors. On a warm night the doors were propped open. Patrons stepped onto elegant flooring of black and white marble through a velvet roped-off entry to the right. The check room was directly across from the doors, with a lavish ladies room to the right. The bar with its leather and chrome stools and large banquettes was just inside the entrance, and a few stairs led you down to the showroom. The actual stage was a small curtained area behind the dance floor with the band occupying most of it. Just before show time two busboys would pull a large platform out from under the stage to cover the dance floor. It brought the headline performers right up to the audience and gave intimacy to the large room.

There was a smaller room off the bar called "The Ciroette," which had its own outside entrance as well as one from the bar. A few steps up from the showroom was a small banquet room with a window overlooking the stage. The business offices and a huge banquet room that could accommodate two hundred people or more were located on the second floor. For an additional fee the banqueters could be led downstairs and seated to see the show. Show times were at ten and twelve, and two a.m. was closing time. Dinner was served starting at eight. Farrell, the hoity-toity maitre d', told me any food served after 8:30 was not dinner; it was supper!

I was now an employee at Ciro's, the hottest nightclub in the country. All my fantasies about moving in the world of glamour were becoming a reality.

Don't sell the steak; sell the sizzle
Elmer Wheeler

26 What I planned to do at Ciro's was make it sexy to buy cigars and cigarettes. After all, the benefits of smoking were being touted in TV ads like, "Manly men smoke Marlboros!" My pitch worked best when I was strolling through the show room or standing at the bar. Dim lights, throbbing music, and beautiful showgirls all helped raise the "temperature" in the room so I could maximize sales.

When I was called to a table or signaled to, it was always a man who beckoned. As I approached the table I would lift the tray chest-high, as though I was offering a rare gift of incense and myrrh. Once I was standing near my "caller," I would lower the tray slowly, so he could inspect the selection and also my chest. "Do you see anything there you like?" I asked throatily. *Remember, I was a paid radio actress.* If he chose a pack of cigarettes, I would open it, hand it to him, and then ask if he would like me to light a cigarette for him. Generally he would agree. Then, with a book of Ciro's matches in my hand, I would tear one out slowly, strike it, and hold the flame near my chest as he bent forward for the light. Not only did I get a good tip but men at nearby tables suddenly realized they too needed a pack.

Cigars required a different approach. Of course, I pitched the one in the metal tube. When I recommended it I would hold the tube in my hand and caress it gently. I explained that these were from a factory where they were rolled by hand against the thighs of young Cuban women. If I was asked to remove the cigar from the case, suffice it to say I did not use my hands to do so.

I have always loved selling, even before I knew what I was doing! The summer when I was twelve years old, World War II was still raging and everyone in Seattle who was able to get out of bed was either in the service, working for Puget Sound Shipyards, or on the production lines at Boeing. Meanwhile, the downtown stores were in trouble. Thousands of people had left their farms in Minnesota and Nebraska and other places to fill the well-paying jobs in Seattle. But when they wanted to spend their fat paychecks in the stores, there weren't enough salesclerks to wait on them.

This is how, at the age of twelve, I was hired to work in a clothing store on Second Avenue. It wasn't the Bon Marche or Frederick & Nelson, but I didn't care. I needed a new used bicycle (no new ones were made during the war time). With my recently acquired love of fashion I was happy to stock, tag, and yes, SELL! My salary was 32.5 cents an hour and I was worth every penny and a half of it!

Three days after I started work a woman I helped the day before came in and asked to see the manager. She produced a jacket from her shopping bag and said she wanted to return it because, "That girl over there MADE me buy it!" Of course she was pointing at me, and in that moment I knew that I had a career in sales ahead of me.

27 It didn't take long to realize that the cigarette girl was as important to the ambience of a club as the name entertainer on stage. Waiters and other employees expected exciting things to happen to the girls at the front desk. The most famous cigarette girl was Marjorie Steele who was pursued by Huntington Hartford, heir to a grocery chain fortune. She married him, and Herman Hover gave them a star-studded reception. Marjorie's successor, Reggie Drew, was offered a sex-for-jewels deal. Since the proposer was the Shah of Iran, I assume the jewels were his part of the deal. The story is that she turned him down, maybe waiting for a better offer. Since I now had this infamous position, I was very aware that the pressure was on. I must refuse or accept a comparable offer or the waiters and other staff would think I wasn't keeping life interesting enough for them.

One evening when Lynn actually showed up to give me some help, I asked her whether she had ever had any tempting offers. She said she had not (probably because she had thin legs and wore a training size 32-A bra). Ironically, the next act booked at Ciro's was the very hot vocal group, the Hi-Lo's. Their name came from both their individual vocal ranges and from their sizes. Two were tall and two were short. They were a popular attraction and were helped by the fact that Rosemary Clooney and then hubby Jose Ferrer were sort of sponsoring them. They had written a tribute on a Hi-Lo's album and were in the audience almost every night.

Lynn struck up a friendship *cum* relationship with Bob, one of the "high" ones and a really nice guy. I hoped for the best but had my doubts that this was a *MMIH* (match made in heaven). He was a sweet guy, a minister's son, and Lynn was... well, a little strange. At any rate, although she said they were not ready to "make an announcement to the media," things were getting pretty serious. So she said she was willing to give up her cigarette and hatcheck concession to me if I wanted it.

Whoa, baby, did I! The first thing I did after letting Mr. Hover know of this prospect was to find a place where I could buy cigarettes next to wholesale—less than two dollars a carton. Lynn had been buying them retail at grocery stores. Another thing that I brought in as part of my takeover was a showcase full of Ciro's mementos: Ciro's glasses, boxes of matches and a selection of expensive "Perfumes of Ciro," a company which happened to have the same name as the nightclub. The fragrances I offered were "New Horizons" and "Danger". (When I sold cosmetics at Magnin's I was told to pronounce it "Donjey." There wasn't much one could do with the pronunciation of New Horizons.) I put all of these items on sale.

Mr. Hover seemed to be pleased to have a new girl in charge. He told me he had just two rules for me. One was to keep my hair blond and the other was to never do anything to tarnish the name "Ciro's." I took the oath and to this day I try to live up to it. The next thing he did to show his appreciation of my new status was to order a costume for me. Don Loper, one of my favorite designers, came up with a beautiful gown. It was a ballerina-length gold pleated dress with a white angora, low-cut top. The top had a few tiny rhinestones nestled here and there, just to show some glitz. The effect of my new position on me was instantaneous. I got relief in my feet, which were always sore from walking around in mesh stockings. And I got more respect. Even the Mexican bus boys who used to get me to say dirty words in Spanish started to call me "Ma'm" or "La Rubia" (The Blonde), and they said it with respect and affection.

My income was increasing, so I said 'yes' when Donna called to tell me she wanted to move away from home and wondered if I could use a paying roomie. In fact, there was a really nice house for rent just a block and a half up Camrose Drive from Broadview Terrace, and it had a bathtub! A friend of Kenny's was looking for a place, so I moved out of my old place and he moved in, practically overnight.

The house Donna and I rented was a Spanish style bungalow with a wrap-around covered porch. It was furnished with bamboo pieces that I swore came from the same shop where the Seven Seas had bought their furniture. It was spacious and had a fireplace, French doors, and, best of all, there was a huge avocado tree in the cozy back yard. In an import shop in Hollywood I bought tatami mats bound in black cotton and then pinned Japanese woodblock prints to them. It not only showed that I had a decorator's touch, but also that I carried no grudges against the Japanese for unleashing Takiko on my husband. Besides, with all the wild tropical print on the furniture and drapes, the Japanese prints offered a respite for the senses. Of course, I called John to let him know that I was making money, had leased a beautiful house in the Hills, and that there was room for a piano in the large, airy living room.

I hadn't heard from John in several months. I had hocked

197

my wedding ring two months before. I even thought about having my wedding dress shortened to cigarette-girl length and wearing it with lace stockings. Mr. Hover wouldn't even notice because of his own personal crisis. In a move that devastated Hover and sent shock waves through the business, Hover's wife had left him for Dr. Weller, his sister's husband. *Maybe Hover and I should get together some night after closing,* I thought. *We certainly have a number of problems in common.*

To my great astonishment, John arrived a week later, no doubt drawn by my alluring descriptions of the new rental house. Donna had not moved in yet, so John and I were like honeymooners all over again. It was all that I had hoped for. Unfortunately, I had spent the remainder of the insurance money, after John's raid of the bank account, to pay for necessities, like beauty shop appointments, make-up, clothes, and rent deposits. I had no savings, and I didn't have time to pursue other income possibilities. So when a tall, young, blond woman with an honest face approached me one evening at Ciro's, I listened to her pitch about why she wanted to be my assistant. She said she had a boring secretarial job in Thousand Oaks and would be available to work any time to relieve me. She wasn't trying to break into show business; she just wanted to work at Ciro's.

I gave her the same conditions Lynn had given me. I explained that the costume I was wearing was made for me, but she could wear a nice cocktail dress and that would be adequate. Fine, she said. Well, it was fine with me too. I liked Beverly. When I asked her if she was single or in a relationship, she said she was overnight dating (a new term to me) a nice young cop. I told her she could start the next night.

Things got better and better for me. One night after I arrived at Ciro's I found a message to call comedian Lenny

Bruce. He was appearing on the Strip at the Interlude. Mystified, I returned his call not knowing what to expect. The conversation was carried on in pieces between his shows that night. He asked whether I would like to be part of his act. It would go something like this: he would call Ciro's at ten thirty sharp each night. I would answer and he would mike our conversation so everyone at the Interlude could hear it:

"Good evening! Ciro's!" I would begin.

"Say, I was there the other night and I think I left a blue jacket there," he would say.

"Could you describe it please?"

"It's blue."

"Does it have sleeves?"

"Yes."

"How many?"

"Well, two, of course. How many three-sleeved jackets do you get?"

"You'd be surprised, sir. Do you have any other way of describing it?"

"It has a zipper."

"Was the zipper in the up or down position when you left?"

"Say, am I talking to that dumb blonde cigarette girl?"

"I may have helped you, sir. I'm always happy to do that. Sir, I'll have you know I've got a Ph.D. from USC!"

"Well put him on!"

This silly bit seemed to go over well. I could hear the audience roar with laughter as I was hanging up. Of course it led to much kidding, because the Interlude crowd also came to Ciro's. One guy even volunteered to pose as my Ph.D. if needed. I was happy. I was appearing nightly at the Interlude with Lenny Bruce. How about that in my résumé!

Besides, every time he used this bit he would drop off an envelope with a fifty dollar bill inside.

As the weeks flew by I was feeling I had made the right decision to stay in Hollywood. John occasionally dropped by Ciro's in the early evening and played the piano in the Ciroette Room for an hour or so. It seemed he might soon be selected to do the show's opener. He had already proved he was popular, as people flocked to the piano whenever they heard him play. Some nights he picked me up but, if not, I would ride home with one of the valets, usually Zollan.

One night when Zollan drove me home, I noticed that John's car was gone. Puzzled, I ran inside. There was a note on the dining room table. "Sorry I had to leave. Taki tried to kill herself. I'll call you."

That was it? Just like that? Twice now he had done this to me. Why? What's wrong with me? Guys are hitting on me all the time. I had to stop my sessions with Bob Kane because he was getting too serious about us. And there was Cole. I knew if it weren't for John, we would be an item. So why had John abandoned me?

I sat down. I couldn't even cry. I stared into space for a long time and then I remembered the fable about the frog and scorpion I had heard in my childhood. And like I always did as a child, I made up my own version.

Once upon a time, a frog encountered a scorpion at the edge of a large pond. As the frog was about to enter the water, the scorpion asked politely if he could hitch a ride across the pond on the back of the frog. After a brief consideration, the frog agreed.

During the long journey across the pond, the two creatures became close emotionally. They even discovered they had a mutual love of music—particularly Beethoven. They seemed to be a well-matched pair. The frog was young and strong with a sense of where she wanted to go and now she had a partner with an apparent similar goal. She was happy in this new relationship and looked forward to good times when they reached the distant shore.

Midway across the pond, the scorpion suddenly stung the frog. "Why have you done this to me?" the frog wailed. "Now we will both drown." As they began to sink beneath the surface, the scorpion answered, "Because it is my nature."

With all her waning strength the frog struggled to the surface and finally made it alone to the shore where she lived happily ever after. Sometimes she cried, but only when she heard "Fur Elise" played softly on a piano.

In time the frog forgave the scorpion because, after all, it was in her nature.

I had to start all over, and I did the thing I always do in times like this. Even though it was 3 a.m., I started trying on clothes. It was my addiction. *I should have switched to heroin*, I said to myself. *It would take up less room.* Finally I slept.

The next morning I awoke at noon to hear a knocking at the front door. *Who could it be? Could it be John? He changed his mind! He's back! But he has a key. Maybe he left it here.* All this went through my mind as I struggled to find my Japanese kimono with the dragons on it. Swathed in gold dragons I went to the door and opened it.

"Oh," said the man at the door jokingly. "We're not going to that new Japanese restaurant today; that's next month."

I groaned inwardly. It was Jimmy, a Phillip Morris rep I'd met at Ciro's. We'd been having lunch together once a month, always at some posh hotel or restaurant. I was looking for extra work and he liked to chat and ask me if I needed anything. *Today, I need a husband,* I thought.

Anyway, I smiled, "Come on in, Jimmy. I'll just be a minute." I excused myself and threw on some makeup and a new strapless linen sheath with a white bolero zebra striped jacket. I was not so broken-hearted that I didn't want to make an impression at the Beverly Hills Hotel.

In the car coming home Jimmy said he'd like to tell me about an opportunity to make some good extra money. My ears perked up. After all, Jimmy did have connections in the industry. He visited studios to try to get them to use Phillip Morris brands in shots where the stars were smoking. *Maybe he had me in mind for a Marlboro ad! Maybe they want to start to appeal to women. Hmmm, the Marlboro woman! That could be me. I knew just what I'd wear.* Suddenly, I was aware that he was still talking. "I thought you would be so good in this film," he said.

"What film are you talking about?"

"I have a friend who is a producer. He is always looking for girls who look like you to appear in his films."

"Oh, what films has he made? I might have seen one."

"I rather doubt it. They are just distributed in South America."

"My Spanish is fair and getting better, but I don't know if I could handle a very big part in it."

"Oh there's not much speaking. It's an adult film and if you have a partner you would like to have as your companion, that's fine. If you don't, I would be more than happy to take that part myself."

"Jimmy, I'm not going to be in a porno film!"

"But it would only be shown in South America."

"Ask the cigarette girl at the Mocambo. I think she's more the type."

With that I hopped out of the car and decided I needed a shopping fix. But first, I called Morgan Lee. I had sort of avoided him after our desert island picnic because I felt I was not being fair to him. I asked if he had any ideas of what I should do next. Ciro's was wonderful and fun, but it was not a serious career. It was a stepping stone, and I was looking for that next stone to appear.

Morgan was sweet as always. He said that, although I had broken his heart by giving him only a kiss on the cheek after our island outing, he was my friend. He said one of these days he would get a sponsor for *Dollars for Scholars* and I would have a role in it. Meanwhile, he gave me the number of Phil Berle, saying I would get some direction from Phil. His second referral was a big surprise. He said to call Mae West.

"Are you kidding? She's from another century," I exclaimed.

"Don't sell her short. She's an old friend of my dad from vaudeville days. She's smart. She's written plays and she knows a lot."

Morgan gave me both numbers. Phil's was his office number and Mae's was her apartment. She lived in an elegant building on the same street as the Casbah motel. In fact, Morgan had just finished visiting her when he stumbled on me at the bus stop that day. He warned me that she lived with three muscle men, two of whom had won body building titles. They screened her calls, but I was just to mention Morgan or Pinky Lee.

I called Phil Berle first, but his secretary said he was out for the day, so I called Mae. The phone rang three times, and a male voice answered, "Miss Mae West's residence." I explained who I was and gave Morgan's name. He asked me to please wait. A few minutes later he came back, "Miss West is entering the room. Miss West is approaching the phone. Here is Miss West."

Whoa, what an intro, I thought. *Did he previously work for Queen Elizabeth?* Mae answered in her familiar sultry voice. I explained who I was, and before I knew it, I was telling her my troubles. Things I wouldn't tell my own mother, I was spilling out to Mae West. She gave me twenty minutes or so of her time. I wish I had taken notes, even though I wasn't treated to any really Mae West-type quotes like, "Goodness had nothing to do with it" or "I used to be Snow White, but I drifted."

Instead it was damn good common sense. She said I was like Frankie in the song "Frankie and Johnny." He was my man, but he done me wrong. She said Frankie made her mistake in hauling out her old forty-four and shooting Johnny. There are better ways to get even. Independence is what women need. Your own bank account, a good job. If they walk out on you, what have you got? More closet space. (She was talking my language there.) She told me that when a girl is in her twenties she can make the most mistakes of her life. So be careful whenever something is offered to you that looks like it's tied with a gold ribbon. That ribbon could turn out to be a noose. I said I would always remember those words, and I always have.

Oh Thou, who didst with pitfall and with gin
Beset the road I was to wander in,
Thou wilt not with predestination round
Enmesh me, and impute my fall to sin?
⌒ *Rubiyat of Omar Khayyam*

28 With my new Mae Westian philosophy I decided the first thing I needed to do was establish myself as a woman who didn't need a man to be happy. Shopping seemed like a really good first move, and there was a sale on at Nancy's on the Boulevard. I had made quite a bit of money a couple of nights before. *Might as well put it to good use. Besides, with John gone, I'll have more closet space.*

Years ago a friend of my father had given me a very old Chinese porcelain figure. He called it a Buddha, but I learned later it was Ho Tai, the God of Happiness. There was a round hole under the base. If you put the seated, smiling figure over an incense cone, the smoke would come out his nostrils and his ears. As a kid I found this a kick. Now I used Ho-Tai to guard my money. I rolled up the large bills and stuffed them into the base of the figure. Every week or so I'd take the bills out and deposit them in my account at Bank of America.

John was not a signer on this account, the way he had been on the one he cleaned out when he left the last time. I told the banker I was single when I opened the account. In a way I was. Whenever I handed over a stash of bills to the teller, incense would waft up. The tellers at this Hollywood branch surely must have believed that I worked in an opium den. I enjoyed the image. I thought it would be fun to make a deposit some time wearing my dragon robe.

All set for shopping, I reached up into Ho Tai's base and felt nothing but sandalwood-scented emptiness. It was gone! All of it! John had robbed the God of Happiness. Surely a curse would follow him for years to come. I still had Donna's check for her half of the rent and enough in my account to pay my half of the rent and the PGE bill. But I'd have to make more, and quick, for the month's other necessities.

In desperation, I thought of someone who might help me. A few nights before I had gone to a party at the home of a woman called Halo Meadows. She lived on Fountain Avenue and was married to a sort of mentalist. He went by the name "The Amazing Criswell Predicts," though the things he predicted were local disasters that never happened, such as "Cockroaches in Cucamonga!" and "Fire ants to invade Fresno." There was always a suspicious alliteration to his predictions, but he was a frequent guest on *The Tonight Show* as well as at local store openings. His wife Halo was a weird, amusing person. A couple of friends and I had gone to her home to hear her play the piano (very badly) and sing her "sad songs" (also very badly.) That night she made the announcement, before it got into the trade papers, that she had decided to live forever. That's all there was to it! She just decided she was going to live forever! This statement started a lively discussion, led by a philosophy professor from Stanford University, on the true meaning of life, religion, morality and how one might achieve happiness in Hollywood.

I struck up a conversation with a muscled Italian-looking guy. He was not particularly interested in the turn of the general conversation, so he asked me if I had ever been to a horse race in L.A. I admitted that this had not been one of my experiences so far. He said anytime I wanted to go to give him a call. His pastime was handicapping horses.

I decided to postpone calling Phil Berle again until I had fixed my money crisis. I needed a good handicapper much more than an NBC executive, but I had forgotten his name. When I found his business card it read Angelo DeRosa, Investment Counselor. Perfect. I called him and he said we should plan on tomorrow because they'd be running a special race, "The Miracle Mile," at Hollywood Park. I thought to myself, *Isn't that what they call a section of Wilshire Boulevard? Well, who cares. I needed a miracle.*

When he picked me up in his T Bird convertible, I was glad the car was a pale sand color, since I had worn a beige safari jacket and pants and I wanted to make a good impression. The pants were loaded with pockets, perfect for stashing betting tickets and cash. The racetrack was not as classy as the Longacres track in Seattle, but what it lacked in refinement it made up for in palm trees. He led the way to an area of box seats, just stopping to pick up a racing form. When we were seated, I asked to look over the entries for the first race.

"We aren't going to bother with any race but the Mile," he said.

"Why?" I wanted to know. "I brought a hundred and forty dollars with me and I want to bet on all the races. You just need to tell me which horses."

He leaned over and whispered in my ear, "The Mile is

going to be a boat race."

Not wanting to seem unhip in these things I said, "Oh, good. I love to watch horses run in water."

"No, no," he said with impatience, "A boat race is when the jockeys get together and decide who the winner will be."

"You mean it's a fixed race?" I asked too loudly.

After hushing me up he leaned over and explained, "Not really. It's just something the jocks occasionally do amongst themselves. Nobody else knows about it, so it's fair. They set up a pool and someone places the bet for them. That's all it is." My ethics warning system was going off, but what could I do? Tell the waiter who had just served us drinks?

The next several races went slowly. If you have no bet on a race, it's not much fun. Finally they announced the Miracle Mile. I reached into my right leg pouch pocket and pulled out all my money. I handed it to Angelo and said, "Please bet it across the board." I had learned this term from my dad and always bet that way at Longacres. It means that whether the horse wins, places or shows, you win something. Of course, you don't win as much as you do when you bet just to win. My dad's way appealed to my financial conservatism.

"We'll do it the way real players play," he said. "Besides, I told you it's all set."

He went to place the bet on a horse named "Good Friday." When he returned with the tickets, he said, "You'll thank me tonight when we have dinner at Chasen's." The race was close. Good Friday did his best and came in second. Angelo tore up the tickets, cursed, and then we headed to Tiny Naylor's for burgers. We didn't say much on the way home. I was furious. But I was already working on plan B.

I turned to my friends for help and guidance. Over a

few cups of coffee we came up with a few ideas for raising money quickly. One of them was Zollan's old proposal that we help him shave his body for the role he'd won as a native in a segment of "Ramar of the Jungle." Two dollars a minute for the opportunity to help him get hairless. He would supply razors and shaving cream.

All that was quickly forgotten when Kenny came up with a fantastic plan. We would host a rent party. He said they do it all the time in New York. You have some cheap wine and a keg of beer, put up signs around the neighborhood and people come. I asked the group if there was any celebrity we could get to help us out for publicity's sake. I thought I could get an item in the *Hollywood. Reporter*, now that they counted on me to tell them who was with whom doing what at Ciro's. I threw the idea out there, warning everyone that otherwise I would demand they pay back immediately the money various ones of them owed me. Maybe that did it, because Kenny jumped up and said, "I'm pretty sure I can get Nick Adams."

"Nick Adams would be perfect, with all his TV work and being in those Japanese monster movies," I shouted. "Do it, Kenny. Get Nick Adams."

Two days later Kenny said Nick had agreed. I used the tips from my last two nights to buy the stuff we needed for the event. Donna made signs. The party would be held in six days. We posted signs everywhere: at Hughes Market on Highland, at the Ranch Market, and all over the palm trees on Franklin Avenue. I passed out notices to the valet parkers at the clubs on the Strip. I was being rescued with a little help from my friends.

The day before the party we got the bad news that Nick Adams couldn't make it. He was called to do some additional location shots for the monster movie he had just finished. This was a devastating blow. We had already accepted advance money from people who didn't want to miss out on our 65-person party limit. What could I do? I called Kenny who had set this up originally. Could he suggest anyone else?

"Yes, me!" he exclaimed. "People mistake me for Nick all the time. Once I told a woman I was his twin brother and she said 'Fine. I still want your autograph'." I said to Kenny, "That's brilliant! Will you do it?" He answered, "If I can play a green leprechaun in *Brigadoon* I can sure play Nick Adams."

So it was set. Kenny had invested in an M.G. sports convertible after receiving his pay from *The Diary of Anne Frank*. He planned to have Zollan be the driver/manager for the party. It sounded like perfect casting. I knew Kenny could pull it off.

On the scheduled day, a crowd arrived. They wandered around the house, porch, and back gardens in wild anticipation of their chance to mingle with a popular movie star. Suddenly, I heard a shout from the front porch. "He's here!" Everyone rushed to the front of the house, onto the wrap-around porch and down to the street. What a show Kenny put on. Zollan, wearing a sort of chauffeur's cap, was at the wheel. Kenny, dressed in jeans with a black tee-shirt emblazoned with a dinosaur-like creature, was standing up and waving. He jumped over the car doors and into the midst of cheering fans who thronged him with autograph books and cameras.

I was worried for a moment about what those pictures might reveal if circulated. But ever since Kenny's nose job, he was a walking duplicate of Nick Adams, except that he sang and danced better. The party was an MGM happy ending. We made enough money for the rent and to cover the cheap wine and chips. There was even enough to pay Kenny something for his stand-in appearance. I learned afterward that Nick thoroughly approved of the deception. In fact he told Kenny he might need him again soon. He had an appearance coming up on *The Tonight Show* that he really didn't want to do.

I went to bed that night with the relief that I had enough money to live on the rest of the month. But when I tried to fall asleep I couldn't. I was now deeply complicit in the illusion that was Hollywood. I thought about my poor Norwegian mother, if this hoax were exposed in the papers: "University of Washington drama major arrested on fraud charges."

29 When my mother's family emigrated to the U.S. from their village in Norway, they settled on a homestead in Minnesota. For some reason unknown to me, they discarded their traditional vows to the Lutheran Church for the far more rigid evangelical denomination called the Pentecostal Church. Even when they left the rigors of the Minnesota winters (far harsher than Northern Norway even) they came to Tacoma, Washington, bearing their stringent beliefs.

With her Pentecostal standards intact, my mother left her teaching career in the early 1930's to marry my law-enforcement-officer father. At an early age I was taught about the fires of hell that awaited those who committed sins that included not only violating the Ten Commandments, but in a Pentecostal "amendment," the sins of drinking, smoking, dancing, wearing make-up, and (maybe worst of all) going to the movies!

On the prison island, where my father worked as a guard, Sunday school for me was in the small community hall. The hall was intended for use by families of the prison employees, so my mom had put dibs on it for a Sunday school facility for the children. It was tiny and folksy, and my mom was always nearby—playing her guitar and leading us in choruses of songs like "Jesus Loves Me, This I Know" and

"If You're Happy and You Know it, Clap Your Hands." We had snacks and Kool-Aid afterward.

At the age of four I had my first experience in an actual Pentecostal Sunday school when we went to visit relatives in the city. I somehow sensed that being in this big brick building at 12th and G Streets in Tacoma was going to be different. For one thing, I was separated from my mom and sent to a room with small wooden chairs and a blackboard. There were ten or so other children bigger than me, but friendly-looking. I sat down, and a lady in a dark blue dress and round glasses had us all say the Lord's Prayer. Some of the kids didn't know the words, so I spoke them out loud and clear. The teacher smiled at me over her glasses.

Then we heard a Bible story (I knew the ending but I kept quiet.) We sang another song and then there was a moment of stillness. I was very still too. The boy sitting next to me suddenly handed me a basketful of money! There were pennies, nickels and dimes so I took a handful. Tittering laughter broke out around me, and the lady who had been smiling at me looked angry over her round glasses. "That's the Lord's money you have taken. It is a sin to steal." Somewhat reluctantly I released the coins from my clenched fist back into the basket. I did not cry, even though I really wanted to. My dad had taught me real men don't cry and little girls don't either.

An eternity later my mom picked me up and asked how I liked Sunday school. I mumbled "fine" or something, not wanting to tell her I was on the road to hell for trying to steal the Lord's money.

Several years later we were again visiting our relatives in Tacoma on a chilly Sunday. We couldn't play outside, so my older cousin Marcheta (named after a song, and pronounced "Marketa") suggested she and I go to the Real

Art Theater on South Tacoma Way and see a Deanna Durbin movie. Marcheta loved Deanna Durbin. I had never seen her, since I had only been allowed to see Shirley Temple movies—and then only if I would pray for her to leave the evil movie industry. I really, really wanted to see Deanna, who was a teenager like my cousin and also a good singer—like I hoped to be. I begged my mom, "Please, please, please." She answered "You know movies are sinful and it's Sunday. Besides, how would you feel if the Lord came back to earth on this day of days and you were in a movie theatre? I decided to chance it. My cousin and I went to the Real Art Theater, sat through a boring newsreel, and then Deanna came on the screen with her long brown curly hair and beautiful voice. I was totally enchanted. *Could this be me one day?*

Suddenly, the film stopped and several ushers came into the aisles with flashlights. Over the loudspeaker a man's voice made an announcement requesting that all service personnel return to their bases immediately. When the movie came back on I asked Marcheta, "What was all that?" She answered "Probably McChord or Fort Lewis is having a drill. They do that all the time. Here, have some more popcorn."

My vague uneasiness increased when a few minutes later the movie stopped, the lights came on, and guys in uniform marched up and down the aisles, yanking out anyone wearing a uniform. Even though I wasn't wearing one I wanted to hide. I was pretty sure I knew what was happening—the end of the world had come and I was in a movie theater! The gates of hell awaited!

Suddenly, I too was jerked up and out of my seat. It was my Dad. Maybe he was going to hide me. All he said was "We're heading home NOW!" I called to Marcheta as I was propelled up the aisle "Are you coming?" The movie had come back on as she said through a mouthful of popcorn, "No, I'll let you know how it ends."

I knew how it would end. Me in Hell! My mom was waiting in the car and hugged me as I tried not to cry. I managed to ask my Dad as we sped back home, "What's happening?" In a deep, serious voice he said "This is War. We are at War!" I had never been so relieved in my life. War? That's all? I had escaped the fires of Hell once again. The date was December 7, 1941.

It was a long time before I went to a Sunday matinee again, but the image of the gaping mouth of Hell for people like me stayed with me a long time, and it was back now. The Nick Adams shenanigan really bothered me.

I will choose a role and play it constantly until I become it
⌁ *Brandon Morrison*

30 One night at Ciro's a producer of *The Helen Morgan Story* approached me, saying he thought he had a small part for me in the movie and would I be interested? "Of course!" I replied, "Isn't that going to star Ann Blyth? She's one of my favorites!"

He gave me a card and wrote my name on it and a date. I decided it would be important to dress appropriately for an Ann Blyth movie. I chose a Mr. Blackwell empire-style black dress with a ribbon band at the raised waistline. Two ribbon steamers hung down the back. I did my hair in a French roll and left two blond tendrils above each ear. I was a cross between Grace Kelly and Audrey Hepburn, with maybe a hint of Mae West.

When I arrived at Warner Bros. Studios, I was thrilled to be walking through the gates that so many famous stars of today and yesterday had entered. The man at the gate told me to go down "Main Street" to the bank building. It was like being in a small town with an impressive oversized bank! When I reached the entrance of the bank building with tall brass doors, I was worried that I would not know where to go once inside. I pulled open one of the tall doors and found myself in a small room with two card tables, five folding chairs, and not a teller in sight. It was a movie set!

A man stood up and greeted me. He explained this was to be a table read. I always had read well at auditions, so I asked who my character was. "You are auditioning for the cigarette girl scene," he replied.

What? I thought, *Talk about type-casting?* I was really disgusted!

"It's just a couple of lines," he said, "but you will wear a sexy costume; and, who knows, it could lead to other parts." *Sure,* I thought, *no matter how hard I try, I come across as a blond bimbo. "* I spoke up and said, "I am recently from the University of Washington School of Drama. I have done a lot of radio drama, and I am an actress!" With that, I shoved open one of the fake doors of the fake bank on the fake street and decided to go home immediately.

As I headed toward the gate, a young man driving a golf cart called to me. "Hey, how would you like to see Jimmy Stewart making *Spirit of St. Louis?*" I stopped short and answered, "Sure, why not?" and jumped aboard the cart. He took me to a large sound stage filled with lighting, sound, costume and make-up people, directors, and cameramen. No one noticed us. The young man motioned me to an area where I could see what was about to be filmed.

Stewart, dressed as Lindbergh in goggles and helmet, was ensconced in half an airplane which was resting on poles. A pair of grips rocked the poles to simulate movement of the plane. Behind the plane was a large screen on which was projected blue sky and moving clouds. It was unbelievable to me that this hokey set, when shown in theaters, would look real. However, Stewart—in the pilot's seat—showed a weariness and integrity that was very believable. He was truly Lindbergh in this movie and in his real life was one of the most respected stars in Hollywood. As I became absorbed in his acting, I quickly forgot the grips and the screen behind the half plane. I saw a hero on a quest. I felt moved and respectful.

On the city bus going home I pondered my own identity once again. In the evening I would head for my job at Ciro's, changing into my sexy outfit and playing my provocative cigarette girl role. Why had I turned down a role playing myself? Was I a lady playing a bimbo or vice versa? I hoped that in the coming months I would find out.

31

My remorse over the Nick Adams hoax faded quickly when the next exciting invitation came along. It was a party at the white stucco duplex on Broadview Terrace where Cole, Kenny and Zollan had the upper unit. I walked down the hill carefully in my fitted white cotton sheath dress. The white and gold bracelets on my bare arms showed off a lovely California tan. My high-heeled, strapped sandals weren't the best for hillside strolling, but it was only a couple of blocks.

In my wildest imagination I could not have guessed that the evening would end in tragedy.

I turned off Camrose Drive onto Broadview and could hear music from a Sinatra record wafting above the lush greenery all around me. Broadview Terrace was not a street but a walking lane with no cars—something I often referred to later as a way of life. I paused before starting up the white staircase. The building was so beautiful, engulfed as it was in tropical foliage and seductive fragrances. A tall palm tree stood guard over the oleander and jacaranda shrubs. Slender vines of lavender-colored blossoms had wound themselves through the ornate iron grills that covered the lower floor windows. This could be North Africa, I thought, except for the voice of Sinatra. In that moment I realized I would rather be here in the Hollywood Hills than anywhere else on earth.

A handsome and familiar face appeared at the open window. I smiled up at Cole. In the six months I had lived in Hollywood we had become good friends. I took one last look at the beauty of the garden setting, never imagining that in less than seven hours it would be completely destroyed by fire.

"Hey, come on up and join the party. It's more fun inside than out there. And Rusty Tamblyn's here," Cole said in his husky, throaty voice. Russ Tamblyn had recently finished "Seven Brides for Seven Brothers," and his career was off and running. He was still living in that incredible triplex perched on the side of the hill above us, and I was still hoping that one day, if he moved out, John and I would move in. Seattle had nothing to compare with living high above the smog on High Tower.

I walked into the smoky, crowded room and looked for Cole. There were groupings of attractive young people all around, smoking, drinking and name-dropping. Recently I had come to understand that if you spoke of a celebrity, you did not use his or her professional name. Russ was Rusty. James Dean was J.D. There was Nat Wood, Sandy Dee, Nicky Adams, etc. Cole spotted me; and as he came to greet me, I was struck as always by his stunning appearance. In a town full of good-looking guys and beautiful girls, Cole still stood out. Half Irish and half Italian, he got the best of both worlds with dark, thick, wavy hair and creamy skin with a hint of pink on the cheekbones. In spite of his dark eyes, thick lashes, and strong blue-white teeth, he seemed unaware of his good looks and just wanted to be a serious actor.

"I hope there's some good food in this place," I said. "I was on a photo shoot all day and I'm starved."

"Kenny's passing around a tray of pickled octopus. How does that sound?" he asked.

"Not as good as Zollan's mom's Armenian stuffed grape

leaves," I said. "Besides, I've had enough pickled octopus today. My client was pickled, and when he insisted on hugging me I felt at least eight arms."

As fate would have it, Kenny came by at that point with the dreaded tray of octopus tentacles. He insisted I try one, so I took the smallest piece I could find, pretended it was tuna, and popped it into my mouth. It didn't have the remotest taste of tuna, and I knew I had my work cut out for me chewing it up.

Someone put on a Latin record, and I began gyrating—slowly. It was because I was moving in time to my chewing, but Cole invited me to dance. When I asked where, he suggested the kitchen hallway. "If you will let me spit out this damned octopus, I'll follow you anywhere," I said. I concealed the little tentacle in a napkin and bid it a fond farewell in the garbage can, hoping that Kenny wouldn't swoop by and get his feelings hurt. Cole grabbed two bread sticks from the counter. "Here, this should help get rid of the slimy taste. It helped after I spit mine out. They're rosemary bread sticks. You'll like them."

The next thing I knew we were doing some kind of flamenco in the hallway with the ten-inch-long bread sticks clenched horizontally in our teeth. Within a few minutes a small crowd had gathered around us. And then everyone got into a breadstick fandango. "Now that we've started a craze, I think it's time to move on," I said, entering the living room. "Besides we are clearly actors, not dancers."

"Speak for yourself," he said. "I just lost a part in a movie to Warren Beatty."

"Ah, but if I were your sister, Shirley MacLaine," I said, "you would have gotten the part."

"I would rather lose the part than have you be my sister," he quickly objected.

Sure it was a line, but still I felt that sort of tingling that I had not experienced in a long time.

"I think I'd better see if I can find Donna. Do you know where she is?"

I thought I detected a fleeting look of disappointment with his answer. "I think she's downstairs. The two guys she was with were up here for a while, and I think they invited her to their place to talk music. She found out they were members of the Red Norvo Trio, and she was bowled over. I guess she's a big fan. Why don't you let her be for awhile?"

I nodded "yes" and wandered around the room. In one corner our paperboy Eduardo Cansino had drawn quite a crowd. His dislike for his sister, Rita Hayworth, fed the gossip-hungry listeners as he told infamous tales about her. I called to Kenny and told him how delicious his octopus was. He offered more, and I ran for my life toward a group where Zollan was getting coached on the accent he needed for the jungle TV show. His dark, handsome, Armenian looks made him perfect for desert or jungle. The only problem was his hairiness. Phil Dixon said, "Zollan is the only guy who leaves a ring when he takes a shower. Forget about the accent, Zollan," he said, "and go buy a case of Nair."

Eventually I made my way outside and went down the stairs. The door to the lower unit was ajar. I tapped on it and went in. "Donna, are you here?" I heard voices. One of them was Donna's, so I entered the living room. Donna was lounging on a sofa and chatting with a young man who was holding a trumpet. "Jack, this is my friend Karoline. Jack is with the Red Norvo Trio," she said to me. We nodded to each other and I sat down next to Donna, careful not to upset the overflowing ashtray beside her. I kept telling her she smoked too much. Not good for the voice, I warned her. She frequently retaliated by saying that Elvis smokes two packs a day and his voice is a "finely tuned instrument." So I gave up. Maybe her doctor had recommended cigarettes to her the way mine had told me to wear sexy Merry Widows. The world of medicine was certainly changing.

In a very short time, I could see I was out of my depth with their discussion of tempos, rhythm and something called *flam*, a diddle that requires a drum. I thought about mentioning the Breadstick Fandango that Cole and I had introduced to the world, but felt I might seem frivolous in their serious conversation. I said my good nights, which went mostly unnoticed, and went out the door. As I stepped onto the walkway I saw Cole in the shadows of the yard. "I thought I'd walk you home," he said. "Are you okay walking up the hill in those shoes?"

"I always go home with the shoes that brought me," I drawled. "But do you have a suggestion?"

From behind his back came a pair of flat woven leather shoes. "My mom keeps these Texas flats here for when she visits," he said. I slipped them on and instantly became four inches shorter.

"I thought everybody in Texas wore cowboy boots," I joked.

"Just the tourists," he said.

We started up the hill, with me flip-flopping my way. Trying for my best Texas drawl I said, "Only barn dance I ever saw that served octopuses." He answered in his authentic drawl, "Why, in Texas we serve near anybody." We laughed and kept up the banter until we arrived at my house near the top of the hill.

On the veranda I bent over to remove my loaner shoes. As I straightened up he suddenly put his arms around me, and I found myself responding to his kiss. Waves of various emotions washed over me. Warmth, pleasure, maybe gratitude, and then guilt and sadness. The last two emotions prevailed, and I quickly stepped back and said goodnight. I hurried into the house, worried that I might change my mind and ask him to come in.

I went to bed, but couldn't sleep. Was I about to be unfaithful to John? *Just because he is unfaithful to me, does that mean I'm to be absolved of any guilt? What if I ask his permission? Wait a minute! This is the land of the free! Women can even vote now, haven't you heard?* I heard Donna come in. *Should I talk to her about it? What kind of example would I be?* Suddenly my brain collapsed and I fell asleep.

Three hours later I was suddenly awakened by wailing sirens and shouting voices. Half asleep I stumbled out onto the veranda. The sky was ablaze with flames shooting up from Broadview Terrace. Acrid smoke stung my eyes, and I could feel heat like an intense Santa Ana wind. In my short nightgown and bare feet I raced down the hill toward the inferno.

Must we ever be slaves of these
The flames that burn, the winds that freeze?
⌒ Laurence Hope

32

Camrose Drive was choked with smoke, fire engines and frightened people. The heat was palpable, even a block away. Shadows from the flames in the pre-dawn darkness were like images from Dante's inferno. I joined a group of sleepy-eyed people who, like me, were dressed in nightclothes, though no one else appeared to be representing Frederick's of Hollywood. Shivering behind the fire department's barricade, I asked an elderly man if he knew what was burning. From where I stood it was impossible to tell. "Probably that party house at the end of the Terrace," he grumbled.

Fearing the worst, I worked my way toward Broadview Terrace. The closer I got the more I felt an overwhelming foreboding. Scrambling onto a neighboring rockery I was able to see what was burning. The pristine white stucco duplex was defiled with soot and water. Worse to me was the sight of fire hoses stretched across the once beautiful foliage crushing the fragile blossoms. Flames suddenly started to shoot out of the top of the building and at the same time an ambulance made its presence known with screaming demands through the crowd. White-coated men jumped out carrying stretchers and disappeared into the nightmarish world that Broadview Terrace had become. I tried to get closer. It was either that or run screaming back up the hill.

A woman suddenly pointed upward. A new horror engulfed me as I looked at what she was pointing to. The stately palm tree that graced the entrance to the building was on fire! Its burning fronds trembled as though in pain. How can a palm tree burn? I wondered. Was this the last thing Lot's wife saw as she turned to look back on the burning Sodom? Was this the image in her brain before she turned into a pillar of salt? Was God's vengeance for the evil personified by that city manifested in a burning palm tree? Was this a message to me from God? Not a scarlet letter, but a scarlet palm because I had kissed one man while married to another? Will I carry this image in my mind, if not on my sleeve? Was Cole to be punished too? I started looking for him frantically, just as the men in soot-streaked white coats appeared carrying two stretchers. I heard a woman scream and realized it was me. The stretchers disappeared into the ambulance as I sank to the ground. *Have I lost Cole when I had just found him? I had experienced a tenderness with him that my soul cried out for. Was it wrong? Whatever John was doing, what I had done was wrong. Perhaps Hollywood is another Sodom or Gomorrah and I was seduced by it. Please God help me,* I prayed.

My answer from God came in the form of a familiar furry body beside me. "Rocky! Rocky, you're okay!" It was Zollan's friendly, shaggy German Shepherd licking my hand. He smelled of smoke, and the ashes were like black dander in his fur. If Rocky made it out, maybe Cole and Zollan did too. Kenny had gone to another party where he had planned to spend the night, so I knew he was safe. "Where's Zollan, Rocky, please show me," I begged. I stood up shaking and grasped his collar to follow him. Behind one of the fire trucks stood two dark-haired handsome guys wrapped in fire department blankets. I rushed toward them. I was sobbing. Rocky was barking. We were both happy beyond belief.

The next few days passed in a blur of activity. Late in the afternoon the day after the fire, Cole and Zollan were allowed to return to their apartment to gather up personal items. The damage to their unit was primarily from smoke and water. The owner's insurance adjuster said he thought they would be able to move back in about a month or so after repairs, painting, carpeting and new furnishing had been completed. The lower level was another story, literally. The damage there was so severe it would be months before it would be habitable.

While the guys and I were bringing out their personal belongings we happened to go around the back side where we made a tragic discovery. The bedroom windows were blown out from the heat of the fire. The iron bars that were part of the Spanish design were still intact. However, inside the window of one of the bedrooms lay a battered brass trumpet. Obviously it had been used by Jack in a futile attempt to get out of the room where he was trapped. That trumpet and the burning palm tree were forever etched in my memories of that tragic night. We were shocked the next day when a story appeared in the *Hollywood Reporter* detailing the death of a member of the Red Norvo Trio. His roommate remained in intensive care, but was expected to survive.

Two hours later we were settled in the comfortable living room of my house drinking strong coffee while Cole and Zollan took turns describing the time before the fire broke out. Apparently, Zollan had been awakened first by Rocky's barking. He described how terrifying it was to wake up in a dark, smoke-filled room and not be able to find the bedroom door. Cole described the same feeling. They both followed the sound of Rocky's barking outside the kitchen door where he slept on the back porch. They groped their way down into the back yard. Screams were coming from the lower unit, but they felt there was nothing they could do, the fire and smoke were so intense. They had each grabbed up a pair of jeans, but had no time to save anything else. The fire fighters arrived, and they were treated for smoke inhalation and given blankets.

I asked if anyone knew the cause of the fire. One of the firemen said it apparently started in the living room and quickly spread throughout the apartment. I remembered the overflowing ashtray on the couch next to Donna. Was it possible that was the cause? Should I have said something or dumped it out? I felt sick at the thought.

Donna was up when we got back to the house. She was devastated at the news. She said everything was fine when she left, and both of the musicians were going to bed. We invited Cole and Zollan to bunk in with us. Donna and I took my room and they had hers. With a false bravado we joked about a *ménage de quatre* and who was going to be assigned to what household duties. I suggested we nominate Rocky for a doggie hero award. Zollan said Rocky would probably prefer lasagna, his favorite dish. We did all the necessary things like getting sheets changed and finding a bed for Rocky. It all seemed very normal to me, like a family surviving a crisis together. I actually was able to go back to sleep. The burning palm tree was there, but off in the distance.

This aura of death affected us deeply. Donna announced that her parents needed her to help in their restaurant.

Kenny said he was moving in with another actor and would not return to Broadview Terrace. Zollan decided to take Rocky and visit his parents in Salinas for a few weeks. He said he needed to be around Armenians for a while. Rocky seemed to agree. Since I was left without a roommate and Cole was room-less, it was natural that he would replace Donna. It was also natural that we would become lovers. Escaping death, it has been said, has an aphrodisiacal effect. Nature is to blame. For me, it was natural and guilt free. I had not been punished. I had been given a chance to experience warmth, affection, and tenderness Ozzie and Harriet style. I was happy.

33 Gradually the images of the fire started to fade. My life had become almost normal. The relationship with Cole blossomed into a comfortable familiarity that was unlike anything I had ever experienced with John. We were friends. Perhaps John and I were never that because he was so charismatic, charming, and talented. I was his groupie, just grateful to be in his presence. Cole and I were like people who had been in grade school together. Better yet he made me feel attractive and desirable in a way none of the men who had pursued me in Hollywood ever had.

Ciro's was a showcase for women, the setting glamorous, the music exciting, and the atmosphere of mingling with celebrities intoxicating to everyone. We who worked there were affected by it as were the tourists. When I sat perched on my stool under an amber light in the elegant foyer I felt a return of my former self-esteem. Herman Hover told me to remember that I was the first person customers saw when entering Ciro's. I must live up to the legend. Cole had helped me find the best make-up and hairstyles. The new costume Mr. Hover had designed for me featured a mid-calf-length gold pleated bouffant skirt with crinoline underneath to make it stand out. If *Swan Lake* is ever performed in Las Vegas, I think this is probably what the ballerinas will wear. I loved it. Sexy yet elegant. It was shortly after I began wearing that costume that the *Hollywood Reporter* referred to me as the "Queen of the Sunset Strip." The Strip was my yellow brick road, and Ciro's the Emerald City. I was a cross between Dorothy and Glinda the Good. Glamour plus innocence. This was for many men a seductive combination.

For the most part I loved the attention. When I got home around three a.m. Cole would be waiting, and I would amuse him with my descriptions of the events of the night. I had many stories about Manuel, my glamorous coworker, who was always nearby if I needed him. He would indicate who was okay to talk and flirt with a little and whom I should avoid. Occasionally a man would "accidentally" drop a tip on the floor expecting me to bend over to pick it up and thus offer an enticing view of a half-bra Merry Widow. Manuel told me to casually step on the bill and wait for the man to leave before picking it up. If Manuel were nearby he would pick it up for me; and if it were less than a five-dollar bill, he would say, "Chipp pipple!"

About a month after the fire, the upper unit of the burned building had been repaired, repainted and re-curtained. The furniture had been cleaned, so it was time to end our house-playing. Zollan came back from Salinas with new Armenian recipes. Kenny had decided to live alone, now that his career seemed to be taking off. Donna was not ready to return, and I was faced with the prospect of living alone. My mom suggested she come down for a visit. I loved the idea. She was such a great mom and I missed her. Also, I wouldn't be tempted to call John and urge him to come back.

Not only was it great to have my mom there, I returned to my old habit of going to a nearby deli, the Gaiety, after work to hang out with musicians and showgirls from the other nightclubs. Mom did not wait up for me, so I could spend a couple hours swapping stories with the show crowd. One night I sat near a table occupied by a young, slender dark-haired man who looked pale and sad. I smiled at him, and we started a conversation. He was from the East Coast (that explained the paleness) and had come out West with his mother to make a movie. Apparently, it was true. The movie was called *Crime and Punishment USA*. I told him my mom was here too and that I was a model, cigarette girl, and actress. I said I know that sounds like the typical bio a hooker gives, but it was true. I did not mention my Queen of the Sunset Strip title. He wasn't bragging, so I wouldn't either. It became a sort of regular habit to meet and talk. I told him about my situation with my husband, and he sympathized. It was pleasant talking with him, and I thought maybe my friends could give him some tips about which studio was looking for what type and so on.

One night George wasn't at his usual Gaiety table. I missed him. I hoped he hadn't gotten discouraged and gone back East. The following evening I walked past a photo studio near Ciro's and noticed that every picture on display was of one guy in various poses. There was a small placard in the center of the photos that announced "George Hamilton, Hollywood's Hottest New Star."

This gorgeous guy, my Gaiety tablemate, clearly did not need my help.

235

34 At Ciro's the next night Manuel came over to tell me that a very nice man would like to have his picture taken with me. This was not unusual. I frequently posed for pictures with guys and then autographed the pictures. Nancy, the Ciro's photographer, would take a picture for her price and have it printed on a giant matchbook. I would charge five dollars to be in the picture with the client and usually get a tip as well. The bigger the tip, the warmer the message I signed. "Loved that week-end in Rio!" Something like that, for a five dollar tip. One man asked me to sign it "Jayne Mansfield." No weekend in Rio for him!

Manuel told me this man would pay for the picture, but he also would like to have coffee with me after closing. Coffee? And what motel would serve us this coffee? Manuel assured me it was okay. This was a very nice man who said he would go anywhere I named for the coffee.

I trusted Manuel, so I said okay. The picture was taken, and the man asked for two prints so we could each have one. I thought that was sweet. I told Freddy (that was his name) that he could come home with me and we would have coffee and conversation there. He seemed delighted with the idea. I also mentioned that my mother was staying with me. He liked that too.

We left together and I directed him to Camrose Drive. He was driving an expensive Mercedes. I examined him as we drove. He was probably in his late thirties, small build, wavy hair. A nice, ordinary guy. Lonely, but not looking for a hooker. I made us coffee, and we talked about nothing in particular. Actually, I think I did most of the talking about growing up on a prison island, being a drama major, musician's wife, etc. I was getting more out of this than he was. He listened sympathetically and quietly. After an hour and a half I yawned and he took the hint. He asked if I would walk out to his car with him, as he had something for me. I felt very comfortable with Freddy at that point, so I said "Sure."

He opened up the trunk of the car and inside was a large round, metal Scotch tape tin, packed with bills. Large bills. He said apologetically, "I've just gotten back from Vegas." He gave me a handful and said goodnight. No hug, no kiss, just "Goodnight." I went back into the house with my handful of bills, dropped one on the porch (it was a hundred dollar bill), and sank down on a living room chair. Seven one hundred dollar bills. *Who is this guy?* I wondered. This incident was repeated often over the next few months. I didn't get it. I talked to my mom about it. She thought he sounded like a very nice man and was probably a good Christian too. I talked to Cole about it. He thought I was giving him coffee therapy. I told Cole that I was the one getting therapy. I was telling him my problems. Cole saw no problem, mom saw no problem. Why did I? And I was getting wealthy off this guy, sort of. Actually, so was mom. I gave her ten percent of my tips each night. She loved this. Since I kept my money stuffed in my beloved Ho-Tai, she decided to put hers in a box she labeled PENGA, which is Norwegian for money. Clearly Mom believed there was no such thing as a Nordic burglar.

One night Freddy told me I was the type of girl he was looking for: moral, kind, smart. I couldn't disagree. But I added, "How about married?" He told me my husband didn't deserve me and that he thought he could make me happy. To prove his feelings he asked me if he could buy me a beautiful full-length mink coat!

Oh, get thee behind me, Satan! I murmured to myself. If there was one thing I would love to own in the world it was a mink coat. In the checkroom at Ciro's I handled, and sometimes tried on, the most beautiful minks in the world. And they belonged to women who didn't even care about them. Zsa Zsa Gabor would drop hers on the floor when she arrived at Ciro's. I would pick it up carefully, comfort it and put it on a special hanger. *If I could have a mink coat, I could handle any crisis in my life,* I often said to myself. *It would be my therapy coat. If John were to divorce me and marry Takiko, I would wear it to their wedding.* I told Freddy I would have to think about accepting such an expensive gift. "I know I take money from people, mostly men," I said, "but that's my job. A mink coat is not exactly a tip."

He asked me to meet him the next day at I. Magnin. Two o'clock. Fur department. Then he said goodnight. I slept that night with visions of sugar plum fairies dancing in my head and they were all wearing dark ranch mink coats. But my decision was made for me at my mother's knee when I was a child. Everything tastes better when you've earned it. *I am not the woman Freddy is looking for,* I said to myself. *I am not a trophy. One day I will earn my own trophy. And it will be a full-length ranch mink coat.*

Two o'clock the next day came and went. I did not go to Magnin's. Freddy probably did. I didn't see him for a few weeks. Then one night he came into Ciro's alone, as usual.

He smiled at me and nodded. I told Manuel what had happened. He said, "Karolina, you are too good for this job. Freddy Scott is the heir to the big Scott Paper Company. He is worth millions."

35 The next day I heard that Russ Tamblyn was giving up his incredible apartment on High Tower Drive. It would be available in a month. I knew I had to see it. It was Sunday, and I had nothing better to do than look at that apartment with its sweeping view of Hollywood. I dressed in my most prosperous looking suit to impress the manager and took the ride in that awesome elevator to the top of the hill. It was so peaceful up there. No cars, no streets, just winding lanes. It was like looking into the future or the past, I didn't know which.

I found my way to the building only to discover a note on the manager's door saying that, due to an emergency, he had been called away and to get in touch with him later. I was disappointed, but managed to see a little of the apartment from the lane side. It looked as if it was built into the hill and appeared to hang in space. I loved it. I turned to go back to the elevator when I heard someone call my name. *Who would know me here in this isolated community?* I wondered.

I moved closer and recognized the bartender from Ciro's. I called back, "Igor, is that you?" He came over to me and gave me a hug. He was dressed in a traditional Russian costume, complete with high black boots. "Welcome! You are just in time for the party. I'm so glad you got an invitation!"

"I didn't get an invitation," I said. "I'm here to look at the apartment, but the manager isn't in."

Igor took me by the arm and escorted me to a nearby home. "Of course you are invited. We Russians invite all beautiful blondes to our parties."

Inside the house there were delicious aromas of exotic cooking and on the patio two musicians playing what I learned were balalaikas. I had heard of them, but never before experienced such sad then happy music. I decided then and there that from now on I would have balalaika music at all my parties.

The inside of the small house was full of guests drinking vodka from an enormous samovar and smoking strange redolent cigarettes. If only I had known, I would have worn the perfect outfit: "Rich Russian Peasant," as the dress I had seen at Saks was described. I compromised by taking off my suit jacket to reveal the low cut white blouse underneath. I was able to pull the neckline down to reveal my nicely tanned shoulders. Fortunately, by wearing a Merry Widow (doctor's orders), I never had to worry about pesky bra straps. *If only I had worn my new high black boots. Oh well.*

Soon there was a great flurry and much excitement. A special guest was arriving. It was the noted restaurateur and royal personage (and one of Hollywood's most famous imposters), Prince Michael Romanoff! Ta-da! The collective guests, obviously in awe of such stature and fame, proved their disdain for Bolshevism by treating him royally. I, too, was impressed. I had read for years about the famous Romanoff restaurant in Beverly Hills. Now to have the proprietor almost at my elbow made my natural instincts for promotion come alive.

I pitched John to Mike Romanoff. I extolled his talent, his charm and mentioned the very distinct possibility that there was Russian blood in his heritage. When the toasts began I was the first to jump to my feet with a solid "Na zdarovye!" which was echoed by the other guests. When one guest had to leave early, I was first with a "Do svidanya" farewell. I think I had one word left in my Russian vocabulary and that was "Nyet!" Those three expressions—to your health, goodbye and no—I thought could take me a long way in this happy setting.

I was suddenly overwhelmed by a Russian memory from my youth. When I was a teenager, I had an incredible experience one summer aboard half a Russian tanker (yes, half) docked in Anacortes, Washington. The name of the ship was the "Donbass." It was one of the many ninety-day wonder ships built and then lend-leased to the Soviets. Unfortunately, these ships had a problem that caused a few of them to break in two when they went from tropical waters to frigid northern waters. The situation, as it was later explained to me by a marine engineer, was that the extreme heat from the welding of the quickly-built sections weakened the steel around the seams.

The Donbass had come from southern waters to northern waters where it broke in two. A nearby American tanker, the "Puente Hills," rescued the stern, where all the oil was, and now claimed salvage. At the time, my father was a U.S. Marshal and he was ordered to remain on the ship (which was now U.S. Government property) until the owners of the Puente Hills arrived to pump out the oil.

What a summer it was! The ship had been in the local papers for weeks and was a big tourist attraction at the lumber mill dock where it was moored. My mother and I and our cat joined my father for a unique vacation experience. A school friend of mine joined us too. My friend and I became "Russian." When tourists approached,

I greeted them in my newly perfected Russian accent. I told them of the great storm which rent the ship in two and how those on the bow perished in the cruel sea. I held my audience breathless (I was already a radio actress and union member). Some of them took pictures of the oil-drenched half ship with me in the foreground.

One day a journalist from a national newspaper found me out. He knew there were four women aboard working as cooks in the galley, but had no information on teenage Russian girls. He did not blow my cover, however, and I retained the words I was now using in my blatant effort to schmooze Mike Romanoff.

When I finally said my "Do svidanyas" to the party guests, full of hope, confidence and vodka, I was on a high apart from the vodka. I was back on track. I was promoting John. We would live up on High Tower and hang out with our Russian neighbors. I would learn to play the balalaika, and work on my Russian accent. Life, after all, would have a Hollywood happy ending.

If that weren't enough, the elevator stopped on the lower level of High Tower and two well-dressed Asian men stepped in. To my great delight I recognized them: Richard Loo and Philip Ahn. Both of them had gained fame during WWII playing evil Japanese officers. Since the Japanese residents in the U.S. had been interned during the war, Chinese actors were in demand to portray Japanese in the propaganda movies of the 1940's.

Full of my new Russian persona and my old Nordic bravura, I smiled and said, "I have seen you in a lot of old war movies. You both played evil men very, very well."

Richard Loo replied, "I hope you are not frightened now being alone with us. "

"Of course not! " I replied indignantly.

"Then we weren't doing our job very well, were we?" Richard Ahn gave his famous leer as they stepped out of the elevator. I decided that I must move to High Tower. What great neighbors John and I would have!

If we can put a man on the moon,
why can't we put them all there?
　～ *Refrigerator magnet*

36 Aristotle Onassis, the Greek shipping tycoon, was a guest one night at Ciro's and was sitting at Table 5, the V.I.P. table. He had requested a cigar, so Manuel called to me to take my cigarette tray over to him.

As I approached the table, where four men were seated, I easily recognized Onassis from his newspaper pictures. He was a bulky, gray-haired man with large glasses through which his eyes glittered. The man next to him turned to me and said, "Mr. Onassis would like a panatela—one that has recently been dipped in something hot and moist, if you understand." With that he waved a fifty-dollar bill at me. I was taken aback by this lewd request and ready to walk away, when I had a brilliant idea.

Earlier, Manuel had asked if I would watch the roped entry and answer the phones, since his assistant, Al Garza, had not come in yet. The Mexican waiters had used some special hot peppers to make a super hot salsa they called "salsa diablo." Manuel had just eaten some and thought he might need to make a sudden trip or two to the men's room.

I went into the kitchen and spotted the bowl of wicked salsa. When no one was looking, I cautiously touched it with the tip of my finger and put it up to my mouth. My lips started to burn and so did my finger tip. *Que calor*! *Think what it must do to your tongue and throat unless you're Mexican and well accustomed to it,* I thought.

I gave the cigar a good, quick dipping. Then, gingerly holding the dry end, I returned to Table 5. The man who had spoken to me handed me the fifty as I handed Mr. Onassis the cigar. I was tempted to say "Enjoy!" but thought that would be overkill. I hurried back to hide in the checkroom. A moment later I heard male laughter erupting in the show room. I began to worry. Would I be fired, arrested, or sued? Possibly deported to Greece for prosecution?

Two hours later the foursome left the club. The man in charge of the party came up to me and handed me a hundred dollar bill. "Mr. Onassis says he enjoys a good joke and hopes to see you again." *Not if I see him first,* I thought; *although, to be paid by the victim of a prank is unusual.* I decided to forgive him for his crudeness, since he had obviously forgiven me.

37 Whenever Sophie Tucker or Cab Callaway were booked at the club you could count on all the greatest stars and comedians to reserve a table. What I never expected was that, on one of those nights, I would get a proposal from a Saudi prince.

Tucker was a legend from the old vaudeville days. Two nights before she opened, I came in early to handle a banquet and discovered a large overweight woman with garish make-up and garishly-dyed red hair sitting at Manuel's station near the entry. She was making endless phone calls. It was Sophie Tucker!

I watched her show on opening night and was thoroughly disgusted. A woman who might have been my grandmother (if my grandmother had run a bordello) was delivering a monologue that seemed to rely mostly on references to pubic hair. But she brought out the legendary comics that had their roots in vaudeville and were now famous in Hollywood. Jack Benny was there. He told his waiter in his inimitable style, "That was the best glass of water I have ever had," a jab that sent George Burns, seated next to him, into gales of laughter.

George Jessel, the acting head of Columbia Pictures, arrived early in a limo. Ray, the doorman, signaled me to come help. I ran outside to the passenger side of the limo to find Rita Hayworth, one of Hollywood's most glamorous, reclining inside. Once the great star of Columbia Pictures, she had done a Grace Kelly and married Prince Ali Khan. Now she was back in Hollywood on the arm of George Jessel. *Only in Hollywood!* I thought.

"Miss Hayworth is having a little trouble getting out of the car," Ray whispered to me. "Perhaps you could help." I stuck my head into the interior of the limo and was overcome by the cloying fragrance of expensive perfume, whiskey and perspiration. I recalled a famous quote by a film director to a news reporter, "Horses sweat, Miss Hayworth glows." Well, she was really glowing that night. I stretched out my hand to her which she graciously accepted, murmuring, "I may have a little trouble getting up, but once I'm on my feet, I'm hell!" These words have continued to inspire me ever since.

Milton Berle showed up that night. And Danny Thomas... all the greats from the vaudeville era! I was entranced. They all smoked cigars, my most expensive item! And they were excellent tippers. Even Jack Benny, who told me that, since he had a terrible reputation for being cheap, he did the opposite and was a most generous tipper. He had a famous skit in which he is being held up by a thug who repeats his demand for money several times then says, "I SAID – YOUR MONEY OR YOUR LIFE!" and finally gets a response from Benny who answers: "I'm thinking! I'm thinking!" These men, like Benny, whom I had listened to on the radio when I was a kid, were gentlemen in the finest sense of the word. I loved them and they respected me.

Swim star Esther Williams was a regular at Ciro's and one of my favorites. One night she arrived at the marble entrance area wearing a dress that looked very familiar. It was a black, short-sleeved Bouche dress with a long split up the back that was covered by a long floating panel. I realized it was identical to a dress I had recently purchased from Little Turk's inventory. Turk and I had haggled over the price. He insisted it was a perfect knock-off of a designer original. I challenged him the best I could, but Turk was the better judge of quality with those young-old eyes. I bought it, though there was a trick to wearing it.

Ms. Williams went to the powder room and when she emerged, the long, floating black panel was wet and dripping. I knew what had happened. She had used the toilet without making sure the panel did not fall in. So, smiling at fans, she walked proudly, confidently, and dripping, into the showroom.

Zsa Zsa Gabor loved Francis Faye, the iconoclastic gay performer. One night Gabor arrived to a packed house at the club. She asked me who all those people were. I informed her it was a group of Swedish tourists who had chosen to have a banquet at Ciro's. "I don theenk zees Sveedes vill deeg Frawncis," she replied. She was right. Midway through the "Frawncis" act, half of them left.

On another occasion Zsa Zsa emerged from the powder room and started signing autographs. I noticed her left shoe was trailing a strip of toilet paper. I walked over to her quietly and stood behind her so that, when she moved away, I could put my foot on the toilet paper and detach it.

One evening, dancer Ann Miller asked me to meet her in the powder room and bring her fabulous sable coat with me. When I did, she told me she had just called a cab and was going to sneak away from her date. He was a very rich and powerful Mexican businessman. The coat was a gift from him. I don't know what had happened, but she was clearly frightened. She was one of my favorite celebrities, and I was very concerned. She stayed in the powder room until I told her the cab had arrived. Then she hurried out, and I never saw her again.

One of the saddest incidents involved Judy Garland. When she came in one evening with two men, I was thrilled. As a child, the only movie I had seen from beginning to end, other than one Shirley Temple film, was *The Wizard of Oz*. I was totally beguiled by Dorothy in the film. She was pretty, brave and resourceful, just the way I wanted to be. I loved her dog Toto too. I hoped I would get a chance to speak to Garland. Manuel seated her party at Table #5, a banquette just a step up from the stage, but private. She was wearing a simple black dress with a small black veiled hat perched jauntily on her head. (Dorothy in a cocktail hat. I loved it!)

About an hour or so later, Manuel frantically signaled me to follow him into the showroom. I was horrified to see Judy/Dorothy sprawled on the floor at Table #5. Even worse, her hiked-up skirt revealed she was not wearing underwear. I quickly grabbed the tablecloth from the table—glasses, candle, and silverware flying. I threw it over her lower body and removed her hat which had slipped down over one eye. Manuel was checking her vital signs. He picked her up, tablecloth and all and I followed him to the powder room, carrying the hat. Anna, the powder room attendant, had been alerted and was holding the door open. He gently laid Garland down on the pink and gold Louis XVI sofa. She was stirring and seemed to be okay. One of her escorts stood in the doorway and said he was her agent and would take over. We put a closed sign on the door and Anna told me she would see to Garland's needs.

Half an hour later, one of the valets told me a limo had arrived. Anna and the agent helped an unsteady Judy out the door. I realized I still had her hat. For a moment I thought about keeping it, but I just couldn't do it. As I ran it out to the limo, I said to myself that, after all, Dorothy never wore a hat. Now if the ruby slippers had been left behind, that would have been different.

Cab Calloway's Cotton Club show at Ciro's was an extravaganza with gorgeous black performers and the incredible Cab Calloway singing "Minnie the Moocher " and other hits like my personal favorite, "Saint James Infirmary." We sold out both shows.

On one of those nights I noticed that the best ringside table, Table 5, was not only reserved, but roped off. I asked Manuel who the V.V.I.P. was who had snagged that favorite spot. He told me it was a Saudi prince and his entourage. Intrigued by my memories of reading *The Arabian Nights,* I could hardly wait to see the jeweled turbans, silk trousers, and shoes with turned up toes. I was disappointed when the group arrived dressed in English Savile Row suits and Countess Mara ties. Where is the Sheik of Araby? Or Ali Baba? These men looked like expensive trial lawyers. I was called to their table for cigars just before show time.

I don't know what I expected, but it wasn't that. A very charming man with incredible dark eyes under serious eyebrows asked about cigars for His Highness. I looked for a man who could possibly qualify as a "highness" and was baffled. A very young man who resembled Zollan without the hairiness looked soulfully at me. I thought, *He's just a kid. Maybe a high school senior. What's he doing here?* I apologized for the pathetic selection of cigars. I suggested the ones in the metal cases, the Imperials, and said, "I don't know how great a smoke they are, but the case could be used to carry your toothbrushes while traveling." When translated, this got a big laugh. They all bought Imperials.

After the first show they made their departure, smiling

at me as they left. I think the toothbrush case joke had impressed them. One of the group lingered for a moment to speak to me. I thought maybe they wanted to take Imperials home to Arabia as souvenirs.

"His Highness has asked me to offer you an invitation on his behalf."

I said, "Of course. I would be happy to hear the invitation. By the way, which one was His Highness?"

"He was the young man next to you on your left at the table."

That kid? I almost said, but saved myself, saying instead; "Of course, I knew that must be His Highness because of his royal demeanor."

"His Highness was most impressed by you and your blond beauty. He would like to extend an invitation to you to accompany him on his tour of the United States."

"That is very kind. I myself have never toured the United States, except for North Dakota and Minnesota, and they don't really count."

"He would also like to tell you that you, as his companion, would be compensated by payment and jewels."

Suddenly I remembered the story of the cigarette girl who preceded me, who was offered jewels for sex by the Shah of Iran. I was overcome by the same awful feeling I got in college once, when a nerdy guy who sat next to me in geology lab invited me to a dance.

"Please thank His Highness for the honor, but I am unsure of my schedule at this time." I spoke in what I felt was the height of diplomatic language. He handed me his card with his name and a telephone number. I took it and smiled sincerely while thinking, *Wait 'til everyone in Seattle hears about this! Especially John.*

Later in the evening, my assistant Beverly came out of

the back of the checkroom where we kept our personal things. She was holding the card, which I had stuck on the mirror as a memento of sorts.

"What's this?" she asked.

"Oh, I've been offered an all-expenses-paid vacation with pay and jewels."

"Is this a joke?"

"I don't think so. There is a catch, though. I believe the job title is 'Concubine to the Prince.' Of course, I suppose I could pull a Scheherazade and just tell him stories every night."

"Are you going to do it?" she asked breathlessly.

"Are you kidding? Of course not. I'm already spoken for. Sort of."

"What about me? Would he take me?"

"Why not? You're a blonde. But what about your boyfriend the cop?"

"Jose? He's talking about marriage now, as if I would ever want to be Mrs. Gomez. "

"Well, there's the card. Call him tomorrow."

I never saw or heard from Beverly again.

Jose, the policeman, stopped by Ciro's one night looking very nice in his neatly pressed LAPD uniform. He said he hadn't heard from Beverly in two weeks and did I know what had happened. I said I thought she had a family emergency somewhere back east. He nodded and thanked me. As he walked away I thought, *There is a nice girl out there who will be very happy to be Mrs. Gomez one day.*

The next day at work Manuel was waiting for me with a big grin on his face. "Karolina, joo joost made me twenty-five dollars." I bit. "Okay, what did I do or say now? " It was not uncommon for the waiters to place bets on who could get me to say a vulgar word in Spanish, not knowing what it meant. Once I was given a message in Spanish to relay to Mr. Hover. The message was supposedly from his wife and it was *No chingas con miga!* I knew all the words except "chinga" (Don't blank with me.) Of course it was an "F" word. Fortunately, Mr. Hover didn't know the word either and thought it was his wife's cute attempt to make up with him. Why Yvonne would leave a message in a language she didn't speak didn't occur to him, but I guess he was under stress. Anyway, there were a few other attempts like that by Manuel and friends, and I assumed this was another one.

I was right. The waiters had a betting pool. The servers who had handled the royal table got wind of what was going on. They noticed I had brought cigars to His Highness three times and that many gestures and words were exchanged. They were sure I was going to be offered a golden opportunity. They all threw money into a pool about my decision. Manuel was the only one who voted no against twenty yeses.

"You just proved you know I am a good and pure woman," I told Manuel. "Tacos and a movie tonight! But no hanky-panky."

"I theenk I like to try hahnkee-pahnkee, but okay."

A month or so previously there had been an incident in which Manuel had come to my rescue. A customer waited after closing and attacked me in the checkroom. He had torn my costume and had his pants unzipped when Manuel heard my cries. Manuel was very skilled in a type of Mexican judo where the feet are the weapons. He finished the guy off, and the sheriffs removed his battered body to jail. Manuel opened a bottle of wine from the bar and soon we were in the star dressing room on the chaise. I adored Manuel. He was handsome, charming, and funny and he cared about me. But I knew it was a mistake. I didn't know who I was cheating on. Cole? John? All I knew was that I wanted a friend, not a lover. And that's what Manuel and I were from then on.

Every now and then we would change our clothes and go to downtown L.A. to an all-night movie. He would be dressed in jeans and a plaid shirt. I would be in cut-offs and a well-cut tee shirt. We rode in his pickup truck. One night I pointed out to him that, since we had both been written up as the most glamorous people working on the Sunset Strip, should we go out looking like this?

"When joo look as good as we do, *no hay de que!*" In other words, clothes don't matter. He was challenging my mantra—the lesson I learned in grade school. When I looked at him in his jeans and faded shirt, he still looked like an Aztec god. As for me, I needed the right clothes. Then and forever.

One late morning my mom brought me a cup of coffee. She called it *kaffe po sange*, "coffee on the bed," an old Norse tradition. Usually the husband brings it to the wife. *That'll be the day for me*, I thought. Anyway she told me John had called the night before and the two of them had a talk. She said he realized that he had made many mistakes and that he wanted to come back and try again.

I was stunned. Maybe I hadn't gotten over John, but I had given up any hope of working things out. I had a life of my own now. I had friends. Hell, I even had a boyfriend! Mom knew all this. She often commented on how happy Cole and I were together and how much we laughed. She said I really should think it through carefully. I thought about it. That night John called me after work. I felt tingly all over again at the sound of his deep beautiful voice.

The song has ended, but the melody lingers on
You and the song are gone, but the memory lingers on
                Irving Berlin & Beda Loehner

38 By the time I finally reached the manager of the property on High Tower, Russ Tamblyn's apartment had been rented. I was determined. I would wait. I was young, and there was always tomorrow. The good news was that John was coming back to stay. He asked me to rent a small Steinway grand.

I made a place for the piano in the corner of the living room near the fireplace. The French doors opened out to a side garden almost as beautiful as what once graced Broadview Terrace. John was very excited when he called. Kenny announced that he had been cast in *I Was A Teenage Werewolf* and had a couple of musical numbers John could help him with. John would be paid but not credited. When I left for Ciro's in the evening my head was ringing with the song, "Eeny, Meeny, Miney, Moe, I Want a Gal with a Lot of Dough." Actually, with my income from Ciro's and the Sunday sittings with Bob Kane, I really could be called a gal with a lot of dough.

A few days later the piano arrived and so did John. Suddenly the house was filled with music and laughter.

There were also incredible nights of lovemaking. John would sometimes drop by Ciro's and play the piano in the adjoining Ciroette Room, which had a carousel motif and was reserved for private parties. *He could be a straight Liberace*, I thought. One night I popped into the room when he was playing a song he wrote, called "Karalise." I was surprised to see Joan Collins leaning over the piano in obvious enjoyment. I was not jealous; I was proud. He was my husband, and I was responsible for his being there.

Whenever John picked me up early we would usually stop at one of the Strip nightspots. It was amusing that everybody knew me. The valet parkers, doormen, bartenders, and waiters—everyone waved hello. I was now part of that clique that forms among people working in clubs. The gossip was part of it. Ricky and David Nelson, sons of Ozzie and Harriet, and two of Bing Crosby's sons had once included me in a conversation about whose dad was the worst. John was an outsider. It was a new experience for him to lose the spotlight to me. Laughingly I reminded him that I was the Queen of the Sunset Strip and had the papers to prove it. I thought he would be proud of me, but I wasn't sure.

John still had not contacted Mike Romanoff. There was time, he said. The *Werewolf* gig was nearly finished, and I felt he should be looking for another. What about doing a demo for a record company? He talked about Vegas. I didn't want to go to Vegas. Ciro's was my job and I also had occasions to model with the Peck Agency in Hollywood. Besides, I knew enough about Vegas and the Mob who ran it from some of Ciro's showgirls who had worked there.

I called Cole to tell him my relationship with him was over, but I hoped we could stay friends. He answered, "I just want you to be happy. If this it what it takes, okay. I'm going back to visit my folks in Beaumont for a month or so.

Maybe we can have a cup of coffee when I get back."

Kenny asked if I'd like to give a party to celebrate the finish of *Werewolf*. Since the awful night of the fire there had been no parties at Cole and Zollan's. The lower floor was still not ready for occupancy and there was a sort of pall over the whole lane. The blackened palm tree was a solemn reminder of what had transpired that night. It had also marked the beginning of my affair with Cole. Now that John had returned I found myself having moments of painful regret for my actions. I was sure John knew about Cole and me; I think, if anything, he found it amusing. He was not jealous or possessive. In fact, I wouldn't have been surprised if he had suggested a threesome. I shuddered. Had we all "gone Hollywood"?

I loved the idea of a party. Michael Landon was such a fox! I would be hosting my first Hollywood movie star party! All the old group pitched in to help. Zollan called his mom in Salinas to ask her to make Armenian stuffed grape leaves and send them down by Greyhound, an arrangement that had worked well in the past. Zollan also fixed a few Armenian delights of his own. I had a favorite chicken, rice, and vegetable casserole to make. I christened it the "Michael Landon Casserole." Cole thought it should be the "Werewolf Casserole," but I prevailed. Cole and I selected the wine—Chianti in straw containers (we thought we could use them for candleholders afterward) and bought some beer. We were ready to party! I even did some superficial dusting.

The party was a great success. Lots of fun people. Some stars and some almost stars. Vince Edwards, who had a hit TV show as Dr. Ben Casey was there. He and Zollan had become friends when Vince was valet parking at Ciro's. I even forgave him for putting a cigarette out on the rug.

Connie Stevens made it. She had just finished a movie with Jerry Lewis called *The Babysitter*. The buzz over Connie was, "When is she going to get that nose job?" Donna was there, and she and John performed some of their old numbers from the radio show they did together in Santa Maria in the old days. Donna seemed like herself again. She was not going to be moving back to Hollywood, since she had started giving voice lessons in a music studio in the Valley.

Michael Landon made a brief appearance to thank us for throwing the party. He was so young and handsome and seemed to be a very nice guy. *Would he ever "go Hollywood?"* I wondered? I remembered the stories I had heard about Errol Flynn and Tyrone Power, arguably two of the handsomest men ever to be in the movies. They could have had any woman they wanted and yet the stories went that they preferred each other. Were they gay or had they just "gone Hollywood?" Would this happen to me? Was the burning palm tree meant to be a warning to me? From now on I was going to be a true and faithful wife.

The next evening, when John did not show up at Ciro's to pick me up, I felt an old sinking feeling. I phoned him. No answer. My good friend Ray, the doorman, picked up on my concern. "Hey," he said, "how about you and me going to the Gaiety for a cup of coffee, and I'll drive you home. Like the old days." I thought to myself, *yes too much like the old days*. I remembered that night at the officers' club at Camp Roberts when John left me twenty miles from our hotel in Atascadero. At least this time I had Ray, who often drove me home. I accepted his offer—all but the coffee. I needed to know right away whether John was really gone.

He was. Car gone, clothes gone, shaving kit gone. I went to Ho-Tai and reached into his hidey-hole. Surprisingly, the money was there, but so was a note. Just one word: *Sorry*.

Now what? Or, as Mrs. Peusa would ask, "And den?" This time I had no answer, not even "tapioca." I walked over to the piano and slowly brought down the lid over the keyboard. It was like closing the lid of a coffin. The next day I called the piano rental people to come and get the Steinway. They came quickly, put the piano on its side, removed the legs and strapped it on a big hand truck. When they were gone I sat down on the floor for a long time staring at the empty space in the corner. The music was gone and this story was not going to have a happy MGM ending. I thought briefly of entering a convent. No burning palm trees there! The problem was the shoes. Nuns aren't allowed to wear high heels. Even on doctor's orders.

Love for Rent: A Preview of Coming Distractions

39 I kicked off my high heels the minute I climbed on my stool at Ciro's one balmy evening after John's departure. I was watching the elegant cars drive up and elegant people emerge. It was a Monday. That night and the next three days of the week were when the rich and the famous went night-clubbing. The weekend was referred to by them as "famers' night out." In other words, the nights when nine-to-fivers and weekend tourists hunted for celebrities.

I loved those nights. The checkroom would be filled with fabulous furs and designer men's trench coats. Frank Sinatra's raincoat had a Savile Row label in it. Even if the weather was mild it was a chance to show off your stuff. It always amused me when some little old lady would reluctantly check a pathetic little squirrel scarf with little paws and heads still attached. I would have to promise that the grubby fur piece would be carefully handled and guarded. After giving her a check number, I would squeamishly take the fur by one paw and hang it on a coat hook in the far reaches of the checkroom. I didn't want to cause the little fellows embarrassment by putting them next to Ann Miller's lavish silver fox coat or Lana Turner's sable. The checkroom could be a cruel and competitive place.

I thought a lot about the owners of those fine furs. I hated Lana Turner's boyfriend, Johnny Stompanato. He treated her with little or no respect, snapping his fingers at her to pay for his cigarettes and not helping her with her coat. What made it even more disgusting was that she was one of the all-time great and glamorous Hollywood blondes. She had sunk to the depths of being with a two-bit mobster who was just a gofer for Mickey Cohen. When I read the screaming headlines of his murder at her house I thought that, no matter who had committed the crime, it was well deserved.

On that particular Monday night a middle-aged man approached my stool and asked if he could have a word with me. I was ready for my usual comeback to the question I anticipated in one form or another: "How much do you cost?" My standard answer was, "I'm priceless." Instead he handed me a business card with his name on it and the Twentieth Century Fox logo. He explained the studio was looking for the right young women for a program to develop them for movie roles. There would be a two-year contract.

I was startled. *Does that mean I am being discovered like Lana Turner sitting on a lunch counter stool at Schwab's Drug Store?*

"Is this for real?" I asked, remembering my experience with the snake and bullwhip.

"Just call the number for the casting office there on the card, and my secretary will arrange an appointment that works for you." With that he turned and left. I looked at the card again for any suspicious signs of counterfeiting. No. It looked like a card from 20th Century Fox—with the twin searchlights sweeping the sky.

Flashback! I remembered a convict at McNeil Island who made my dad some beautiful facsimiles of an old calendar of my mom's that had suffered water damage. Except for the stain you couldn't really see any difference from the original. The counterfeiter was a trusty and worked in the prison library. He had made a beautifully lettered sign over the library door that read: *There are a lot of books you have been meaning to read when you have the time. Now you have the time and we have the books!*

I decided there was only one way to find out whether the card was for real or a beautiful facsimile. *Make the appointment,* I said to myself, *and if I am asked to go to room 745 at the Roosevelt Hotel, forget it. If I am asked to go through the gates of Fox and proceed to a certain bungalow, that's okay.* I would take some scripts from my childhood radio experience and college classes to show off the versatility of my voice. One was from a Tom Sawyer radio series in which I played Becky Thatcher. This voice was high and sweet and sounded like a ten-year-old. The second was from an old, idyllic poem I had read before each chapter of a radio series based on Marcus and Narcissa Whitman. For this I used a mellow and somewhat sexy voice. The third was from *Elizabeth the Queen,* a harsh, commanding threatening voice.

The following Wednesday I arrived at the gates of 20th Century Fox and gave my name. The guard looked at his list, made a check mark, and directed me to a bungalow about a block away. It was a very pleasant scene. Little white houses were scattered around, some with green lawns and flowers. A guy was cutting the grass near the bungalow I was headed for. It reminded me a little of the south Tacoma, Washington, neighborhood where we lived after leaving the island. It was as far removed from a downtown Hollywood hotel room as anyone could imagine. *Why had I gotten so suspicious? Forget about that bullwhip and snake incident. I am going to be very happy to have a chance to work or be developed into a starlet here.*

I was glad I had worn my best audition outfit. It was perfect for this occasion—a simply cut black crepe dress with a stand up collar. My hat was black velvet circled with a matching chiffon scarf that draped under the chin and hooked on the other side of the hat. A little touch of Marlene Dietrich in an old movie I had seen called *The Garden of Allah*. Basically, classic Grace Kelly with a little touch of Dietrich. Both blondes. Perfect!

I knocked at the door and a female voice told me to come in. Very neighborly. I might have been dropping in to borrow a cup of sugar.

A middle-aged woman was sitting at a desk piled high with papers. Scripts? Maybe I will be asked to read from a script. I was good at cold reading. A few times when I was doing radio in Seattle I would be asked to step in for someone at the last minute and did quite well. My problem acting-wise was that, even after weeks of rehearsal, I was not much better than the first read through. *Oh, well*, I thought, *time and practice will take care of that.*

Without looking up from her work, the woman gestured to a half-open door down a short hallway. I approached the door, tapped lightly, and walked in. A different man than I had talked to at Ciro's was seated behind a large desk. He gestured toward a chair. Removing his glasses he looked me over.

"You are Karoline Morrison?"

"I am." I wanted to add "in person," but thought the better of it. He seemed very serious.

"Fox is looking for a few girls like you to be in a two-year program. There will be some small movie parts for those who qualify." He mentioned the salary and I thought it was generous, but not overly so.

"There will be opportunities for you to augment this from time to time with additional duties."

"I was a drama major at the University of Washington, and I started doing professional radio in Seattle when I was fifteen," I stated eagerly. "I am also a member of AFTRA. Would you like to have me read something?" I reached for my bag of monologues. Outside I could hear the sound of the lawnmower. The window was open a little.

"That won't be necessary. Would you stand up please and turn around? And remove the hat." I did so, feeling a sense of *deja vu*. This was a little like the days I worked as a model in L.A. I thought: *If he pulls out a measuring tape, I'm climbing out that window.*

Instead he said, "Very nice."

"Is that it? I don't need to audition?" I asked.

"You have the right look. That's what's important." He reached into a desk drawer and pulled out a document. It looked like a contract. *This is just too easy,* I thought. *Maybe they are looking for stand-ins.*

"I will point out one paragraph in the contract. It refers to times when the studio is entertaining businessmen, particularly from the East Coast. One of your duties will be to help us entertain them. We will expect you to cooperate with this." The sound of the lawn mover was fading away. I heard voices coming from outside, but couldn't tell what they were saying. Suddenly I wanted to be outside.

"Does the word cooperate mean what I think it does?"

"You're a bright girl. I'm sure it does."

"Then I must say no thank you." I stood up and put my

hat back on. This time I did not hook it, but let the scarf trail down my back. It was flimsy armor, but it helped.

"Miss Morrison, do you know how many girls in this town would give anything they own for the opportunity you are turning down?"

"I'm not one of those girls," I said. And then, determined not to leave without delivering one of my prepared monologues, I turned and proclaimed:

"I am a queen! Where I walk is a hall of torture, where the curious gods bring their racks and gybes and stretch me there to writhe til I cry out." Then I stuck in my own line in the same deep and powerful voice, "I will never cry, flinch or ever want to see you or this evil place again! " With that I strode out, firm in my red high-heeled sling back pumps and shut the door forever on "15ᵗʰ Century Fox."

On the bus back to Hollywood I thought of things I might have said. *Give up everything I own? Like pride? Self respect? Virtue? To become a piece of meat you throw like a foil-wrapped Hershey Kiss to businessmen? (I rather liked the Kiss comparison.) Maybe I should write this out and send it to the president of Fox. No, maybe I can contact the Secretary of State. I have been a victim of bait and switch.* Instead, I told Manuel and Cole about it. They both said I did the right thing. I thought about phoning John to tell him. The trouble there was he might tell me to call back and say I'd changed my mind. A steady income in this town is not easy to find, he would say, and on that he would be right.

Later that week Cole and Zollan had a party to celebrate the completion of *The Diary of Anne Frank*. Kenny had a part in it where he had to wear giant lifts in his shoes. For some reason the director felt his character had to be taller. Kenny had suffered backaches as well as the ignominy of being considered short. "Remember Alan Ladd?" he used to remind us. "He did love scenes standing on a box, and he did okay."

They invited other cast members to the party. By mid-evening only Diane Baker had showed up. I held forth on my Fox experience complete with a re-creation of my exit scene, complete with heavy dialogue. It garnered hearty applause with a few boos which I was sure were meant for "15th Century Fox". It was nice to have the support of my friends.

Suddenly Diane stood up to deliver what she said was an important announcement. She had met with the head of Warner Brothers who offered her a three-year contract with NO STRINGS ATTACHED! She said she would be starring as Tess in *Tess of the Storm Country*. Another round of applause followed, in which I joined, even though I was furious at this insult added to my injury. To make it worse she looked directly at me when she spoke. I looked back at her and saw a slender, dark-haired young woman with slightly patrician features. She was dressed in a simple cotton peasant- style dress and brown flats, as flat as her chest. I was wearing a white jersey low-cut halter dress a la Marilyn Monroe. My shoes were white with high heels made of cork which gave me a somewhat bouncy walk. I felt a need to fill the quietness that had suddenly enveloped the living room.

"When I'm older and wearing cotton dresses, I'll rely on my acting ability; but for now I'm doing okay with what I've got."

Cole quickly steered the conversation in another direction by mentioning that Paul Newman should be coming by soon, and to be sure there was some pickled octopus left for him. The octopus was gone and Paul Newman wasn't showing up, so we had a welcome chance to gossip about him. The crowd seemed to find this more delicious than either octopus or a catfight.

271

The Landscape of my Bed

40 I awoke one morning at 10 a.m. to find that a strangely beautiful landscape had appeared on my bed. Rising near my feet was a purplish blue mountain range tinged with gold. Below these mountains a serenely placid lake reflected the majesty of the purple mountains. In the distance white smoke erupted from a tall volcano, while ice crystals glistened atop twin white hills off to the left. Next to the two hills was a narrow black abyss—leading perhaps to Dante's inferno! "Abandon hope, all ye who enter here," it seemed to say. A sparkling river slithered past the abyss.

I reached over and raised the blinds on the window near my bed. The sun beamed in and ended the illusion. In the full daylight I discovered what my late night undressing had created. The mountain range was my long purple chiffon party dress and scarf I had worn to a party at Kenny Miller's new digs. An oval hand mirror lake peeked out from under the scarf. Beside it a tall, square Kleenex box held a white tissue that moved in the breeze from the air conditioner. Rhinestone earrings lay on my white Merry

Widow. My black bikini underpants were near the bra with my unclasped rhinestone necklace stretched out beside the black panties.

I picked up the mirror-lake and looked at myself. Blond hair out of a bottle, eyes made larger with Kohl eyeliner, and body shaped by my Merry Widow. I too was an illusion, a product of Hollywood's special effects industry. And at that moment it dawned on me what I had attained with my "special effects." It was glamour! Yes, glamour.

I grabbed my Funk & Wagnall's to look up the word and cheered when I read its origin and definition:

Glamour: Scottish/Gaelic for beauty where none exists. Alluring charm or fascination, often based on illusion that transforms a person or things.

Exactly! This is something attainable by most any woman who wants it. The first thing one needs to achieve this goal is confidence. There is no glamour without it. To be comfortable with herself a woman needs the right clothes, make-up, and weight control. I had all of these. I felt that I had already handled many personal challenges in Hollywood with success, including being abandoned several times by my husband. My dramatic clothes, my make-up, and the body enhancement of my Merry Widow had made all of it possible.

So, what's so bad about special effects? I asked myself. *Jimmy Stewart looked pretty darn good in his leather helmet, though he was flying in only half a plane parked inside a Hollywood sound stage.*

I was seeing glamour created by special effects every night in the many stars I greeted and served at Ciro's. I even kept my own list of the best (who were my models) and the worst. The most glamorous women ever seen in Ciro's (myself excluded) were:

Top three: Audrey Hepburn—true elegance; Lena Horne—true beauty; Marilyn Monroe—true sensuality.

Bottom three: Debbie Reynolds—makes own clothes and not very well; Shirley MacLaine—not recognizable to tourists due to mundane appearance; Sophie Tucker—where do I start?

Most glamorous men ever seen in Ciro's were: No contenders! Only El Cordobes, famous Spanish bullfighter. The look, the walk, those dark eyes… and he almost kissed me! I would have followed him to the ends of the earth—even to Forks, Washington.

Glamour and special effects, in myself and others, were keeping my life interesting and bearable!

I love The Mob, The Mob loves me
We'll be together for eternity

41 On my first day at Ciro's I had been told that many "connections" had been made in Ciro's checkroom. The checkroom was actually composed of two adjoining rooms. One was a large square room that was quite private with a doorway connecting it to the front reception area. This room was lined on both sides with coat racks and shelves above. Connected to it in the rear was a smaller room which was mostly for storage. I kept my stock of cigarettes and cigars there as well as my costumes and personal items. There was a nice mirror and makeup table. Hanging on the wall was a beautiful mandolin made of inlaid wood. When I asked about it I was told that it had been given to Mr. Hover by José Carioca (I later found out he was a cartoon character), and that Mr. Hover occasionally strolled around the bar strumming it. *Now, that I would love to see!* I thought to myself. He just didn't exactly look the part of a troubadour.

At the checkroom, when you were given an article to be checked, you handed the person a numbered ticket and placed a matching ticket on the hanger. Or, in the case of hats, it would go on the hatband. If the item belonged to a celebrity you did not give that person a ticket, just as Ray the doorman did not give celebs a check when the valets took their cars to be parked. I never quite understood this, since the check was a receipt acknowledging you had something of theirs for safekeeping. But I was learning all the secrets of how to properly deal with stars, and I wasn't always succeeding.

One evening I was filling in at the showroom entrance when a man came up to me and said he had reservations for nine o'clock. I looked at the reservation book and asked him his name. He answered through clenched teeth, "Hugh O'Brien," and then began to lecture me on the importance of Ciro's employees being able to recognize well-known people. I replied smugly that I did recognize movie stars, and that TV actors were not in the same category. Manuel fortunately returned to his post just in time and gave O'Brien a bow of recognition and a "Good evening, Mr. O'Brien." I was not asked again to fill in at the reservation podium.

Something much more challenging took place one night when my then assistant, Beverly, had taken in two identical gray felt hats. Neither one had a check or name tucked in the band. The correct procedure was to place the guest's name somewhere on the item. Beverly said she couldn't tell which was which because both men had entourages with them. She knew they must be famous, so she did not give them checks. She left work early that night, saying she had a date with her boyfriend. *It was my problem now. Oh, the pain of being a boss!*

An hour later a gray-haired man came up to the counter and asked for his hat. I realized it was Walter Winchell, the country's top radio and TV announcer—*Good evening, Mr.*

and Mrs. North America and all the ships at sea, let's go to press, was the staccato opening to every one of his famous news commentaries—who always wore a fedora. I took a chance and handed him one of the gray hats. Smiling, I said, "Here you are, Mr. Winchell," and prayed silently that it would fit him. He placed it on his head and tipped me. The last time he had come in he was with Marilyn Monroe, and he seemed to have a new spring in his step. He smiled and waved as he left. The hat really looked a little small on him. I was glad there were no mirrors in the lobby. Relieved, I went back in the checkroom to examine the remaining hat. A chill went down my spine. Inside the hat in gold letters were the initials. W.W. I knew then who owned the hat that was sitting on Winchell's head. It was the "Head Mobster" himself, as he was called. Mickey Cohen.

I should have known. The only guys who wore hats in L.A., with the exception of Frank Sinatra, were from the east coast or were mobsters. When Cohen came for his hat, I took a deep breath and confessed that I had given Walter Winchell his hat. I showed him the initials inside the hat I had and waited nervously for his reaction. He burst into laughter. He thought it was hilarious. "Well, does it fit?" he asked, as he slapped it on his head.

I said truthfully, "I think it looks really good on you. And I don't need you to give me a tip."

"For giving me Winchell's hat?" he said, handing me a large bill. "Wait 'til some of the guys I know get a load of this. Hell, they'll want to buy it off me."

Apparently this really brought me to his attention because he stopped to chat with me every time he came in. He had taken over operations in mob-ruled Las Vegas after Bugsy Siegel was killed. I heard about his newest project there, a Playboy Club. A lot of the showgirls were talking about it. "That's where the money is," they all said.

And then I started getting this money—dropped off in envelopes, which would be left with someone at Ciro's to pass on to me, with the only message being "somebody left this for you". I figured out who was doing it—it had to be THEM! But how would I give it back? Who would I give it back to? I didn't know what to do, so I took it and put it in a separate bank account.

Girls who had been part of the song-and-dance line at Ciro's dropped by occasionally to rave about the money to be made in Vegas. The Las Vegas Strip had everything: high rollers, big-name entertainers, and gambling. They knew Mickey Cee was trying to lure me there, and the girls urged me to sign on.

One early evening I was called into the Ciroette Room. I brought my tray of cigars and cigarettes. When I entered I saw seated around a long table several men, many of whom looked familiar. They were smoking Cuban cigars (not my Imperials) and whispering amongst themselves. I was struck at the contrast between these men and the décor of the room, which was generally used for private parties. It had a carousel theme. There were painted horses under the red and white canopy and paintings of balloons and clowns decorated the walls.

Mickey introduced me, but did not tell me their names. I was being pitched to. One man said Las Vegas would be a great opportunity for me. I asked if he could give me a clear idea of what I was being offered. I said that, although I had done some dancing, that was not what I was best at. I started to give them a pitch about John's talent, calling him better looking than Liberace and also a better musician. They quickly made it clear that it was me they wanted. Mickey spoke up and said, "I like the way you handled that

hat stuff. You showed me you're honest." He turned to one of the men and said, "I love this kid."

Another man spoke up. "Good-looking dames are a dime a dozen, but you're smart and that's what we want." He went on to describe casino hostesses who are assigned two or three big spenders. They act as gambling companions, having drinks and dinner and making sure the guy has a good time at the tables. They receive a percentage of their guests' losses, plus the generous tips they will surely receive besides. The way it sounded to me was that I would cozy up to these guys in whatever way necessary while encouraging them to keep gambling. I would be a white geisha! I felt like I was back in the agent's office at Fox, but I had no exit line except, "This is a very generous and interesting offer, Please let me think it over and get back to you." I picked up my cigarette tray and put the red velvet rope around my neck. I felt it was strangling me as I left the innocent circus room and made my way back into the sanctuary of my checkroom. It wasn't Seattle, but it was close enough.

I tried to smile and chat with guests, knowing that nearby in the cozy Ciroette were some scary men who looked at me like I was raw meat in a butcher's showcase. Oddly enough, Mickey did not scare me. I kind of liked him. He was short and a little swarthy. Only his eyes showed something I didn't like. I tried not to look into them. There were times I almost felt comfortable enough to tell him how I had grown up on the prison island where he too had spent some time. I would have loved to ask him if he had run into my old pal Rain-in-the-Face who was a trusty and used to carry me around when I was young. I hoped Rain-in-the-Face was out by now and back home in Alaska. I thought about trying to get a chance to talk to Mickey alone. I would tell him about my Fox experience and how

I didn't want to find myself in another situation like that. However, he was spending more and more of his time in Vegas where the mob was a major presence.

*A Legend Dies: It has been said that
it is not death but dying which is terrible*
⌒ *Henry Fielding*

42

The mass exodus of Ciro's talent was in full gear. First to depart was Mr. Wolters, the diva-like chef who ran the kitchen with an iron skillet. He was replaced by an underling who created a simpler menu that a small staff could handle. Then Bobby, the delightful and jolly head bartender, was replaced by his assistant Sam, who was a student of modern art. Many of his paintings adorned the walls of the bar. (I thought they were awful.) Nancy, the camera girl, who wore her "I've seen it all and photographed most of it" expression announced that she was retiring to Palm Springs where she kept an apartment with a pool. She invited us all to come and visit, but we knew we never would. Anna, the powder room attendant, left in tears. She loved Ciro's but her tips had dwindled too. Even Zsa Zsa Gabor, who she said was her best tipper, rarely came in any more.

Jerry Gallien (actually Galliano) left for a better gig in Vegas. The acts now coming to Ciro's did not need a nine-piece band. Cab Calloway was not coming back. He was replaced by a small, gray-haired, handsome man with great capped teeth who called himself Felix Martinique. He had done some solo work in the bar at times playing various instruments. Now he was joined by two leggy young ladies who looked like they played the field. The trio was called Felix and the Martiniques. No one paid them much attention. The biggest blow to me was when Manuel announced he was leaving to be the maitre d' at the Star on the Roof atop the Beverly Hills Hilton. I was devastated. He was my friend and comrade-in-arms against the drunks and womanizers.

I hung on, hoping maybe George Schlatter would give up producing TV shows and come riding up on a horse to revive Ciro's. No such luck. I became a one-woman show. Although I did not cook or serve, I filled many other slots. I sat on my perch in my beautiful Valentino dress and greeted the customers as they came in. Then I sold them cigars and cigarettes and took their pictures. If they wanted me in a picture with them, one of the waiters would oblige and take the picture. I also answered the phone and took an occasional reservation. I also lied. When someone phoned and asked if any stars were there that night, I would say that someone just called to make a reservation and he sounded just like Brando. Or I'd say Rock Hudson, or James Garner. Take your pick. Since the showroom was quite dark, it was easy to give out-of-towners a thrill by saying, as they were leaving, that that was Elizabeth Taylor seated near your table. Did you notice? They would generally say that they thought that was who that was, and wait 'til they tell the folks back in Nebraska about THAT! "We were with Liz Taylor at Ciro's!" I was now thoroughly ensconced in Hollywood's illusion factory. Somehow I didn't care.

One day I was startled to hear from my good friend Kenny that he was headed for Vegas to appear in a musical revue. He said, "I know I'm not an actor. Oh, I can read lines, but I'm a song and dance man. Vegas is where I belong now." I suddenly had a rush of nostalgia back to a time when John and Kenny and I were all at Camp Roberts and Kenny told us about the movie he made just before he was drafted. *Fearless Fagan* was a comedy about a lion who had escaped to a military base. A group of us went together to the Oak Theatre when the movie played there. Kenny had <u>one</u> line in the show: "Over here, sir." That was it, but we were ready in the audience. When the scene came up and Kenny said his line, we all burst out with wild applause, totally baffling the others in the theater. At that time I thought Kenny showed so much talent that he would surely have a long career as a movie actor. So it was disappointing that he too had bailed on Hollywood and was headed for Vegas.

I told him about the meeting with Cohen and his offer to me. He said only, "Be careful." Then he added, in Elmer Fudd's voice, "Be vewy, vewy careful!" Later I heard he was doing well, but I never saw him again.

So life on The Sunset Strip limped along. Mocambo closed. Fifi D'Orsay's closed. Besides Ciro's, only the Largo still hung on. We had a momentary reprieve when Francis Faye was booked at Ciro's. The tourists didn't know who she was but the hip crowd loved her. Francis was an amazing performer. She looked more like a homely gay man in drag, but when she sang and played the piano in her hoarse raucous way, she was terrific. She and Mel Tormé had just come out with an album, so Mel would drop by occasionally and do a couple of numbers with her. Francis' rendition of "I Love You Porgy" from *Porgy and Bess* was a showstopper. There was such feeling of anguish and pain in her deep raspy voice that even Gershwin would have loved it. When she sang the words, "I love you Porgy, don't let him hurt me. Don't let him handle me with his hot hands," it made me want to cry. She was there for three weeks, often interrupting her repertoire with a mournful refrain, "Gay, gay gay; is there another way…?" When her gig ended we went back to the downturn that was accelerating daily. "There's <u>no</u> business like <u>no</u> business," was the tune we were singing.

The party's over, it's time to call it a day
They've burst your pretty balloons and taken the moon away
⁓ *Comden & Green, Styne*

43

Two months after John's departure I gave notice to vacate my lovely house on Camrose. It had been the scene of so many good times full of friends and laughter. Now it was cold and lifeless. I moved in with a girl friend, Chris, who worked as a film editor and had rented a small cottage on Gardener Street. There was only one caveat: every Saturday her married boyfriend spent the night. Chris suggested I could spend that night with Cole.

Sure, why not? It made perfect sense. I, like the boyfriend, was married so we were equal in our adulterous lifestyles. I thought about designing a T-shirt with a burning palm tree emblazoned on the front. Lots of flames, too. I was sure any T-shirt shop in Hollywood could produce this for me. I'd wear it like a modern day Hester Prynne. I would accessorize it with a pair of old jeans with strategically placed threadbare spots. I was sure Nathaniel Hawthorne would approve. It might even catch on, once people knew the meaning of it. A lot of adultery was going on in Hollywood according to the *Hollywood Reporter.* Maybe I could make a profit from this venture. *Uh-oh! Profiting from sin! Like a madam?*

The fateful demise of Ciro's was an earthquake that was uprooting a lot of us. After Cole's visit to his folks, they convinced him to forget movies and offered to set him up with a nice beauty salon. He agreed and was moving to Santa Monica, where the salon would be located. After John's most recent visit, Cole's and my relationship was a little strained. He said something about not wanting to play a supporting role in my drama. I couldn't blame him.

Zollan had already moved to the Valley where he had a job as assistant cook in an Armenian restaurant. His stuffed grape leaves and pilaf were his résumé. Donna had fallen in love with a cook at the restaurant and was making marriage plans. Kenny felt he had found his niche in Las Vegas doing musicals. Even Phil Dixon had given up his show biz aspirations by doing freelance comedy writing. Buddy Hackett was never as funny again. Phil had a job in Sy Devore's exclusive men's shop on Vine Street. He loved fashion almost as much as I did. Once he had to spend a week in jail due to a zillion overdue parking tickets. Cole and I visited him and were impressed at how he managed to put a little style into his jail uniform. He belted it in the back and made cuffs on the pants with the clever use of hidden paper clips. If they ever gave an award for jailhouse costume design he would walk away with it.

Meanwhile, the money in the mysterious envelopes kept coming in to me, and the balance in my special account grew substantially. It got to the point where it was coming in once a week, not once a month. Ciro's had a funny relationship with The Mob anyway. There was a hatbox that went out once a week and everybody knew it was money. It didn't really seem to affect us in any way, but we were aware of it.

288

One night a valet handed me an envelope that looked different. I opened it with trepidation. The money was there but so was a printed note. Before I even read it I thought; *This looks like a ransom note.* It said: "We have made an investment in you and now we need to collect."

It was tapioca time.

I called my father in a panic. I told him about the money and that the pressure was building and Ciro's was almost ready to close. He said, "Get out of there now! Like TODAY." The fact that I was pregnant helped me decide to take his advice.

No one knew when I came to work that it was my last night. I didn't want Mickey C. to know or anybody else. After closing, I walked around the rooms—the kitchen, show room, upstairs banquet room, bar, Ciroette Room, powder room and lastly the checkroom, my personal domain. My costume was hanging there. In recent days I had been wearing my own clothes as I was playing many roles. The long gold pleated skirt with the white cashmere jeweled top looked as sad and forlorn as I felt. I thought about keeping it. I had paid for it, but somehow I couldn't take it. I was shutting this door and taking no souvenirs. I left a note for the young man who developed the pictures that I was gone and to give away the cigars and cigarettes that remained. I walked out into the evening air, listening to the familiar sounds of Sunset Boulevard and thought I might cry. The taxi I had called was waiting. I got in and never looked back.

To my good fortune, my roommate Chris was about to drive up to Vancouver, Canada, to visit her family and said she could drop me off in Seattle. There was only room for my clothes and for Ho Ho, the god of happiness, to ride in my lap, wrapped either in a cashmere sweater or a silk kimono, depending on the weather.

I moved everything else—my photos, records, books and other memorabilia—into a storage shed behind the café in Encino, planning to get it shipped up later. Time went by and I never saw my stuff again.

Saying goodbye to Cole was the hardest part. When I told him I was pregnant and going home, he smiled and touched my hair. "I knew one day you'd go back to your roots. I knew too that you'd never marry me." Tearfully I got up to go. He put his arms around me and repeated a line from *Tea and Sympathy*, a piece he had done at The Player's Ring: "Years from now, when you speak of this—and you will—be kind."

I never thought I would see him again.

Home is where the art is
⌒ *Kari Field*

44 Three days later I was sitting on the patio of my parents' Green Lake home pondering my next move. I, of course, was welcome to stay with them as long as I wanted. They knew they were going to be grandparents soon, and they were very excited, but worried—though only my dad knew about the Mob factor.

"Does John know about the baby?" my mom asked. "Not yet." I answered. "I want to get settled first. I think I will take an apartment in the new building up the street. It's the right size and has a balcony overlooking the lake. And it's just a ten-minute stroll from here."

I told them I would be using my stage name, Kari Field. Mom was pleased that I was using her grandmother's first name. She warned me, "Be sure you tell people to pronounce it 'Kahree' not 'Carry' like some people do." My dad said, "Good idea. We'll make sure you aren't bothered by anyone." I was glad my mom didn't know my secret. If she had, she would have spent even more hours on her knees praying for me. My dad was glad I was using the last half of his last name, Field. I trusted his years of law-enforcement to make sure no one he didn't know found me.

When John learned I was back and why, he was surprisingly pleased. He did not ask me who the father of the baby was or any really personal questions. Maybe it was because he really didn't care. Nevertheless, he showed up the next day driving a 1950 green Plymouth instead of his silver T-Bird. He explained that he had bought it from a Japanese dentist. Of course, that made alarm bells go off in my head. *MY war with Japan was not over! Could there be a pipe bomb attached under the car? Set to go off when someone other than John was at the wheel? Were the Japanese clever enough to have figured out how to do that?*

I decided to take a chance. So I got behind the wheel and drove around the block. The comforting sound of a Coke bottle rolling around on the floor in the back was very reassuring. *Besides, a dentist?* Anyway I loved the car. It was so the new mom-to-be rig. It had a stick shift, which is the way I learned to drive as a teenager. I drove back to the house, and my dad looked it over. Suddenly, like a magician he produced two knives from under the back seat. They had wooden hilts and were in wooden sheaths. I quailed in fear. Maybe this dentist was one of the Japanese spies who hadn't surrendered yet. My dad chuckled and said to John, "Your dentist friend hid these from us Marshals when we took the Japanese into internment camps."

John was startled too. "What'll we do with them?" he asked.

"Give 'em back. Down at the Marshal's office. We still have a lot of this stuff, including fireworks that were never reclaimed after the war."

"Can you hang on to them, Jim?" John asked.

"Sure," my father answered. "I've got quite a few already, but I can always use more. How you going to get back to wherever you're going? Can I give you a lift somewhere?"

"Thanks, but I'm ok," he said. "I'm meeting a friend at the Twin Teepees in a few minutes. Enjoy the car."

And with that he walked off. I had a moment of disappointment about not being invited to go along. I loved the Twin Teepees, a landmark restaurant built in the thirties. They were two big concrete buildings shaped and painted like Indian teepees and with open fire pits inside. In my mind they were "cooler" even than the famous Brown Derby in Hollywood. But I consoled myself with the fact that now I had wheels.

After signing a lease as Kari Field, I started the exciting project of furnishing my new home. I decided I wanted it to look like a movie set for a Marilyn Monroe movie, very chic Manhattanish, very Kari Fieldish. My shopping spree was a little like the one I had at Magnin's with my insurance windfall five years before. Part of the fun was spending money I had not actually earned. Or perhaps in a way I had earned it, if you count pain, suffering worry, fear and having to wear a Merry Widow in perpetuity. However, I had a great time cruising around in my Plymouth to yard sales, department stores, art galleries, and Seattle's Ye Olde Curiosity Shop on the waterfront.

What I ended up with was beautiful. In the entry was a tall, carved Chinese stand with a marble top. Ho Ho sat upon it in style. There was a little more of a smirk on his face these days; but, after all, he <u>was</u> the god of happiness. The living room was graced by an elegant white leather sofa of a simple design resting on slender teak legs. I added two black cushions. In front of the sofa was an ebony coffee table with a white Italian marble top. On the long, elegant tabletop rested a copy in white of a Tang Dynasty horse. Between two matching coral shell-shaped armchairs was a matching lamp table. On the table were an Italian lamp and a white fruit pyramid under a white silk lampshade. On the far wall was a combination TV, radio and record player with wooden folding doors that could be closed when those items weren't in use. On the wall was a collection of unframed modern art and Asian prints. Above the sofa was a four-paneled screen of white lotus blossoms on a soft gold background. I felt Ho Ho was pleased

The main bedroom was very nouveau Beverly Hills with a Hollywood bed (elaborate quilted plastic headboard and no footboard). The bedspread matched, as did the bolster pillows. A white and gold dresser with enormous mirror gave the room a true look of the bedroom of a kept woman. Not quite the look I was going for, but the bedding was on sale at the Bon Marché. The baby's room had a crib, chest of drawers, and, best of all, an old rocker my mom had rocked me in. I found some great French Mother Goose prints in a little shop in Pioneer Square run by the Salvation Army. All in all, it was a treat to have a place like this while I waited for the baby, plus it had a deck where I could tan. Oh yes, my mom furnished me with boring things like pots, pans, dishes, and towels. A proposed baby shower would help with some baby requirements. I was ready!

"Ready" came early on a chilly Seattle morning. I awoke to strange pains in my back, and I thought this might be it. When I called the hospital they told me to come in right away. I got up and went to my closet to find an appropriate outfit. Shopping for maternity clothes had been a distasteful experience. Every time I shopped I could only say "Ugh!" no matter what I looked at. *These company designers of maternity wear must think that only fifty-year-old fundamentalist librarians get pregnant,* I thought to myself. One baggy navy blue dress with little white polka dots on the collar made me realize too late that pregnancy was not meant for such as I. In my vast wardrobe collection, stored temporarily in my parents' house, were some things that worked for awhile; but by my eighth month I needed something else. Fortunately I had gained a minimal amount of weight, so I found the perfect dress style. It was called the "trapeze" dress, and it was in high fashion. The cut was like a triangle with small shoulders slanting down at an isosceles sort of angle so the dress covered many figure faults, including final-month pregnancies. The one I chose to wear that morning was cornflower blue with a scalloped hemline. I called a cab as I slipped on my matching high-heeled shoes. Over it all I wore a black swing back raincoat. As I snatched up my monogrammed Chanel purse, I realized that I had only twenty dollars left to my name. The rent was paid, and the hospital charges were being paid by John's insurance. But after that cab ride, my baby and I would be broke.

"And den?" Once more, Mrs. Peusa's voice asked the eternal question.

A man of words instead of deeds
is like a garden full of weeds
        ⌒ *Nursery Rhyme*

45 The joy I felt when I first looked at my newborn son was indescribable. He had brown hair, fair skin, and a deep cleft in his tiny chin. Everything I had experienced in the past—the hurts, the agonizing hours waiting through the night to hear a car door shut and the front door open, the pain of smelling Tabu perfume on the jacket John dropped on the chair—it was worth it now for this gift that surpassed all else. I was a proud mother of a boy named Brandon. But could I be a good mother without a good husband?

John gave Bandon and me a ride from the hospital to my parents' home, where my mom greeted us with liberal open arms and where I would stay for a few weeks. She had turned my old room into a nursery, complete with a rocker and a single bed for me. My dad was grinning from ear to ear. At last he had a grandson. I always knew he had wanted a son, and that's why he taught me *judo* and how and when to use a pistol. When John was ready to leave us, I walked him to the door. He glanced over toward the baby and said, "Now you have someone who will never leave you."

I loved staying in my old room, and I learned baby care skills from my mom. When Brandon was asleep, I began trying on some of the clothes I had left stored there. I couldn't wait to return to wearing many sorely missed pieces and even my old friend, Merry Widow. Within a week I was back to my same old measurements. Two weeks later I moved back into my movie set apartment and landed a job at a new downtown club called (of all things) "The Casbah." The manager didn't need any references, which was good because those were in my real name. The only thing he cared about was how I looked in the harem costume. My job was to greet patrons, check coats, and sell cigarettes. He said I would get the best costume in the place since I was a "showgirl."

When I tried on the costume, I was pleased that it fit perfectly. It was a gauzy, sexy, two-piece affair. No Merry Widow with this! The pants were sheer, with baggy legs that fit tightly at the ankle. The slippers with turned up toes were quite comfortable. A jeweled headdress completed the harem girl look. All the female servers wore a simpler version. I really liked the look of the two bartenders who wore tunic tops, large turbans and authentic-looking mustaches that dropped nearly to their chins. Guests had the option of sitting at iron and glass tables or on large, silky cushions around low round tables with brass hookah centerpieces. I found the whole effect more fun than the sets in the movie *Casablanca*. Maybe John could get a piano gig there. I could hear it now, "Play it again, John."

A pang shot through my chest. *There I go again, looking for jobs that would showcase John. Will I never quit?*

John dropped in one night, "to see how you are doing," he said. As an afterthought, he asked about the baby. I told him that Brandon was fine and that I was leaving him with my parents while I worked at night and then picking him up in the mornings. I told him about my piano idea. He said the drawback would be the turban. The mustache was okay, turban no.

He went to the bar to have a drink. When I passed by with my cigarette tray, he looked down at my curled-up shoes and asked, "Why are you walking so funny? Is it the shoes?" I explained it was the damn elastic at the bottom of the pants. They were really tight, so I tucked the back parts under my heels and had to shuffle to keep them in place. "I see you do the harem shuffle," he joked. "That could be a new dance craze."

I put my tray down and did an experimental combination belly dance and shuffle. He said, "All you need is a snake draped around and you've got a hit." I shot back, "I think I know of a perfect snake—you!" We both laughed, and for a minute, it was like the old days when we used to laugh together. I picked up my tray and said, "I'd better be shuffling off." When he stopped by my perch in the entrance he handed me a folded up bill. "Here's a tip for you. Keep the belly dance and the snake. Forget the shuffle." After he left, I looked at my tip. It was a hundred dollar bill. With a wink and a nod, he left.

A month later I was fired. The manager said, "You got a great body kid, but the owner doesn't want no blondes. He says they don't fit the decor."

Wow, I thought, *the blondes stigma has made it to Seattle.*

*Idiot's Delight: The game that never
means anything and never ends*
 ❧ *Robert Sherwood*

46

The next club that fired me was called "The Roaring Twenties." It too was a theme park club that featured music, dancing, food, liquor and fun. Before I was fired, though, I had some good times both inside and outside the club.

The decor was early speakeasy. The guys working there looked like hoods and the girls like brain-dead flappers. Some were servers and some were playmates. I was a playmate. Once an hour the playmates made a dramatic entrance by sliding down a brass pole accessed from a hidden area above the dance floor. There was much whooping and squealing from both the sliders and patrons. The fact that the girls were all in short flapper dresses made the descent harder but the male attention intense. Minimal underwear was encouraged by management. I chose to wear one of my favorite Ciro's dresses. It was white with overlapping rows of fringe. The low neckline was outlined in rhinestones, as were the straps.

One of the favorite games available to customers was to shoot baskets with a playmate on a small court located near the entry. The girls who were picked to participate were tipped well. I was frequently chosen, partly because of a dress problem. Whenever I shot a basket or made a throw, one of my straps usually broke. Eventually, the other one gave up too. I joked about a new rule for the NBA— once a girl's uniform goes strapless, the game is over and the opponent wins. Many times my opponent would offer to tip generously if I would go for overtime, strapless or topless. It reminded me of an incident at the L.A. country club pool, where I was modeling bathing suits. Thanks, but no thanks.

One night after I played several games in high heels and dangling straps, I left early. As I waited at my bus stop, shivering in the midnight wind and rain, a familiar car drove up. I thought, *If they offer a ride, I just might be tempted.* As I looked more closely at the car, I realized it was John's. And seated in the passenger seat was my old enemy, Takiko!

The next thing I knew I had yanked the passenger door open and started pounding on Takiko. I got in a couple of good licks before John got out and came around and pulled me off her. I thought to myself that my athletic talents ran more to boxing than basketball. John flagged down a passing cab, gave the driver some money, and not too gently deposited me in the back seat. As he closed the door he muttered, "I'll call you."

The next night the manager of the club told me he was sorry, but he had to let me go. "The other girls are complaining about you. They say you think you are better than they are and make more tips." I couldn't disagree. And, besides, I was ruining one of my favorite dresses.

47 Two weeks later John called and said we needed to talk. I expected I was in for a lecture about how brutal I was, beating up on Takiko, just because I was standing in a cold, midnight rain waiting for a bus while she was being chauffeured around town in a car that legally was half mine.

I agreed to meet him at the Twin Teepees the next day. It was a nearby and neutral place to talk, and I loved the central fire pit. At one o'clock, dressed in what I considered a power black suit, I arrived, ordered a cup of coffee and prepared to wait the usual half hour for him to show up—if he did.

Amazingly, he was there after just five minutes. What did this mean? Did he want to borrow money? He was casually dressed in slacks and a zippered jacket. He was showing a serious beard shadow. I smiled to myself as I thought about a guy at our old grocery store who once asked me whether John had a good-looking brother who played piano downtown. John didn't shave until just before going to work (the deep cleft in his chin required special shaving skills.) Once he emerged shaved, showered and in a well-cut dinner jacket, it was quite a transformation.

He signaled for coffee while I waited to hear the reason for this impromptu meeting. He took a swig of black coffee and said, "I'm through with Taki! When I saw you standing there in the rain at the bus stop, something happened. I knew that I wanted to be a husband to you and a father to Brandon. I know I've made mistakes. I'd like a second chance."

Second chance? I thought. *How about fourth or fifth chance? I've lost count.* A confusion of emotions swept over me. One was fury that he could snap his fingers, say a few nice things, and I would fall into his arms (or trap). The other feeling was one of elation. He had changed. This was the real John I had met in college and fallen for who now expressed a sense of responsibility toward Brandon! *He needs a father*, echoed in my head. So I took a big chance and said okay.

John moved into my posh apartment, and I was very happy. He got a job at a new, very classy downtown club called the Viceroy. He played an early gig in the saloon-style bar on a piano with tacks in the hammers to give it a honky-tonk effect. The outfit he wore was a striped vest and sleeve garters. For the dinner hour show he changed into a black tie and dinner jacket to play standards on a black grand piano. Everybody loved him, and the tips were generous.

The increased income made it possible for us to buy a charming, two story Cape Cod house near my parents. I fell feverishly into scouting for antiques. A friend of John's advised me that, once you pay for a piece of new furniture it immediately begins to depreciate; but if you invest in antique pieces, they begin to appreciate right away. This appealed to my frugal, yet extravagant ways.

I haunted consignment shops, thrift stores, moving sales,

and mom's attic. In no time at all I had a classy living room with a baby grand in a corner by the fireplace, just the way it was on Camrose Drive. There was a 1920's burgundy, cushioned sofa with matching armchair, both with caned backs; and my prize—an oriental rug with burgundy background and simple but intricate designs. I think it was called a "Bukhara." I loved the name and planned to call our next cat Bukhara. The downstairs bedroom was now a den with a color TV. Brandon's room had French Mother Goose pictures on the wall and a coordinating bedspread. The master bedroom across the hall was spacious, and, best of all, it had TWO closets. Perhaps my favorite room was the breakfast nook off the kitchen overlooking the pleasant backyard with a sandbox and swing. The nook was furnished with a Blondie and Dagwood chrome breakfast set with yellow vinyl seats and backs. It was not an antique, but it was getting there. All my dreams had come true. We were a family!

We had two years of Leaving-it-to-Beaver bliss. The Queen of the Sunset Strip had morphed into the Queen of the Casseroles. No tuna could hide in a can and be safe from a role in one of my Good Housekeeping recipes. I was cast in a part, however, that I never expected—*housewife*! I went back to my roots in more ways than one. I was now a cute brunette mama. The church ladies smiled proudly at me. Their prayers had been answered, and I was safe. No drugstore blonde anymore!

I was not used to being alone at night, so, in addition to reading, I decided to paint. I wanted to do a painting of John. As we sat at our early dinners before he went to work, I would study his face carefully. This unnerved him somewhat, but I told him I was painting him from memory and he didn't need to pose. Each night I went into the den after Brandon was asleep and painted. I had only a palette

305

knife, an eyeliner brush and a few tubes of oil paint from a moving sale. I found a piece of fiberboard and got started. I decided to show him from the waist up in a tuxedo, similar to some publicity posters he had ordered in that style.

What emerged on the board was somewhat disturbing. John looked handsome but haunted, and tragedy showed in his eyes. Where did that come from? The tuxedo looked phony like those cardboard bodies of Superman or whomever that you stand behind for a photo with your head showing over the cardboard body. "It must be the way I see him," I thought, so I found an old gilt frame and hung the painting over the fireplace.

Life was good and I was enjoying every minute of it. We hosted parties for friends and for my folks, who also joined us for holiday events. It was the dream all girls have in high school, and now at last it had come true for me. I thought about making a career for myself in interior design. I wouldn't have to schmooze with men, and I could be my own boss. I could dress the part easily with my arty dresses and silk shawls thrown casually over the shoulders. It sounded really promising, perhaps something I could launch at the point when Brandon was ready to start school.

As good as life was, John began showing some small changes. He got irritable with me more and more frequently. If I dropped a dish in the kitchen he would swear at me, even though I was the one to sweep up the mess. Then he started getting phone messages. They were mostly from guy friends or regarding radio spots, but then gradually it was more and more a woman's voice. She gave no name. When I asked John about this, he brushed it off saying it was a girl who worked at his last job at the Hilton Inn. She was having some problems, and he was trying to help her.

An old, familiar feeling began to well up in my chest.

Please God, don't take all this away from me, I prayed silently. However, the old pattern emerged bit by bit. Coming home later and later at night, he smelled of cheap perfume. *At least Takiko had worn "Patou's Joy!"* I groaned inwardly.

Back in the Camp Robert's days there was a song I sang occasionally at USO parties. Now the words from "Nowhere Guy" came back to me:

> *Here am I like a fool just listening,*
> *listening for the footsteps down the hall,*
> *Just talking to the shadows on the wall,*
> *Telling them this can't go on at all,*
> *I'm through, for good, forever!*
>
> *Then he'll walk in, he'll smile*
> *And I'll forgive again and I'll live again.*
> *Why don't I leave him?*
> *It makes no sense to even try.*
> *He's just a nowhere, but without him, so am I.*

Mercifully, the end came quickly. On a "Gloomy Sunday" (another appropriate song), he packed up a few personal things, telling me he had to "be there" for this poor girl who was leaving her husband and needed help. I was standing in my beloved living room of carefully chosen antiques. I looked down at the Bukhara carpet. It rose up to meet me. It pulled me down into its bloody burgundy depths. I gasped for breath. I wanted to say, "Please don't do this to me. We have a child who needs a dad." I couldn't speak. I was dimly aware of him stepping over my gasping body as it struggled to stay afloat on the storm-tossed rug.

I heard the front door close, and I was alone once again. As I struggled to breathe, I looked at my painting over the fireplace. The face looked down at me, not with pity, but with distant unconcern. I saw my life passing before me in a story told by the rug. One design was the happy college years. Next to that was the Paso Robles years with a hint of doom when I was abandoned far from home. Then the happiness of dancing in the moonlight at Nina's in Shell Beach. Then I saw the fun turn to pain. The deep red background became a sea of blood. My blood. I had a sensation of something leaving my body. Was it my soul? Had my very soul left me? The answer came to me. I knew in that moment what it was that had left me: hope and dreams.

48 The next morning, after a sleepless night, I got up to see if a cup of strong coffee would help me pull myself together. My four-year old son had spent the night with his grandma, who was going to take him shopping the next day. I wanted to seem normal when he returned home. I stepped onto the balcony and saw that a spider had begun spinning her web on the railing.

I have long held a deep admiration and reverence for one of nature's finest works of art—the spider web. How fragile, yet strong it is! I love to see one gleaming in the morning dew as it hangs ready to trap the unwary. But much as I love the artwork, I am repulsed by the artist. So I was surprised when I started developing an affection of sorts for the orange and black spider who displayed her creations on the iron railing of my balcony. The contrast of the lacy web against the stern, unyielding metal posts was delightful to behold. In fact, I decided to name my new friend "Webster."

It looked as if Webster's creation would end up at least ten inches in diameter. I sat down and followed this work in progress. She had started from the outside and was weaving her way toward the center. I watched for over a half hour, hypnotized by the unfolding of a truly awesome web. I thought, *This is one for the Guiness Book of Records!*

Just as I got up to try to find a camera, my son rushed onto the balcony. I told him I had something amazing to show him and that it was right behind him. He answered by reaching into a shopping bag, boasting that he had something to show me too. "Ta da!" he proclaimed and whipped out a cool pair of jeans my mother had bought him the day before. As he swung them toward me for approval they hit the web and in a nanosecond the incredible work of art and its creator disappeared. I leaped up from my chair screaming, "No, no!" Tears filled my eyes, and I crashed into the hard reality of the iron bars that had briefly held the web. My son was astonished at my reaction and kept saying "sorry" over and over. Then he saw that blood was running down my leg where I had crashed into the sharp railing. *There should be blood,* I thought, *after such a catastrophe.* I banged my leg again and again into the sharp metal. More blood! Let there be more blood.

I sank down into my chair and sobbed. My son was crying too. I knew what that web meant to me and why I had exploded. I had been "weaving" by myself, just like Webster, year after year, caring for John and now Brandon. The fragile web was a symbol of hard work and dedication that can be swept away by chance or design, leaving nothing behind but a few pathetic shreds moving in the breeze.

I couldn't eat that day and sleep came reluctantly again that night. I was at a point where my life was over. I would never again be able to create a strong, durable design for my world. I wondered if Webster was feeling the same way. In spider time she probably had spent as much of her life as I had, working toward goals. My hopes and dreams had been a web as fragile as Webster's. The "big time" was not for me after all. It was time to give up and just watch myself grow old with nothing to show for all my early efforts.

The next morning I hesitated to go out on the balcony where such a disaster had occurred. But I went anyway. To my happy surprise my old friend was hard at work in the corner where the railing made a turn. There she was, busy creating a new, smaller web that appeared luminous and three-dimensional. She was trying something different, as all artists do. I saluted her with my coffee cup and said, "Thank you, Webster. I get it." I went inside, ready to rethink everything and try again.

I looked at myself in the ornate mirror. Who was I now? The answer was; I was Bess dumping Porgy. I was the pathetic girl who found the guts to dump the Nowhere Guy. I felt euphoria in realizing I had dumped John! I was free to be me. I had the locks changed as my first action in taking control of my life. What a sensation to know that no man would ever have the power to hurt me again.

One evening, while I was sitting with Brandon wondering what I could afford to make for dinner, the doorbell rang. It was a pizza deliverer with a pizza. I told him I had not ordered one and asked if he had the right address. He said he did, and the pizza was paid for.

Two days later a taxi delivered a box of groceries. Same answer. It was paid for. *It must be John*, I thought. *He feels guilty, leaving us with no food.* The next time it happened, I asked the deliverer of Chinese *dim sum* if he could describe the person who ordered this and paid for it. "I dunno ", he said. "It was a real good-looking Asian girl, maybe Chinese or Japanese." My mind reeled. *Could it be Takiko? Was the food safe to eat? Well, Brandon and I had scarfed down the pizza with no ill effects. We could surely use these care packages. But what did it mean?*

Next, our benefactor phoned and invited me to meet her that night at ten o'clock in Chinatown. She would send a cab and meet me at 14th Street South and Jackson. *Did she think I was crazy? Did my longtime mortal enemy think I was so stupid as to go to my doom at her request? Or were we now a sisterhood, both of us having been dumped by John? How do I deal with this? Would I go like a lamb to the slaughter in Chinatown or, at best, let myself be shanghaied into white slavery?* So, of course, I went.

My biggest problem was what to wear. I remember what Marie Antoinette wore to the guillotine. But even if I had an ornate gown like that, I wouldn't wear it on the back streets of Chinatown. I settled on a black leather dress with a zipper from the hem to the waist and another which went from neck to waist. I could adjust the zippers up or down depending on the situation or weather.

I remembered an occasion some years before when my dad and I had gone to a Chinese restaurant for dinner. We had walked back to our car parked on Jackson Street, when we were threatened by a trio of vicious looking men carrying clubs. My dad quietly opened the trunk of his car and took out a tire iron. With his best prison-guard, U.S. Marshal scary grin, he walked toward them saying, "Come and get it, boys!" They quickly disappeared, and we drove home. I didn't have a tire iron for this meeting with Takiko, but I looked scary in black leather with metal zippers. (Or so I hoped.)

Takiko was waiting at the corner wearing a red silk dress. *Of course! My blood would not show up on her red dress. It was a little dated, though, with fifties' shoulder pads.* She escorted me into a dark alley that Hitchcock would have loved.

"Where are we going?" I asked, as casually as I could.

"You'll see," she replied, in her Tokyo Rose voice.

Naturally, it made sense to murder someone in an alley rather than out on the street and then have to drag the body away. At the end of the alley was an old dark building with a big metal door. "Shortcut," she explained. We climbed a flight of metal stairs to another metal door, behind which I was sure ninjas were waiting with swords like the ones my dad and other U.S. Marshals confiscated at the beginning of the war.

She threw open the door as I braced myself. I was instantly overwhelmed by loud music. Jazz! Minutes later I was on a dance floor doing the boogie-woogie with a Japanese man named Hiro. He was such a wild boogie dancer that I was forced to unzip my skirt a little higher, thankful that I had worn my new flesh-colored nylons. Then another dancer grabbed me and we did an amazing jitterbug. I was having fun! As I danced I waved to my new friend Taki, who smiled back.

She had brought me to the Japanese-American post of the American Legion. The men there were veterans of WWII who had served in the European theater with much honor. I felt very privileged to talk with them and thank them for their service to our country. Hiro asked to drive me home. So I said goodbye to Taki (as I called her now), to which she replied, "I want you to have fun." Oddly, she didn't sound like Tokyo Rose anymore.

As I got ready for bed that night, removing my "un-bloodiest leather crime-stopper outfit," I thought about Takiko and the games she played. She was a shrewd woman and perhaps now a little desperate. For over five years she had been able to entice John away from me. Now she faced what I had been suffering for a long time—*rejection!*

Perhaps she felt the pain I had felt and was asking herself the same questions I had asked myself many times: What did I do wrong? What could I have done better? Be a better lover? Cook? Conversationalist?

Since time immemorial women have been locked into rivalry. The man you snagged would determine your place in society and what kind of financial security you and your children would have. "A good catch" was a saying commonly heard in my grandmother's day, but it had been established as an institution long before her time.

Takiko was acknowledging that it was she who had lost the game—not me. I was no longer her rival, so she could afford to be generous. Perhaps the care packages she had sent and tonight's surprise party were her way of saying she was sorry. I mulled this over and decided to accept the apology. I had learned from it too and, like her, I would never be the same.

Could I forgive her? No. Could we be friends? No. Could I feel sympathy for her? Perhaps. Who did I blame for her pain and mine? John Morrison.

Don't cry because it's over, smile because it happened
Dr. Seuss

49 I realized that I needed a job, unless I was ready to become a charity case for Taki. I didn't want another nightclub job, given that the last one almost ruined my white fringed dress. I called a modeling agency where I had been trained and had done a few jobs. Jeri-Dean, the manager, was happy to give me a job as a receptionist and instructor of a class or two in "charm." I thought I'd do better teaching self-defense, but I agreed.

The office was located in a nice building called the Grosvenor House, located near the site of the upcoming World's Fair. I was a blonde again. I enjoyed sitting at a fake French desk surrounded by mirrors. A nice extra treat was that I was encouraged to wear a hat at all times. Jackie Kennedy's pillboxes were all the rage, and I had two of them—one with a half-veil. I felt very chic in these hats, although the one with the veil was inconvenient when I had to blow my nose or sneeze.

Many calls started coming in for models to work at Century 21, the official name for the fair. As the opening day approached, I decided to take a job there myself. I auditioned to be a perfume model. I wasn't sure at first whether that meant girls would stroll around in big cardboard costumes designed to look like bottles. I was relieved that they wanted models who had fashionable wardrobes to walk beneath a canopied runway holding and spraying cologne. Each of us would represent a different fragrance. The perfumes would be sold inside an Arabian-looking tent. I was named Miss Chanel #5—not my favorite but definitely better than Tweed, which another girl got. I had coveted Tabu, mostly for the name, but that went to a dark-haired beauty. *It's the Jackie effect again,* I thought.

I was Miss Chanel for two days and quit. I had already had enough of guys making comments and offers as they crowded along the runway. I thought, *Why aren't they hitting on the lovely brunette girl? Of course they wouldn't. She was Tabu!* One man who approached me, as I climbed down from the runway, asked to talk to me. He looked okay in his suit, beret, and horn-rimmed glasses. So we sat down on a bench, and he asked if I would like to be a "Girl of the Galaxy." This was a spot on "Show Street" next to "A Night in Paradise," where a woman entrepreneur named Gracie Hansen was replicating the Ziegfeld Follies. She was a short, chubby woman with chipped nail polish, but she had gotten more press from her show than anyone. That was quite a success for a middle-aged gal from Morton, a small mining town in Eastern Washington State. I had heard that the "G. G. Girls " (Girls of the Galaxy), as they were called, were a sort of less expensive version of Gracie's Girls, the main show inside that featured a semi-known stripper named "Stormy."

The man's name was Ralph and he explained that I would not have to work inside. He was the pitchman, and I would be out on a platform with him. He said I could wear whatever I wanted as long as it was sexy. I told him that would be no problem. I would be a sort of pitch girl. My mom would approve of that. So I said sure, I can start tomorrow.

I really wanted to work at the Fair. It was so exciting. It was my island in the stream. President Kennedy had inaugurated festivities from Florida, where he was on vacation. He pressed a telegraph key that picked up an impulse from a star and redirected it toward the World's Fair site in a futuristic signal that started the celebration. The grounds were crowded with people of all races, ages and colors. There were fountains everywhere, and the 60-story Space Needle loomed over it all. It was an urban fairyland, and I needed to be there.

As a new Galaxy Girl, I changed into my sexy new dress in the dressing room with Stormy. The room was always crowded with mostly men—agents, managers, and publicists. At first I was a little self-conscious about being seen in a Merry Widow while I changed into my performance dress. I tried to hide in a corner until I realized nobody was looking at me. Stormy made me look downright flat-chested. She must have been a triple D and proud of it. She had meetings and interviews totally topless. Actually, I was relieved to be unnoticed until I was on the stage as a pitch girl.

My costume was a black satin strapless dress that I wore with long gloves and rhinestone jewelry. I stood around mostly smiling and occasionally walking around while Ralph and I exchanged some comedy patter. We even did a couple of magic tricks. It was a little boring, but I was where the action was in Seattle and that's what mattered.

As one part of Ralph's spiel he would say that those who bought tickets to the show would see a lot more of me. At that point I would slowly remove one of my long gloves in a slithery manner and parade around the platform swinging it.

One evening I recognized a lady in the crowd (a rare sight) who was a neighbor of my parents. I walked closer to the edge of the stage and waved my glove to her. I was hoping she would approach me, so I could explain I was not a stripper—that this was just Ralph's way of selling more tickets. Instead, a man moved very close to the stage and grabbed my ankle. I reached down and yanked on his tie while I beat on his head with my glove until he let go. The crowd cheered. Ralph loved it and said we should keep this in the act.

I decided to move on down Show Street to a different job. This one was the "Wild West Show," where five girls ran around a corral in little, short cowgirl outfits with sensors in various parts of the fringe. Men with arcade-type rifles fired at us until they connected with a sensor, at which point we would let out a squeal and drop to the sawdust. When the time limit was up, those girls who survived and those who didn't ran back into the bunkhouse until the next open season was declared. I loved the hat, but hated the job. I was tired of being a quarry for men, so I left Show Street for good.

My next job was at the Spanish Village. It was a compound of artisans and artists from Spain who demonstrated their wares in little open shops. In the center was a building in mock Spanish architecture which housed "The Cantina." The atmosphere was most delightful. There was a *tapas* stand redolent with wonderful aromas and musicians strolling around. The Cantina was a restaurant with stage where musicians and flamenco dancers performed. My job was to fill in as hostess and take pictures with a Polaroid camera of guests wearing sombreros of their choice. Everyone who worked there was from Spain except me. I spoke Spanish as much as possible. If I had to resort to English, I used my best Spanish accent.

Most of these Spaniards refused to learn any English.

My Spanish vocabulary improved so much that a visitor from Spain said he recognized my accent. He said I was from Las Islas Canarias! I was so flattered I was tempted to thank him, but added that I was actually from La Isla McNeil. I'm sure that didn't sound quite right to him, and he also didn't know McNeil was *un calabozo!*

One afternoon a young gypsy from the hills of Granada took my hand and, while holding his guitar in the other, led me into the small storeroom at the rear of The Cantina. He shut the door, sat down on a case of Madeira wine, and began to play. The music filled the storeroom and blended with the smell of spices. I knew I was experiencing a rare and magical moment that I would never forget. I was transported far from Seattle and all the problems that surrounded me. For a beautiful moment in time I was in Spain. The fact that, during that time in the dark, I always knew where his hands were, made it even more sublime. When the concert ended he opened the door and we exited back into the hubbub of the Fair, my magical journey to his homeland over.

I not only worked with the Spaniards, I partied with them. I learned to love *sangria*, which was made in big washtubs and was present at all events. I dated one of the musicians in the Las Tunas group from the University of Madrid. However, it was the slender young man named Cruz Luna that I had a brief romance with. To see him on stage in his tight, white outfit was tantalizing. He liked *las rubias*, (blondes) but could not understand my need to have a tan. Pale skin is highly valued in Spain. I thought perhaps when I sold my house I could take the money and move to Spain with Brandon. Cruz liked the idea and said I could buy a *segundo-mano* Fiat (second-hand) and live like a *reina* (queen) on my house sale proceeds. At last I had a man and a plan!

The urban fairyland that was Century 21 ended in late October. It was the same month I learned that the house John and I owned was in foreclosure and I would have to pay up or move out. The money to pay up was more than I had or could raise.

"And den?"

Back to Hollywood I went. Spain would have to wait.

*When you hit a wrong note, it's the next note
that makes it good or bad*
    ⌢ *Miles Davis*

50 The rain began gently and then increased. *I'm glad I brought my raincoat,* I thought, forgetting what had happened two nights before, when bandleader Eddie Grady offered me a ride home from the Largo. It was November 1962, and I was back in Hollywood.

I was staying at Chris's house on Fountain Avenue, after deciding not to move in with Cole. Cole and I were friends as always, but we were not in our twenties anymore, and I was a mom! After one night of trying to recapture our old romance, we both knew that too much had changed. I learned how much I had hurt him when I left the last time. He had spent two years in therapy. Guilt washed over me. Had I used him to get back at John to prove to myself that I could be in a successful relationship? We had a special connection, and I knew I would always have a special place in my heart for him. Chris was happy to have me back as a paying roommate. She had broken up with her old weekend boyfriend, so I did not have to be gone Saturday nights. The boyfriend had dumped her for someone else, so we had a lot of commiserating to do about men.

Two nights before, driving home from work, Eddie and I first stopped off at the Gaiety for old times' sake and coffee. Things had changed there too. With the Strip virtually empty of nightlife, the deli was empty of showgirls, bartenders and most of the late night workers on the Boulevard. The crowd was not only smaller, but dull and boring. (George Hamilton was nowhere in sight.) When I entered in my white vinyl raincoat with tiny rhinestones on the collar and wide, waist-defining belt, accompanied by a handsome bandleader, I was gaped at. Although it didn't happen, I was prepared to sign autographs.

After looking around the room, Eddie said, "Maybe we should go someplace else. Any ideas?"

"What about that new place on the Strip? " I suggested. "I think it's called The Unicorn."

"You mean that so-called coffee house where beatniks hang out?" "Sure, why not?" I said. "Everybody else is doing it."

A few minutes later we entered a very different Sunset Strip hang out. The Unicorn was packed with young people, smoke, and noise. We found a tiny table, and I ordered a café latte. I had no idea what it was, but the server said it was creamy and that I'd like it. Eddie ordered a cup of black coffee. On the small stage were two guys in jeans and long beards. One was playing the guitar while the other recited poetry. The crowd loved it. I did too. *Maybe I could read a poem there one day,* I speculated. *Maybe accompanied by bongos. Hmmm.* Eddie finished his coffee quickly and suggested we leave, while muttering about the Strip going to hell.

We left the Unicorn and drove to Chris's house. I knew she would be sleeping, so I was prepared to exit the car quietly and tiptoe in, when Eddie grabbed my arm and said, "Hey, the night is young. Let's cozy up."

"Thanks for the ride," I said. "But I think I'm ready to go to bed."

Alone, I muttered under my breath, as I started to open the car door. He still did not release my arm. "Come on," he begged. Suddenly I heard a ripping sound. It was the sleeve of my beloved raincoat. I think it shocked Eddie too, because he let go and I ran into the house, sleeve dangling beside me. Why hadn't he just broken my arm? That could be fixed, but I knew there was no duct tape in the world that could repair the brutal damage to my raincoat.

The next evening at the club I received a shock to my body and soul. A couple came in, and the man dropped his fedora on my countertop. He looked familiar and so did his hat. Then I realized it was Mickey Cohen. But I had read he was in prison! Had he escaped and come after me? A voluptuous blonde stood next to him. "Hello, Mr. Cohen. Can I check your hat?" I blurted out stupidly. To myself I said, *Of course he wants his hat checked, Idiot, that's why he placed it on the counter.* Another voice in my head said, *Run away! Run away!* The sane voice in my head said, *Where to? Where can you run to?* My crazy voice said, *Who cares? You are in more danger now than you were in that dark alley in Chinatown.*

I think he sensed my unease, because he said, "Don't worry. It's not the same hat; and, besides, I trust you." *What did that mean?* I pondered. He turned to the blonde and said to me, "This here is my girlfriend, Candy Barr. She's booked here next." I turned to her and asked, "Oh, are you a singer?" She giggled and answered, "Hell no, I'm a stripper. Mickey likes to call me an exotic dancer, but I strip!" With that she squeezed his arm.

"Nice to meet you, Candy," I muttered, wondering if she might have a softening effect on him. I hoped so, shaking madly in my shoes (the silver high-heeled ones with ankle straps.)

"Everything going okay with you?" he asked.

"I guess so. I miss my little boy," I said. *It had softened Takiko to hear that. Would my being a mom do the same for a mobster?*

"Yeah, so I heard. Up in Seattle, is he?"

"With my mom," I managed to say through frozen lips. *He knew where I was all along. He knew even about Brandon, and still I was alive!*

As they started toward the show room, he turned back and looked at me. "Why don't you go home to your kid?" he said.

I picked up his hat and holding it to my chest with tears welling in my eyes, I said, "Thanks, Mickey." He gave me a wink and walked away. I knew what he had said to me was that I was free. Free to be me. Kari Field was dead, and Karoline Morrison was alive and kicking!

That night I told Chuck Landis that I was leaving. I was thirty years old and I knew my final tapioca moment had come. Sarcastically, he said, "Oh, you'll be back. You girls always come back." Under my breath I retorted, *Only as a tourist! The Mob had forgiven me, and now I could do and be anything I wanted.*

I didn't sleep well that night. So much to think about. No more men in my life unless I wanted them there. In the morning I called home to say I was coming back, for good, forever. I asked if their upstairs apartment was still available, as it was last time we talked. My mom answered in a happy voice, partly because I was coming home, but also because she had just rented the apartment to a nice young man from Spokane. He was attending the University of Washington and played the banjo! Mom played guitar, so I think she was looking forward to some guitar and banjo nights. She went on to explain that my old room on the first floor was waiting for me, as always, right down the hall from Brandon's. It sounded so good to me. I thanked her and asked if Dad could meet me at the Sea-Tac Airport. I would let him know my arrival time.

As I started getting my things together, I discovered in my make-up case two business cards given to me by TV producers when I worked at the Seattle World's Fair. One of them was Bud Yorkin, who was the producer of many highly-acclaimed comedy and musical shows, such as the Carol Burnett Show and Jack Benny specials. He had promised to find me a "spot" and introduce me to some "important people." I carried the cards into the living room to dispose of them, when I had a great idea. The day I moved back in with Chris, I had noticed something very strange in the living room. It was her fireplace mantel "decoration," a pair of pale, tapered candles in round holders that had softened in the heat and were drooping down with their wicks facing the hearth. "Those candles need jock straps," I had observed. Chris laughingly explained that there had been a heat wave in September that caused the candles to collapse. Since her boyfriend had just dumped her, she decided to leave them that way as a kind of symbol of revenge.

I knew what I had to do. I got a match and newspaper from the kitchen. I laid the newspaper down on the fireplace hearth to protect it. First, I set fire to the business cards in the fireplace. They quickly turned to ashes. Next, I lit the flaccid candles. As I watched them burn, dripping their waxy sperm down on yesterday's newspaper, I felt a moment of deep satisfaction. I was burning in effigy all the men who had hurt me, let me down, tried to use me, lied, cheated, and belittled me. By the time the cab arrived to take me to the airport, there were only two pathetic little stubs left. I extinguished them and my 19th Century fantasy of carrying a candelabrum to light John's way to fame.

On the flight home, I panicked twice as I looked for the bag where I had always carried Ho-Ho. Then I remembered that, for the first time, I had left Seattle without his smiling, familiar presence. Somehow I must have known this was a trial balloon trip. I had only packed four val-packs of clothing, surely not enough for a long stay.

I felt a strong homesickness for Ho-Ho. He had always been there with his little smile (more sincere than the Mona Lisa's). He had been there for me since I was twelve. He had heard my laughter and my tears and triumphs, the disasters, hopes, dreams, and the rejoicing whenever I got a good deal on a dress at Saks. I shared many moments with him. The two times he had been robbed by John of the money stuffed inside him, he was sad but still optimistic. After all, his job description was "God of Happiness."

I glanced at my seatmate. She was an older, gray-haired woman wearing a navy blue polyester suit and very sensible shoes. She told me earlier that she had been visiting her son and grandchildren in Pomona and was exhausted from the effort to coexist for two weeks with teenagers. She was happy to be returning home to her husband and cats and a quiet life of retirement.

Could this be me in forty years? I asked myself. *Would I constantly wonder whether I had made the right choices, especially this last one?* One thing I knew for sure: I would not be wearing a navy polyester pantsuit and walking shoes. Nor would my hair be a tight cap of gray curls. Nor would I be thirty pounds overweight!

I thought about Cole—perhaps the only man who would ever really love me, roots and all. But I needed more. I needed a man who could be the father John could never be. And Cole was not the one.

When I was six or seven I tasted Coca Cola for the first time. I exclaimed that I loved it! My mother told me firmly, "Never love anything that can't love you back."

EPILOGUE

*The twilight has deepened into night. The rule of the mythic
gods (and Hollywood blondes) has ended. A new dawn awaits
⌒ Wagner's "Gotterdamerung"*

On April Fool's Day of 1963 I divorced John Morrison. Two
years later, I had become a successful antiques dealer and
appeared frequently on local TV doing comedy with antiques.
I later married the nice young man from Spokane who
played the banjo. I continued to suffer from closet gridlock.

Straight from an I. Magnin's window display, it was my uniform for eight days when I landed in Hollywood. While the airline searched the entire East Coast for my luggage, I learned to hate that dress.

Blonde entrapment!
Between a rock and a hard place.

Ciro's souvenir matchbook was
four times the size of other match-
books. Patrons could have their
pictures printed on the cover, but
often wanted me in the picture too

If you have a request, just
hum a few bars and he'll
fake it. He's good at that.

John Morrison at a
wedding party in a Seattle
hotel ballroom. This is the
way he looked at work,
a charming keyboard
wizard, playing whatever
you wanted, with flourish.

A painting I worked on in the evenings while John was at work.

Something I did not see across the happy dinner table came out in the painting. If you're an attractive female, his eyes will follow you.

Ho-Tai, Chinese god of happiness. Sometimes he's good at his job; sometimes not so much.

"Ho-Ho" went everywhere with me. My father's friend gave him to me when I was twelve. In Hollywood he guarded my tip money inside his round, porcelain belly.

Karoline Morrison

currently resides in a house overlooking Puget Sound in Seattle, Washington. She lives with three good-looking males: her husband Dennis, her son Brandon, and her awesome cat named Orange Julius Caesar (or Joules for short).

Karoline and Dennis split their time between the Seattle house, an art-filled vacation house on the edge of the continent at Ocean Shores, Washington, and aboard their boat, the Velvet Elvis.

She no longer runs an antique shop in the Carnegie Library Building in Seattle's Ballard neighborhood. She now owns the building and conducts estate sales to keep her hand in the game. She can often be found in the upstairs office of the Carnegie Building, working on the sequel to Twilight of the Blondes. The title of that sequel is My Mother's Was Bigger and Had Roses Painted On It.

Clothing and fashion are still a passion of Karoline's. She continues to suffer from closet gridlock. She still has her very first Merry Widow and it still fits!

Acknowledgements

I wish to express deepest gratitude to my longtime friend, skilled editor, taskmaster and cheerleader, Rosanne Royer. Without her, this manuscript would never have come out of a rag bag and into the light. I am also grateful to my treasured daughter Mei-Ling and my pal Vickie Dillon for their help and encouragement throughout the project. I thank well-known Hollywood TV producer and former manager of Ciro's nightclub, George Schlatter, for conversations in which he encouraged my writing and updated me on people who were part of the Sunset Strip in our day.

My dear friends Joann Nicon, JoAnne Rudo, Yasemin San and Marianne Forssblad cheered me on during many happy hours cruising in the Sound on the "Velvet Elvis." And to Carole Jordan, a kindred spirit on things Hollywood, I owe a debt of gratitude for leading Rosanne and me to Kristen Morris of Tigress Publishing, an outstanding collaborator. Tigress editor Peter Atkins and artist Steve Montiglio's insights and creativity have made the final product a truly beautiful and engaging book.

Finally, I want to raise a glass of wine to my good friends Cole, Donna, Zollan, Manuel and Kenny, who shared my Hollywood years. As my mother would say to them, "May the Lord be with thee and also with me while we are absent, one from the other."